Nonie Sharp has worked with northern Australia's indigenous coastal peoples for nearly 25 years. After obtaining her PhD in 1985, she taught sociology and anthropology at La Trobe University, Melbourne. A five-year Australian Research Fellowship enabled her to travel to Pacific islands, parts of coastal Europe, Canada and the US, and to write a book about people whose ties to the sea pervade their lives.

Nonie Sharp is also the author of No Ordinary Judgment, *the story of the landmark Australian* Mabo *case on indigenous land rights, a book shortlisted in 1996 for the Australian Cultural Studies Prize and for the New South Wales Premier's Literary Awards. Other books include* Footprints Along the Cape York Sandbeaches *(1992), shortlisted for the Victorian Premier's Literary Awards, and* Stars of Tagai *(1993). She has also published widely in journals, magazines and edited collections, especially in the Melbourne-based serial* Arena.

An acknowledged authority on the historical origins of rights to the sea, she brings together in Saltwater People *her scholarship, talent for writing and passionate concern for the rights of indigenous people.*

Nonie is married with a son, two daughters and a granddaughter.

saltwater people

THE WAVES OF MEMORY

NONIE SHARP

First published in 2002

Cover photos
Front: Yintjiŋga Sandbeach People, Stewart River, 1929 by D.F. Thomson (courtesy of Mrs D.M. Thomson and the Museum Victoria)
Back: In the waters of Mer, 2000 by Kim Batterham (courtesy of Film Australia)
Author photo: Australian Institute of Aboriginal and Torres Strait Islander Studies
Map: John Waddingham

Allen & Unwin
83 Alexander Street
Crows Nest NSW 2065
Australia
Phone: (61 2) 8425 0100
Fax: (61 2) 9906 2218
Email: info@allenandunwin.com
Web: www.allenandunwin.com

National Library of Australia
Cataloguing-in-Publication entry:

Sharp, Nonie.
Saltwater people: waves of memory.

Bibliography.
Includes index.
ISBN 1 86508 729 7.

1. Aborigines, Australian - Land tenure. 2. Torres Strait Islanders - Land tenure. 3. Aborigines, Australian - Fishing - Law and legislation. 4. Torres Strait Islanders - Fishing - Law and legislation. 5. Native title. I. Title.

343.9407692

Typeset in 10/15 pt New Caledonia by Midland Typesetters, Maryborough, Victoria
Printed by SRM Production Services Sdn. Bhd., Malaysia

10 9 8 7 6 5 4 3 2 1

For my family,
in memory of my father
Douglas John Mainland
and our forebears of the
Shetland Islands

Contents

List of Illustrations

Acknowledgements

THIS BOOK IS BASED ON MY WORK AS AN AUSTRALIAN Research Fellow from March 1995 until March 2000, a time during which I visited many island and coastal indigenous sea communities in north Australia. It draws also on first-hand comparative study of sea communities in other parts of the world between 1995 and 2000 and on my work over more than twenty years with the seafaring peoples of the Torres Strait Islands and northern Cape York Peninsula. I am deeply grateful to many people who have shared with me their knowledge, their experiences and their memories. I thank them too for their friendship and their encouragement.

I thank the late H. C. Coombs, who sponsored my application to the Australian Research Council, and the ARC for awarding me a five-year research fellowship. I acknowledge with gratitude the following people and groups: John Clarke, Grant Duncan, Sue Jackson, Peter Jull, Yvonne Forrest, Merrkiyawuy Ganambarr and Buku-Larrŋgay Mulka Centre, Eses Gesa, Rose Hesp, George Kaddy, Flo Kennedy, Anita Maurstad, Tania MacPherson, the late Dolly Nasslander,

Gobedar Noah, Mary Noah, Dave Passi, Edwina Preston, Colleen Pyne, Ben Scambary, Viv Sinnamon, Mary Yarmirr; the Counsel of Elders and Kowanyama Land and Natural Resources Management Office, Dhimurru Land Management Office, Northern Land Council; John Bradley and Deborah Rose for reading and commenting on the manuscript; the circle of people associated with *Arena Journal* and *Magazine*, especially Paul James in the early stages of the study, John Hinkson and Guy Rundle for their comments on the manuscript.

Special thanks go to Martin Hoare for sharing his knowledge on Irish history and culture; to Jackie Yowell for her professional advice, encouragement and commitment; and as ever, to Geoff Sharp who, for nearly half a century, has shared with me many of the perspectives from which this study arises.

I thank the staff of Sociology and Anthropology at La Trobe University for their professional advice, their patience and their friendship. I thank Bronwyn Bardsley, who typed the manuscript in its various stages with great expertise and forbearance. Without her work this book would not have been written. Merle Parker and Elaine Young kindly assisted with the typing and Mary Reilly and Barbara Matthews gave valuable advice. I thank the School of Social Sciences for its support towards publication of this book.

People in many communities in north Australia offered me hospitality as did those in Norway, Shetland Islands, Netherlands, Ireland, Nunavut province of Canada, New Caledonia, Fiji and New Zealand and at the Northwest Indian Fisheries Commission in Washington State. I am most grateful to them all.

Many scholars have contributed to a vast literature in a variety of fields on which this book relies. Much of their work is exciting as well as informative. My debt to them is unbounded. While the book acknowledges its sources, because it reaches across many fields, it is not feasible to list in detail the progression of work on which these particular sources build. I hope this book will stimulate some people to explore the rich store of archaeological knowledge, the growing body of ethnographic, legal, literary, artistic and cinematic work, and studies on the marine environment, resource management and indigenous fisheries on the tropical coasts.

I thank Geoffrey Bagshaw for permission to cite material from his Anthropologist's Report, Native Title Claim WAG 49/98, prepared for the Kimberley Land Council on behalf of the native title claimants, February 1999. I thank Film Australia and Ian Dunlop for permission to cite excerpts from scripts of the Yirrkala Film Project, A Collection of Twenty-Two Films made with the Yolŋu of Northeast Arnhem Land, 1979–1996. *Saltwater People* draws upon my earlier work published in *Arena Journal*, *Australian Aboriginal Studies*, *Indigenous Law Bulletin*, *Law in Context*, *North Australia Research Unit Discussion Paper Series*, *Pacific Conservation Biology*.

Preface

THE TROPICAL COASTS AND ISLANDS OF NORTH Australia, where the sea and the terrestrial environments meet one another, are areas of great richness and diversity. The marine environment, plant communities and animal life offer food sources as abundant and varied as anywhere in Australia. The indigenous peoples of these areas are themselves rich and diverse. In their world, threads of association join people with the sea as well as the land, imprinting them as sea peoples. They believe their ancestor spirit beings and heroes of the sea endowed their clans with rights to particular reefs, seabed, sites and waters, also conferring a special responsibility to care for them. The ways in which they distinguish themselves depend on contrasts with their neighbours: Sandbeach People, not bush people; island not mainland people; people of the sea versus people of the bush or 'scrub' country. Yolŋu people of northeast Arnhem Land and Yanyuwa people of islands in the Gulf of Carpentaria make a contrast between saltwater and fresh-water people. 'Saltwater people' is used throughout this book to denote the sea people of the coasts and islands.

From the Torres Strait in the far east to the Kimberleys in the west of north Australia, many indigenous peoples live in small communities on clan-owned lands beside the sea. Still today they form a majority of the population in the islands of the Torres Strait, the Gulf of Carpentaria, the coasts and islands of Arnhem Land and the Buccaneer Archipelago in the southern Kimberley. Their present numbers lie in the many thousands, even tens of thousands. This book is about these people, many of whom 'speak' directly in its pages.

This book is also about waves of remembering in the time of dispossession. People's connections with seascapes spring from enduring attachments to place and ancestors. Their stories tell of how recent events have stirred memories carrying feeling and emotion, so releasing the spiritual and practical energies of coastal peoples. There is beauty and grace, strength and fortitude, hope and love, on the one side; on the other, there is ugliness and death, melancholy and weakness, despair and hatred.

THE ISLANDERS OF THE TORRES STRAIT AND THE maritime Aborigines of northern Cape York Peninsula are the first inspiration for this book. I first visited some of their communities in the late 1970s. At that time Donald Thomson's ethnographic writings had given me a sense of the seafaring Aboriginal people of northern Cape York Peninsula and how they contrast themselves with their inland 'bush' neighbours, referring to themselves as Sandbeach People. Thomson's understanding of their spirituality, their prowess and their courage as seafarers and sea hunters, their profound sense of their environment, led me on a saltwater journey of my own.

Through the work of overseas scholars, especially human ecologist Bonnie McCay and anthropologist John Cordell,

I began to grasp the unfamiliar truth that coastal and island peoples in various parts of the world hold customary rights to marine areas adjoining their lands and are bonded with these seas in innumerable ways. Betty Meehan's 1982 study, *From Shell Bed to Shell Midden*, gave me a grounding on the long-term use of the sea and sea-shore in Australia.

In 1992 the High Court of Australia recognised indigenous rights to land in the *Mabo* case. I became suddenly aware of the active presence of sea Dreaming peoples along the tropical coasts and islands. 'Salt Water Dreaming', a paper given by lawyer David Allen at the Surviving Columbus: Indigenous Peoples, Political Reform and Environmental Management in North Australia Conference, Darwin, in 1992, brought home to me the aesthetic wholeness of the saltwater people's relationship with the sea. I knew then I would write a book to help make this relationship known to non-indigenous people.

As it turned out the book became a journey between two cultural traditions of the sea. The cornerstone of Western sea tradition is the notion that the seas are for everyone to share in. Such an enduring and compelling belief makes it hard for non-indigenous people to understand the 'sea rights' of indigenous people.

Saltwater People criss-crosses contrasting sea traditions, identifying differences — and, to my surprise, points of contact — so facilitating people's understanding. Exploration of the origins and history of the ancient Western tradition of sharing the sea may rekindle memory of a time when local groups along the coasts in parts of Europe exercised customary rights to strands and waters they took to be theirs.

Saltwater people today see native title rights to the sea as a stepping stone to a long overdue economic independence. This is happening at a time of major world economic change when even the once sacrosanct Western tradition of open access to the coasts is giving way to property rights-based fishing. The concluding chapter asks burning questions about the future: if individual marine property rights become established along the Australian coasts, will some indigenous people be integrated into conventional entrepreneurship? How might accountability towards others and care for the sea that saltwater people claim as their birthright be built into modern fishing enterprise? These are unresolved questions relevant to indigenous people, to the fishing industry and to us all. Several illustrations of self-regulatory fisheries and fish habitat conservation projects in world settings raise the possibility of finding forms of mutual endeavour in a marine world devastated by the pursuit of narrowly conceived individual interests. Questions about the prospects for finding new ways of living together concern us all. *Saltwater People* searches for answers realistically, respecting the strengths and limitations of different peoples and cultures.

At a time when old Western anchors of sea tradition are being raised, a deeper understanding of different traditions of the sea has become urgent. My wish is to convey a sense of the richness and resilience of peoples who are shaped by and in league with the sea and its creatures, corporeal and spiritual; and whose attachments are to specific locations bequeathed to them ancestrally. I like to think that the understanding I am seeking is close to what philosopher Raimond Gaita means by the word 'lucid': a clear understanding that impels people to act in morally enlightened ways.

Saltwater

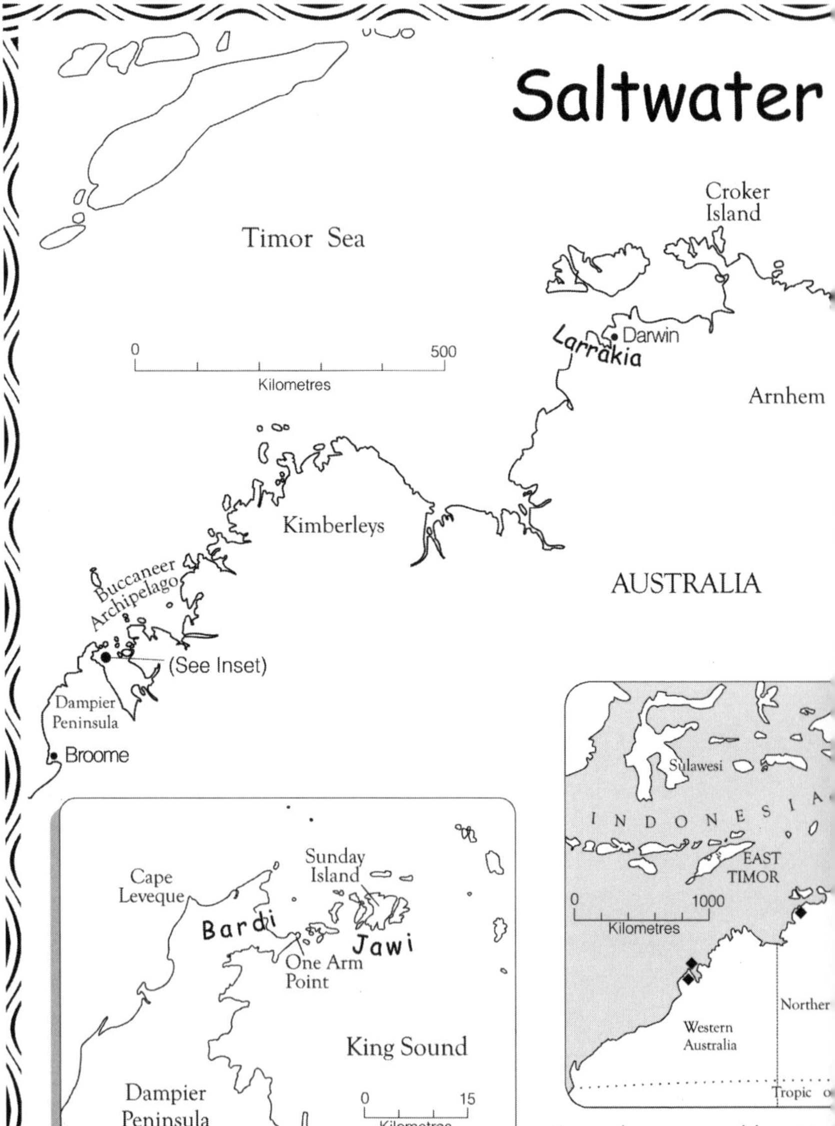

Croker Island
Timor Sea
Darwin
Larrakia
Arnhem
0
500
Kilometres
Kimberleys
AUSTRALIA
Buccaneer Archipelago
(See Inset)
Dampier Peninsula
Broome
Cape Leveque
Sunday Island
Bardi
Jawi
One Arm Point
King Sound
Dampier Peninsula
0
15
Kilometres
Sulawesi
I N D O N E S I A
EAST TIMOR
0
1000
Kilometres
Western Australia
Norther
Tropic

Maps show general locatio
mentioned

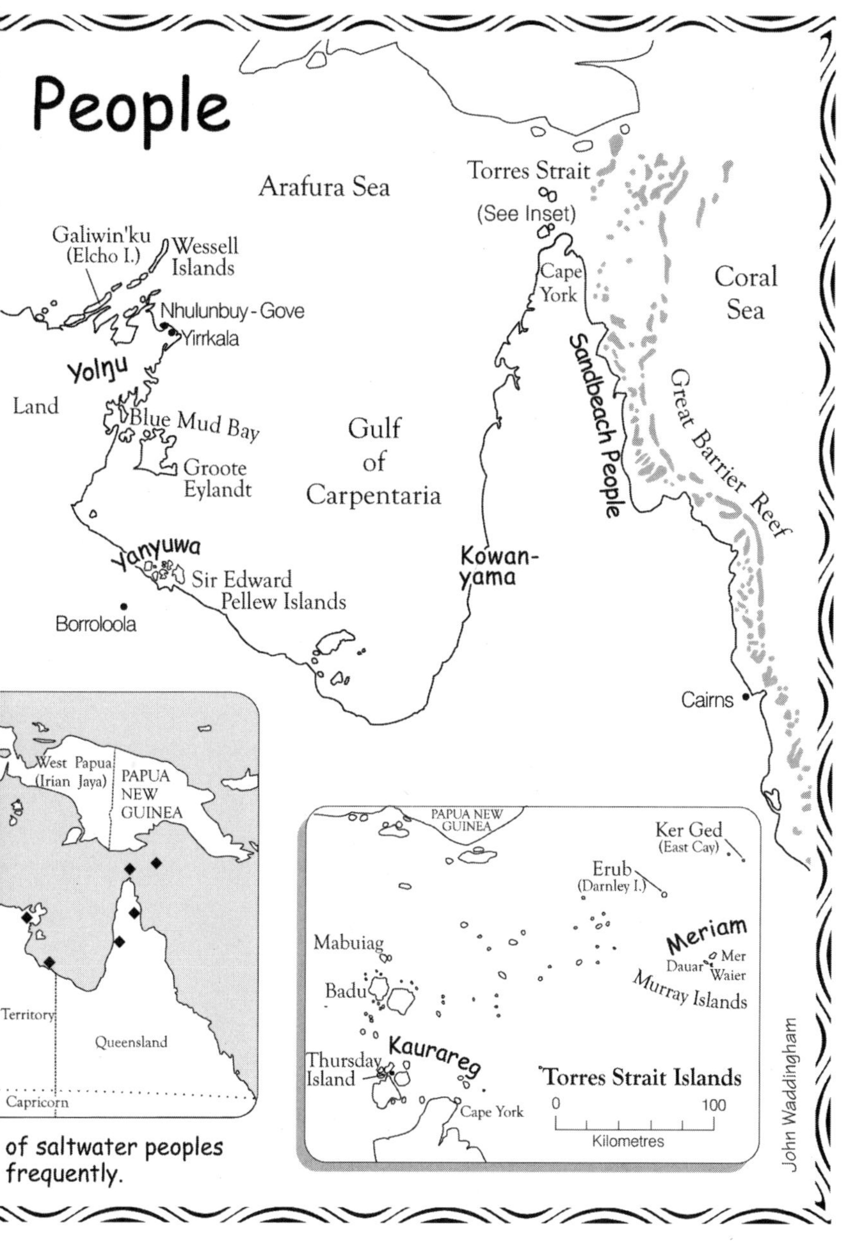
People
Arafura Sea
Torres Strait
(See Inset)
Galiwin'ku
(Elcho I.)
Wessell
Islands
Nhulunbuy - Gove
Yirrkala
Yolŋu
Land
Blue Mud Bay
Groote
Eylandt
Gulf
of
Carpentaria
Cape
York
Coral
Sea
Sandbeach People
Great Barrier Reef
Yanyuwa
Sir Edward
Pellew Islands
Borroloola
Kowan-
yama
Cairns
West Papua
(Irian Jaya)
PAPUA
NEW
GUINEA
Territory
Queensland
Capricorn
PAPUA NEW
GUINEA
Ker Ged
(East Cay)
Erub
(Darnley I.)
Mabuiag
Meriam
Mer
Dauar
Waier
Murray Islands
Badu
Kaurareg
Thursday
Island
Cape York
Torres Strait Islands
0
100
Kilometres
John Waddingham
of saltwater peoples
frequently.

PART I

TRADITIONS

1
Two Traditions of the Sea

Resonances

It was 1978 and I had come to the Murray Islands — Mer, Dauar and Waier — within listening distance of the Great Barrier Reef. I was watching a man cast a sardine net in the shallows in front of his house. His movements were graceful, seemingly effortless. With both hands, he held the edges of a circular net weighted around the edge and flung it a few metres in front of him. As the net described an arc in the light morning air his right arm continued to reach out as though it was helping the net to reach its goal. For a few seconds the man and the freed net formed a silhouette against the pale blue sky and the dappled sea. With his arm outstretched he looked like the statue of a way-finder.

He recovered the net from the sea and soon he and his little son were picking out sardines from the mesh and dropping them

Meriam people performing the Sardine Scoop dance at Mer–Murray Island 1989

into an empty petrol drum. Schools of sardines in their thousands form large bands along the shallows at Mer island. People use them as fish bait and they also provide good food for a rainy day. The Meriam people perform their traditional sardine dance to the beat of the New Guinea drum. I watched the fisher and his son return to their home on the beachfront to prepare for a fishing trip out on the reefs surrounding the Murray Islands. The man and his brothers-in-law would fish for the family, even for the whole village.

This scene is rich in meaning for me. At this moment I sensed an elemental attachment to the sea that the Meriam were able to take for granted. Sardines are insignificant fish in themselves, but everyone knows that they are a ready lure for bigger fish. The five-year-old boy on the sand with his father would already know that trevally are a landward fish and will follow the sardines into the shallows. He would soon learn too that trevally, a fish he knows as *mekmek*, will strike at the sardines each morning but at different places along the shoreline according to the tide.

My memory of the man, the boy, the net flying through the air, and the sheen on the sardines, evokes a scene of tranquillity, grace and beauty. Yet I was soon to learn some important meanings of the saying that calm surfaces may hide turbulent waters. Mer was the island where the nation-shaking *Mabo* case would soon begin its ten-year story. In its famous 1992 judgment the High Court of Australia recognised the rights of the Meriam people to land above the high-water mark: the island of Mer was exclusively theirs 'as against the whole world'. But from a Meriam standpoint this was only half a story and half a victory. The Meriam are seafarers and fishers and for them the sea is life. In the wake of the *Mabo* judgment, leaders at Mer announced to the world that fishing for the family by no means fulfils all their needs. Their aim is economic independence, not reliance on welfare payments, and they see the source of this independence as coming from the sea. But traditional fishing has not met all their needs for more than a century; over five generations ago their forebears began operating clan-owned luggers and earning a living from pearl shell and trochus shell.

Mer is an island of rich and expanding traditions with a long-standing code of behaviour. If you follow good custom, or *debe tonar* in the Meriam language, you take only what you need from the sea and the land, you respect other people's property rights and above all, you share. The Meriam hold their sea hunters in high esteem, and in turn, the hunter takes pride in being generous, for to be greedy is shameful. The Meriam are steeped in the custom of generosity with food: the sharing of harvested food, wild or cultivated, still remains its own reward, and to expect a return in kind is like not sharing at all.[1] Before the Christian missionaries arrived at Mer in 1872, there were other sanctions: people who failed to follow the law of sharing with others and at the same time respecting other people's property, 'didn't see the sun go down' that day.

What were their rules and law? I wondered in those first days. What knowledge guided the daily round I was glimpsing? I learned then in 1978 that every inch of the lands of the Meriam people is owned by someone, even in those village areas that had become public space with a community hall and school. I became aware that the entire perimeter of the island was divided into eight clan territories, as it still is today in 2001. Much later I learnt that the boundaries between these clan lands extend out over the foreshore and reefs and came to appreciate the courteous silence of the Meriam at my unwitting trespass on their clan-owned marine territories. The Meriam are an intrepid sea people who, until the end of the 1800s, made sea journeys of over 150 kilometres for trade, for battle and for fertiliser for their food gardens, often travelling in canoes 15 metres or more which they obtained from coastal New Guinea. They were great gardeners of the rich volcanic soils of their islands. Their law, known as Malo's Law, after their sea god Malo, forbids them to trespass on each other's land, and Malo's Law is also a law of the sea. The Meriam have a form of sea ownership derived from local custom and law. Over the last fifteen years anthropologists have termed this form of ownership 'customary marine tenure'. This marine tenure, the Meriam taught me, is as important to them as land ownership.

When a major anthropological expedition from Cambridge University visited Mer and other Torres Strait Islands in 1898, the scientists were struck by the Islanders' knowledge of their land and sea environments. The local people had a distinctive name for nearly every species recognised by scientists.[2] They observed that the Islanders were competent navigators with a flair for geography. All the islands, large and small, the sandbanks, coral reefs, capes, coves and prominent rocks had distinctive names too. The anthropologists soon became aware of the Islanders' vast mental store of geographical knowledge, demonstrated by the readiness with which they drew maps and portrayed 'the essential characteristics of an island from memory'.[3] Nearly a century later, Meriam descendants drew and named the reefs, cays, islands and passages that mark their sea boundaries. Across this time gap much of their knowledge of inherited marine boundaries had been buried beneath an imposed sea tradition very different to their own. More than 100 years ago, government officials told the Meriam to forget about the clan land boundaries that extended out over the reefs.[4]

Anchors of tradition

THE SEA DREAMINGS, FORMS OF OWNERSHIP, AND SEA knowledge of coastal and islander indigenous peoples in Australia are little known even today. People believe that Aboriginal Dreamings come from the land; that it is non-indigenous people of the island continent who are bestowed with a sea dreaming. Australian novelist David Malouf said just this in his 1998 Boyer lectures. He contrasted the 'vision of the continent' as an island culture of settler Australians to the organising vision of Aboriginal people: 'If Aborigines are a land-dreaming people, what we latecomers share is a sea dreaming, to which the image of Australia as an island has from the beginning been central.' 'Our land is girt by sea,' Australians sing unself-consciously; the image of a blue-bordered island continent brings with it pleasurable thoughts of wave and sand, surf and rollers, reef and sea as a place of free expression. This statement disregards the 'bush dreaming' of settler Australians; it is also born out of a lack of knowledge of the vision of indigenous coastal Australia. Like most Australians Malouf is unaware that indigenous peoples of the coasts and islands are sea Dreaming peoples. Their Dreamings follow the law of each people's coastal territory which extends out into the sea.

Most Australians take for granted their right to free use of the seas around the continent. Certainly this sense of freedom is now qualified by rules curtailing that freedom: swim between the flags, buy a fishing licence, don't take too many fish, care for the coasts. Yet an overwhelming feeling that the beaches are for everyone remains dominant in the minds of citizens. Licensed commercial fishers — men and women — know that there are three maritime boundaries set by Australia and the International Law of the Sea. Within those limits, the coastal seas are available to all Australians. The professional non-indigenous fisherman in the following story is working tropical seas within the terms set by Anglo-Australian law.

Like his father, the fisherman has a licence to fish commercially and has done so for twenty years. He described himself to me spontaneously as a 'saltwater person'. He catches about 40 fish each day and if he doesn't catch this number he moves on. As a responsible producer and an office-bearer in the seafood industry, he has led moves to eliminate what fishers at the port of Karumba on the Gulf of Carpentaria call the 'cowboy element' in the fishing industry. In July 1996 we sat in his office near the Darwin waterfront and he told me how he saw Aboriginal saltwater people. 'I think Aboriginal people just want to be left alone; but realistically I just don't think it's actually possible, and we need to train both Aboriginal people and non-indigenous fishermen just to interact better. But I know Aboriginal people well enough to say they really are very, very easy people to deal with and they have the best interest of the resource at heart.'

A year later the same fisherman was in the Federal Court in Darwin contesting a claim by the Aboriginal saltwater clans of

Croker Island (200 kilometres northeast of Darwin) to a primary right to the waters adjoining their islands. He had been fishing in the waters according to Australian rules. The Croker Islanders believed he required their permission to fish there, and had taken their native title claim to seas adjoining their islands to an Australian court. Theirs was the first claim to sea rather than land in Australia — and became known as the *Croker Island Seas* case.

The fisherman was upholding a powerful and appealing sea tradition, one with ancient origins. It carries an obligation to share the sea. Western sea tradition is grounded in an ancient belief that the sea is open to everyone and cannot be owned. This was the view expounded by Roman jurists and philosophers, who believed sharing the sea arose out of the unbounded and constantly moving character of the sea.[5] Until recently, the view that the public right to fish in tidal waters became part of English law in 1215 when King John signed the Magna Carta, was upheld in major legal judgments.[6] The idea that sharing the seas stemmed from the nature of the sea itself became embedded in the thinking of English jurists. Sir William Blackstone, famed English jurist of the eighteenth century and leading exponent of the doctrine of individual private property in land, wrote in 1789 of how 'water is a moveable, wandering thing and must of necessity continue common by the law of nature'.[7] However, the idea that all citizens may share the coasts is only as old as sovereign states — that is, several centuries — but this way of imagining sea space came to exclude all other perspectives. Today, owners of sea country like the Meriam land–sea owners, who drew their sea boundary markers in the sand for me in 1993, challenge us to recognise that the European cultural perspective on the sea is by no means the only one.

This challenge to the imagination reached Australia's highest courts. In recognising native title rights to the sea on 18 September

2001 the High Court made a ground-breaking judgment. Five of the seven Justices concluded that the rights and interests of Croker Islander *yuwurrumu* or clans exist in some 3,300 square kilometres of sea in accordance with the claimants' traditional laws and customs. In one important respect the judgement is a milestone along paths where two laws meet, for it breaks with the certainty that the sea cannot be owned. However, unlike the High Court judgment in the *Mabo* case on native title to land on 3 June 1992, the sea rights recognised by the majority in the *Croker Island Seas* case in September 2001 are not exclusive: they coexist with the public right to fish and the right to navigate. In this view, 'there is a fundamental inconsistency' between common law public rights of fishing and navigation and native title rights. Although they may coexist they 'cannot stand together' as one.[8]

Sacred design

WHAT IS THE SALTWATER PEOPLE'S CONCEPTION OF SEA property? And why do people like the Croker Islanders or the Meriam feel so strongly about it? First of all, they own areas of salt water in the same way as they own land: on behalf of a patriline or a clan. This joint ownership with or on behalf of others is very different to conceptions of property recognised as institutions in the common law of England. In the *Mabo* case the majority of Justices of the High Court recognised the existence of 'interests of a kind unknown to English law' — words used by Justice Hall in a landmark case in British Columbia, Canada in 1973.[9] In Australia, these interests were designated as 'native title rights', which the High Court took to be unique or *sui generis*, that is, rights which exist according to the local laws and customs of a group of people of a particular locale. We are speaking here of what one authority referred to in relation to Ireland as 'a different concept of property altogether' to that derived from feudal law.[10] In a short paper he prepared in 1969 for a land case brought by Yolŋu people of northeast Arnhem Land, anthropologist William Stanner described a different way of owning to the European one. He said that Aboriginal people's relationship to land was a dual one where 'human corporeal life was indivisibly in pair with spiritual life'.[11] This way of owning where, as Stanner says, people are 'of and with the land' and 'of and with one another', holds true for the saltwater peoples of north Australia — Aborigines and Torres Strait Islanders. Being of and with the sea was made possible by the journeys of founding creator beings, which Aboriginal people call Dreamings or Stories. They marked the seascapes in their travels, giving sacred power to the places they marked.

Yolŋu people of northeast Arnhem Land continue to believe today that their sea rights come from creator beings who shaped the seas. Their conviction is powerful and compelling. Their creator beings gave Yolŋu people rights and responsibilities for the beaches, reefs, seabed, sea life and waters adjoining their lands. They imbued those waters with their spiritual power. Shimmering waters 'speak' ancestral power to Yolŋu who recreate its brilliance in their most sacred paintings.[12]

Their entitlement to this saltwater world finds expression in a profound and detailed knowledge of its geography: the reefs, the channels, the currents. Yolŋu know the habits of the sea turtle and fish, their life cycles and, importantly for Yolŋu, the cycles of seasons and tides. This knowledge is stored in memory, in images, in performance, in song, in sacred regalia, in objects they make. It is also 'written' on the salt waters themselves, so that for the Yolŋu the reefs and waters, the channels and passages, the rocks and beaches, are like vast tapestries or atlases.

Here lies the heart of Yolŋu 'belonging': a two-way interchange between the Yolŋu and their seas, where the people become part of the sea world and elements of the sea world become part of them. This two-sided belonging is a domain of intense feeling and emotion. 'We are sacred design,' Dula ŋurruwuthun, a Yolŋu artist with special knowledge of Yolŋu sacred law, declared in 1999 in a statement on his inheritance of particular seas. His declaration, translated from his native language, accompanies ŋurruwuthun's sea paintings. These became part of a national travelling exhibition and are now held in a permanent collection at the National Maritime Museum in Sydney. The sea paintings were created to help Australian people understand the nature of Yolŋu rights to the sea. ŋurruwuthun's declaration is rich with an identification with the sea that carries feeling and emotion. It speaks of Wulamba, the *sound* of Gapu Dhä-yindi, a body of open sea belonging to his clan. The artist explains that this 'wide open sea has a huge tail of waves. Waters that roar.' It existed in ancestral times, yet it is everlasting, a massive cycle of movement. Out of the sacred design of this body of water, Gapu-Dhä-yindi, comes also 'the tantalising taste of the Green turtle'. Its pattern is 'etched by the smell of the sea'. In Yolŋu understanding, a body of water is identified by the various senses.[13]

In this two-way belonging, the sea is not just waters moving in rhythmic patterns or in tempestuous ways. Like the reefs and the seabed and sea life, salt water itself has its own ancestral and human attachment. When a Yolŋu saltwater person dies, sacred songs are sung in cycles guiding the person's soul over waters owned by different clans to his or her ancestral homeland. It is this ancestral attachment above all that requires the coastal saltwater peoples to say vigorously to outsiders: 'You cannot come into our sea world without our permission.' These seas and their marine life are Yolŋu people's responsibility because the salt waters are 'part of our blood and body'. In these words Mr Weluk, a land–sea owner at Milingimbi off the Arnhem Land

Mary Yarmirr, chief plaintiff in the Croker Island Seas *case at Croker Island, 1999*

coast, sought to explain his sea rights to the 1980–81 judicial hearing on inshore marine rights, conducted by the Aboriginal Land Commissioner, appointed by the Federal government.[14]

More than a decade later, claimants in the *Croker Island Seas* case gave renewed expression to this elemental attachment to the sea. On 23 April 1997 the chief plaintiff Mary Yarmirr explained to the Federal Court her right to speak on behalf of the members of her clan. Mary was born at the place where the white and brown eagle painted himself in a creation story, a place called Minjalang. Her rights to certain named waters come from her father, his father and his father again. She is free to hunt in the waters of her clan estate for the rest of her life because as a member of that *yuwurrumu* or clan her right 'lies in there'. As a baby her father put her in a canoe with him and from then on she travelled with him on the sea throughout her life. From the day she was born she learnt first and foremost to respect the sea. This is the law she was taught and it says her clan has rights and interests as well as obligations; it confers on the clan the responsibility to return the turtle bones to the sea, for instance, to respect and not waste fish.[15]

Journey into memory

In 1995 my saltwater journey began. It was often a solitary path but this was always compensated by rich experiences along the way. My approach to understanding saltwater peoples and their unique relationship with the seas around them took shape around the theme of imagining and reimagining sea space. At first glance, differences between cultural perspectives appear deep-set, traditions miles apart. In the Western tradition the sea is for everyone; in indigenous Australian tradition sharing is restricted: you share with joint owners, that is, clan members, those in other clans tied by marriage, and on occasion, with everyone in your community.

I first explored the different ways in which sea space had been imagined and reimagined at different periods of history. I visited places on the coastal margins of Europe and Canada, the United States and Pacific islands. My first impression was that customary marine rights had somehow been forgotten and when I inquired further I discovered powerful cultural reasons behind this forgetfulness. Examining these reasons became as important to me as understanding what customary sea ownership means. As it turned out, placing these sea tenures within a larger historical and cross-cultural context is highly relevant to an understanding of who the Australian saltwater peoples were, who they are today, and the challenges they face.

I began to ponder some serious questions. The 'public right' of all citizens to share the coasts is commonly known as 'open access'. How had the idea of open access to the coasts come about in Western tradition? Was it because the sea was taken to be a gift from God or nature? Or was it integral with a more general social imagination? That is, at some time in the past did people *will* open access into being? Had there been stretches of the coasts that served as a series of sea commons for groups of local inhabitants? Had clans, or clan remnants, or villages, divided marine areas among themselves according to geographical locale? Had they fought over these portions of strand and waters? In his scholarly and highly readable book *The Law of the Countryside, the Rights of the Public*, environmental lawyer Tim Bonyhady gives a picture of English coasts teaming with locally based fisheries with exclusive rights from ancient times. What kinds of tenures did these fisheries have? Were they customary and informal or held in severalty in a similar way to land? Bonyhady himself expresses some uncertainty about the basis on which these fisheries were established.[16] My questions were outstripping my own capacity to find answers.

Even in England where vast tracts of land had become privately enclosed, especially in the eighteenth century, there were exceptions as for example in the County of Wessex, the setting of Thomas Hardy's novels. The opening lines of *The Return of the Native* take the reader into a seemingly timeless commons that had figured in the Domesday Book: 'A Saturday afternoon in November was approaching the time of twilight, and the vast tract of unenclosed wild known as Egdon Heath embrowned itself moment by moment.' Within this relic of unenclosed land, seemingly 'as unaltered as the stars overhead' from ancient times, local inhabitants were exercising rights to furze and turf even in the heartland of private property at the end of the nineteenth century.

Several discoveries relating to Western land–sea traditions came as special surprises to me. The first related to the paradox between private property in land as the backbone of Western tradition and the doctrine that all citizens may share coastal waters. At first sight there is a glaring inconsistency between private rights to land owned and saleable by an individual sole owner and public rights to beaches and coastal seas. Sharing the seas is a tradition expounded by ancient philosophers — Seneca for example, who lived from 4BC to 65AD, emphasised sharing and inveighed against those who used this freedom for commercial gain.[17] Yet from the 1600s onwards sharing the seas became vital to the rise of capitalism: on land and sea the pursuit of trade and commerce were ascendant. The paradox raises a further question. Did this ancient tradition of sharing the sea become a vehicle for the modern goal of individual acquisitiveness, an aim contrary to the ethic that had originally nurtured that tradition?

My second question was whether there are affinities between the customary tenures of indigenous Australian saltwater peoples and earlier ideas of sharing in Western sea traditions? Unexpectedly I discovered lost stories of customary marine rights in Europe: inherited fishing grounds marked out by custom and fishing rights given to inhabitants as the gift of a king a millennium ago linger on even today. This form of sharing among a group of people who jointly own a portion of sea or land is illustrated readily among European peoples who were not subject to feudal law. In the Tuath or Kingdom of pre-colonial Ireland, 'the public' comprised all the members of that body of people, each of whom had an equal right for instance, to the salmon of the locale of the Tuath. Under the Brehon Law of Ireland, declared to be no law at all by the colonising English in 1607, this equal right of such a group of inhabitants was recently compared by one jurist in an Irish legal case 'to a public right of fishing'.[18] Yet this does not amount to a state-based right to sea space; it is the right of members of a geographically based group to the exclusion of the other inhabitants of Ireland.

Elsewhere, in the fisheries of northern Norway for example, even on the isle of Skye in Scotland, official policies of public rights to state waters have served as a carapace for locally based groups. Under the umbrella of open access, these informal rights have sometimes been passed down through families and groups as rights of inheritance to particular fishing grounds. Lost memories of customary rights to fishing grounds and foreshores are by no means lost altogether. Inherited rights to fishing grounds were passed on in marine areas of Trom's and Finnmark in northern Norway. There, in modern times, small-scale fishers made agreements on fishing practices which respected one another's rights to long-standing fishing grounds.

Yet if informal customary rights had existed in the past or even survived into the present, why was there no literature acknowledging them? And why had English common law no category of ownership of land and sea as the joint or common property of a clan or other geographically based local group? And then again, how local is a local group and how big? Sir Tipene O'Regan, Chairman of the Treaty of Waitangi Fisheries Commission, rightly pointed out to me that the local territory of his tribe, Ngai Tahu with some 30,000 members, comprises nearly 50 per cent of the whole coastline of mainland New Zealand.[19]

A third discovery gave promise of answers to some of my questions. Scholars associated with the International Association for the Study of Common Property, formed in the late 1980s, sought to distinguish common property as a form of property and to show its relevance today. An important starting point was a 1989 collection of essays, *A Sea of Small Boats*, edited by John Cordell, a world authority on customary marine tenure. Its appearance marked the beginning of a period when scholars would debate the character of property rights, old and new.

Transformations?

THE CONTEMPORARY CONTEXT IS A CHANGING ONE. Assumptions about the 'real' Australia located exclusively inside the continent are rapidly being surpassed. As David Malouf's thoughts suggest, the bush image of Australia has changed over the last twenty years; increased leisure and mobility have brought the idea of coastal recreation into the experience and the aspirations of most Australians. The growth of the recreation industry along the coasts and the changing world of northern Australia since East Timor's independence in September 1999 may presage a transformation in the lives of the saltwater peoples on Australia's northern rim.

Suddenly the economic independence I have seen so many people in indigenous communities crave, and which has so often been thwarted by Protectors and 'native welfare officers', has become a subject of active debate. In the name of a failure of indigenous separatism, a simple choice is being posed between assimilation and endless social stagnation. Aboriginal leader Noel Pearson addresses cogently the question of Aboriginal dependence on welfare. Rejecting the notion of the government as a 'welfare-spraying Hydra', he asks how the values of reciprocity and responsibility intrinsic to Aboriginal societies may reassert themselves in modern economic enterprise.[20]

In his book *Belonging*, historian Peter Read remembers how he was sometimes 'overwhelmed by the sadness of our history'. In the first few years of my association with people and communities in the Torres Strait Islands and northern Cape York Peninsula I too had moments of sadness and of anger. I wept at the loss of will and listlessness I saw in some communities. This was toward the end of the 1970s in a world awakened by calls for black power, independence, and rights to land. Some years earlier, in 1973, in a landmark case known as *Calder*, the Supreme Court of Canada recognised that native title rights could exist in Canada. About that time the Inuit began a long and eventually triumphant struggle to establish the province of Nunavut.[21] I could scarcely believe what I saw and heard in far north Queensland. 'Killing them softly' summed up the still palpable colonial legacy behind the words 'protection', 'native welfare' and 'advancement'.

Today there are contradictory tendencies within indigenous communities; citizenship, the formal dismantling of the old 'native welfare' systems and the promise of native title, have aroused hope and self action. However, a lack of self confidence, sense of purpose and spiritual numbness, inherited from a system where people were treated like children, have taken a hold on some people. There are others with the strength of will and the enterprise to break through dependence on welfare. My mind returns to the image of the man and the boy sardine fishing at Mer island in 1978. Today, a generation later, the boy is now a man and there is another boy. The man casts the sardine net, he fishes for his family — but he also goes out in his dinghy and sells his catch to the community-owned freezer facility at Mer. This is modern marine enterprise, Meriam style.

Breaking the silence

Australian historian Greg Dening has suggested that the most difficult problem in cross-cultural research 'between indigenous peoples and intruding strangers . . . is the depth of the silences'.[22] Such a silence exists between the saltwater cultures of indigenous Australia and non-indigenous Australians. We cannot understand or speak of that we do not know and David Malouf is by no means alone in his ignorance of indigenous sea Dreamings. His view may be seen as the reverse side of a growing sensibility about indigenous attachments to land. Many people know the history of the land rights movement, its beginnings in the 1960s among the Gurindji at Wave Hill and the famous 'bark petition' of Dula ŋurruwuthun's people, the Yolŋu: their response to moves for a bauxite mine on Yolŋu land was a petition to the Australian government attached to a piece of stringybark. That petition was followed by the first Aboriginal Land Rights case brought by Yolŋu clans and was followed in turn by the *Aboriginal Land Rights Act (Northern Territory)* in 1976. Most people know of the ten-year long *Mabo* case brought by Edward Koiki Mabo and other Meriam land–sea owners, and the breaking of what William Stanner called 'the great Australian silence' about indigenous people.[23] This occurred on 3 June 1992 when the High Court of Australia recognised native title to land at Mer and overturned the doctrine of Australia as *terra nullius*, that is, land belonging to no one.

That nation-shaking event did not bring with it any public awareness of the existence of indigenous saltwater peoples; even less the modest history of sea rights. It was Yolŋu people themselves who had first brought the issue of customary rights to the sea on to the national 'stage'. Following the Yolŋu land rights case, known in legal terms as *Milirrpum v. Nabalco and the Commonwealth of Australia* (1971), a Commission into Aboriginal Land Rights was set up by the Australian government. In 1973, the Commissioner, Mr Justice Woodward, presented his First Report in which he made a brief reference to Aboriginal sea tenure. In 1977 submissions were made on indigenous marine tenure by several anthropologists who had worked with Yolŋu people, to a federal inquiry by the Joint Select Committee on Aboriginal Land Rights in the Northern

Territory. Yet the first book to be published on the issue, *Customary Marine Tenure in Australia*, only appeared twenty years later. As the editors remark in their introduction, it was not until the 1970s that saltwater people's claims to foreshore, reef and waters and marine life even began to receive attention worldwide.[24] And anthropologists who had worked in coastal areas did not always explore the character and the strength of saltwater people's relationship with the sea. Fortunately, by the early 1990s, the work of scholars concerned with the ecological sustainability of marine resources and the importance to coastal people of customary marine tenure was beginning to influence mainstream thinking. As early as 1984, a report from within a Commonwealth government department brought to government attention issues of indigenous sea rights and fishing, both subsistence and commercial.[25]

Many Australians know that Inuit-Eskimo people have more than 60 names for snow in its various forms and stages. Few know that the Torres Strait Islanders have 80 words for the different tides and their variations according to lunar and solar cycles. Or that these Islanders liken tidal movements to the stages of animal growth and decline: new-born tides are weak, increasing in their range and height towards full moon; they go through stages analogous to adolescence and adulthood and as the tide weakens and the final quarter of the moon arrives, the Islanders give it names likening it to old age and death.[26]

PART II

SEA PEOPLES

2

Saltwater Peoples

Respecting the sea

It was the late 1970s and three of us were sitting together in Thursday Island in the Torres Strait. Flo Kennedy and Fred Ware were speaking. 'When you are on the sea you mustn't say anything bad about it. Not criticise it. Because the sea is alive, like a person. So you must respect it.' Otherwise, they explained, it will claim you. The sea has rhythms — the tides and currents create patterns of movement memorised by saltwater peoples. It also has dramatic and unpredictable moments which lead them to ask, why is it raging *now*?

Flo Kennedy is a leading storyteller of the Torres Strait Islands, a creative woman of spiritual power, personal generosity and political savvy. In the mid-1990s she received an Order of Australia Medal. In 1996 when a book I had written on the historic *Mabo* native title case was being launched, Flo told those assembled at the launch in Canberra: 'Nonie didn't know anything. Nothing. But we decided to teach her.' Taken as a whole this was a compliment.

'When you're on the sea,' Flo continued, 'and a big wind, maybe a cyclone is coming, you mustn't say "Oh, cyclone's coming." Because that will bring it. You must be very very careful. Keep silent. There is the eye.' Fred Ware spoke in a low voice. 'Winds too; they can hear.' In Torres Strait Islander tradition, shipwrecked people have been rejected by the sea, and in days gone by, those who survived shipwrecks were killed by their fellow Islanders. In those times Islanders chanted 'power songs' to assuage what they saw as the dread powers of the sea; in the bows of their canoes they carried certain plants to ward off danger; and no one had the hubris to say 'Good fishing' to departing sea hunters.

On other parts of the coasts and islands of north Australia, the saltwater people also seek to placate and temper the sea. Mary Yarmirr, whose people are from Croker Island, northeast of Darwin, gave the Federal Court a sense of her reciprocal obligations with the sea: 'if you don't know how to respect the sea, the sea claims you'. The Aboriginal people of the Croker Island area believe the Rainbow Serpent lies on the seabed at a particular site and must be respected. If it is given due respect, a person is granted 'special spiritual healing'; otherwise the sea is dangerous. It has the power to wreak vengeance and even to kill.[1] People negotiate this power, seeking to transform profane danger into sacred power through ceremonial rites. Sacred power carries the strength of a host of sea creatures. Among Aboriginal saltwater peoples, from Cape York to the Gulf country, from Arnhem Land to the far west Kimberley coast, negotiating the destructive power of the Rainbow Serpent is integral to their seamanship, their direction-finding and their hunting skills.

The saltwater people 'cooperate' with the sea along the same lines as they cooperate with one another. Like people, waters differ from one another. Some tropical waters are smooth 'like grease', especially in the season of the northeast winds; there are also places of myriad whirlpools, rips and tidal currents like Sunday Strait in the southern reaches of the Buccaneer Archipelago. The Jawi and Bardi peoples of this area live beside seas with fierce tide races of ten or even twelve knots, described by William Dampier in 1688 as 'five fathom tides'. Songs, dances, emblems received by men in dream visits to various locations are often about tides and whirlpools as in the following sequence: 'branching tidal current spinning vessel around, whirlpool getting me.'[2] If you do not respect the sea which, as Mary Yarmirr says, 'holds our life', it will take you. Where the sea has the power to heal or to claim you and you must learn to live with it, its power is felt elementally as part of people's 'blood and body'. 'It is just beyond your understanding,' one land–sea owner said sadly to the Aboriginal Land Commissioner in 1981 as he struggled to find suitable words.[3]

Such expressions of sentiment are emotionally charged, and rarely voiced. When saltwater people are feeling happy or nostalgic about the sea they often break into song — or tears. In times of crisis or challenge — when people are separated from their sea domains or when they must make a legal claim to sea territories they have inherited — they do find the words. When George Kaddy, a Meriam elder, said to me in 1999, 'I am part of the sea and the sea is part of me when I am on it,' I thought, what does he mean? Now I believe he was saying that his sensibilities are shaped by the salt waters to which he belongs so that he and his kin themselves become the salt waters speaking.

Such feelings and beliefs about the sea are by no means totally foreign to Western sea traditions. Irish sea traditions abound with rites placating and paying homage to the inhabitants of a maritime Otherworld, the Tuatha De Danaan, legendary beings with a sea origin. Without the hint of a swell or wind the Tuatha may cause a huge wave to roll up, engulf and overwhelm victims who have offended their law or their wishes.[4] Irish sailors believed that to learn to swim is to display hubris towards the beings of Otherworld. 'Power chants' may help but a person marked by a spell for wrong-doing, or as a victim of malice, will drown anyway. The epic voyages of St Brendan in the sixth century link Irish pre-Christian 'sea Dreamings' with Christian tradition, reclaiming visionary islands in the Atlantic from the inhabitants of Otherworld.[5]

Nor are beliefs about the wilful side of the sea so alien to European culture in modern times. In the late nineteenth century my great grandfather's people, fishermen of the Shetland Islands north of mainland Scotland, were following practices which echo those of Australia's northern sea peoples. As historian John Drever recorded in the late 1930s, when the Shetland Islanders went out to the deep-sea fishing grounds (known as the *haaf*), they were silent about their destination, they avoided carrying ballast stones with white veins through them because white augured white-capped waves, and no one on the shore said 'Good fishing'. At the *haaf* they spoke a secret language derived from old Norse when referring to their gear and their boat. This custom was also observed by fishermen of Norway and the Faroe Islands and many of the words were of ancient Sami (Lapp) origin. The inclusion of 'old worship words' drawn from ancient Eddic poetry for sun, moon, sea, land and fire suggests a language with religious overtones.[6] In *The Tempest*, Prospero, following 'an auspicious star', raises a sea-storm that wrecks a ship, bringing all the men safely to the island 'inhabited' by spirits, to which he himself is bound. As the storm rages a wise old man takes comfort from his sense that they will not die because the boatswain 'hath no drowning mark upon him'.

Those who sailed the oceans from Europe in the last few centuries were often driven by social changes in the Old World. From the 1820s onwards, seacraft reliant on wind and current began to be supplanted by steam-driven vessels. Yet despite tumultuous changes in Europe which created territorial seas around sovereign states and turned land into real estate, the consciousness of European mariners and immigrants invites comparison with the conceptions of those they supplanted in the new lands. Many seafarers and writers of prose and poetry in the eighteenth and nineteenth centuries experienced the sea as a potent force, a living being. European sailors respected what Joseph Conrad called 'the infinite power of the sea', drawing upon its strength yet mindful of its caprices. In *The Mirror of the Sea* Conrad captures eloquently the awesome beauty and deadly playfulness of the ocean during the sinking of a brig. First there came a slight swell so smooth as to resemble 'the graceful undulation of a piece of shimmering grey silk shot with gleams of green'. Then in an 'overwhelming heave of its silky surface . . . a smother of foam broke out ferociously'.[7] A smooth swell ran out from the horizon and the brig disappeared.

In the traditions of saltwater peoples in many places, whatever is dangerous to ordinary mortals may become negotiable through sacred chants and religious rites. The bridges of meaning people build to span the abyss may seem lightly built and fragile. Yet where there is danger there 'grows also that which saves', as Friedrich Hölderlin says in his poem, 'Patmos'. Overcoming danger in this way makes for resilient yet awesome connecting points; this is the realm of the sacred. The great seafaring Gilbertese peoples of Micronesia have sacred sea chants that must be learnt only on the sea. Of such grave and profound import is their subject matter that men lower their voices when they say the secret names of the seaways.[8]

In tropical Australia the sea journeys of sacred beings and their teachings told in song, in narrative and in religious ceremony helped to shape people's lives. Their own sea journeys and their journeys of the imagination fashioned and gave depth to their ways of being human. Today many of the saltwater peoples have accepted new ideas. On my own long journey, I came to understand and admire the resilience of their values, to appreciate how creative some people are in finding renewed expression of their spirituality.

I am sitting learning again in Thursday Island, December 1979. This time my teacher is Harry Captain, an old blind man with a clear mind, from Erub–Darnley Island. He comes from a line of people with the power to read the signs in sea and sky and say, 'Don't go out to sea today. It looks like trouble somewhere.' Harry had just given me a cone-shell (*wauri*), a talisman which sealed across-sea friendships through the power of the sea god Malo. 'When the mission boat *Surprise* arrived in 1871 my grandfather was there waiting,' said Harry, 'He knew in his heart something important was going to happen. New ways of accepting God.'

To outsiders who visited the Torres Strait Islands in the period following the arrival of the *Surprise* and the London Missionary Society — 1871 until the 1970s — Christianity appeared to have completely supplanted old belief systems. Yet, as we will see, in the period of cultural renaissance in the 1970s and 1980s, Islanders reassessed their pre-Christian religious beliefs which had been suppressed and 'forgotten' in the name of a civilising mission. As Meriam priest, Reverend Dave Passi explained to me in 1981, 'the truth is not easy to cross out, as every Christian knows.' I have found that the saltwater people who have sought to teach me about their beliefs are people of developed religious sensibility — men and women with both the sign of the Cross and the emblems of their ancient sea gods imprinted on their hearts.

Diversities

In owning sea territory saltwater peoples are radically different to the modern West. Their ways of owning marine areas are unfamiliar to the European mind: their sea property includes foreshore, reefs and sandbanks, sites of spiritual potency and seabed. It also includes the saltwater itself, stretching to the horizon or even beyond it. These sea territories belong to clans and other groups and these marine areas are not always extensions of clan land boundaries into the sea but may form a patchwork of 'plots' of sea belonging to different groups. In all these respects and probably others, saltwater people's ownership patterns vary from one group to another, even though they follow the same basic principles.

The saltwater people's homes are built upon the land, but their founding figures are creator beings of the saltwater worlds, usually sea creatures whose tracks mark out their sea territories. At Groote Eylandt in the Gulf of Carpentaria, the land is linked with the sea by a founding narrative relating the journeys of the Dreaming figure, Tiger Shark. The sweeping movement of Tiger Shark's tail created bays and inlets. On his journey he encountered less powerful sea creatures, like Porpoise. The narrative links the place he killed Porpoise, and the island to which each of them originally swam from the mainland. Upon death Porpoise was transformed into a rock, at the same time creating other natural features around the area.[9] In this way Tiger Shark's spiritual strength finds expression in sites invested with spiritual potency.

In varying degrees, all the saltwater peoples were, and remain, mobile: the seacraft they made or procured took them further than they could go by foot, and by rafting or rowing they moved with the sea. Seacraft in different places varied greatly: rafts of mangrove wood in waters off the Dampier Peninsula and sewn bark canoes off the coast of present-day Northern Territory. On the coasts of northernmost Cape York Peninsula and the Torres Strait there were dugout canoes, equipped with double outriggers and sails.

Osward Brierly was an artist on HMS *Rattlesnake*. He recorded in his diary on 16 October 1848 the ornamentation of a canoe *Kie Marina* belonging to a seafaring man named Manu, one of the Kaurareg people of the islands of Endeavour Strait. 'I have long admired but never have I seen anything that realised so much the idea of beauty.' Maybe it takes an artist to appreciate an artist. He recorded its 'beautiful workmanship'. The bow sides were painted with red ochre and over the front there 'hung a string of large white cowrie shells' with long reeds trailing into the water, palm leaves hanging each side of the red-painted stern. He sketched *Kie Marina* and wrote down his impressions of the local sailors, their polished shell pendants catching the light as they steered through the strong currents.[10]

In times not long past the Sandbeach People of northern Cape York Peninsula, as they called themselves, travelled long distances in dugout canoes rather like that of Manu, made by their own craftsmen.[11] Like the Torres Strait Islanders with whom they fought and traded, the Aborigines of the Cape York seaboards were splendid seafarers and warriors as well as great sea hunters.[12] The Meriam people of the eastern Torres Strait travelled to the New Guinea coast and to the Australian mainland. They wore sacred cone-shell (*wauri*) armlets and pendants which they exchanged for canoes with their 'cone-shell partners', drawn from neighbouring peoples. The Meriam of the Murray Islands sailed far from home; in June 1841 Captain Stokes of the *Beagle* noted with fear their presence in warrior mode at Restoration Island, more than 300 kilometres from Mer.[13]

The various saltwater clans of the islands of the Gulf of Carpentaria and coastal Arnhem Land were great dugong and turtle hunters, as they are today. In this area hunting dugong was an especially dangerous, even perilous activity, undertaken only a century ago in sewn bark canoes. More recently, the Arnhem Landers made their own dugout canoes with skills learned from Macassan seafarers from the Indonesian archipelago. They fished for trepang — sea-slugs, known also as *bêche-de-mer* — in the waters of the saltwater peoples, and then with the permission of the Arnhem Landers, gathered on their sandbeaches during each northwest season to cook the trepang. In European eyes, even the dugout canoes were unstable: 'you had to part your hair down the middle to stop them capsizing,' said one of Prime Minister Curtin's secret bush commandos, recalling humorously his wartime experience of these boats.[14]

There are major differences in custom between one saltwater people and another. For example, Meriam people of eastern Torres Strait 'farm' the sea, building unique crayfish-raising houses and growing seed clams. The peoples of the western islands of the Torres Strait built 'dugong platforms', from which they deftly roped and then speared dugong. The saltwater country of each group of associated clans varies; it may extend many kilometres inland to country where the rivers cease being tidal and salty. Or, as at the island of Mer, itself totalling only several square kilometres, there may only be some metres of saltwater vegetation inland from the high-water mark.

Similarities

DESPITE THE RICH DIVERSITIES AMONG THE SEA TRADITIONS and beliefs of the saltwater peoples of tropical Australia, four common features stand out.[15] The main one is that their spiritual inheritances from the sea link living saltwater peoples with creator spirit beings, sea gods and culture heroes, whose sea journeys mark out marine territories and who remain ongoing presences. For example, when the Yanyuwa people of the Sir Edward Pellew group of islands on the western side of the Gulf of Carpentaria say, 'We are people who originate in the sea,' they mean they are 'people whose spiritual and cultural inheritance comes from the sea'.[16] That inheritance is the Law which endows them with a responsibility to respect the sea, to follow the paths and marks set down by ancestral figures, to pass on the sacred clan designs to descendants, to protect sacred places in the sea and on the shore, and to maintain balance and reciprocities between clans. The 'Law is first for us,' a senior Jawi man emphasised in his evidence for a native title claim in 1999.[17]

A second feature is the saltwater people's special knowledge about the ecology of their natural habitat. As sea hunters and collectors of seafood the saltwater peoples know the rhythms and patterns of movement in the sea. They are guided by a set of marks in sea and sky derived from the movements of tides, currents, winds, fish, sea birds, underwater luminescence, celestial bodies, and the interrelationships between all these at different times of the year, the month and the day. The ebb and flow of tides, the movement of winds and currents in the sea are associated with paths followed by celestial bodies. For example, the rising of Orion and the Pleiades signifies renewal: for Yanyuwa people this is the cue that certain sea creatures will be feeding near the shore; for the Torres Strait Islanders in the days of canoe travel, it meant that the time was ripe for voyaging. The Bardi and Jawi people's detailed knowledge of the local tidal currents enables them to distinguish what they call 'roads' in the sea. These depend on the movement of the tidal currents, which the people know and can name, some twenty of which lie between the Dampier Peninsula and Sunday Strait. In rafts made of mangrove wood, they used to move from site to site for fishing and collecting by riding a series of these currents.[18]

A third feature common to the saltwater peoples is their systems of property in the sea, today referred to by scholars as 'customary marine tenures'. We are speaking here of inherited clan-owned, saltwater territories that may extend across the foreshore to home reefs, fringing islands, coastal areas, cays and fishing grounds. Customary sea tenure is complex and many of its features are totally unfamiliar to non-indigenous people. The idea that ownership 'goes right to the bottom — and to the shore', as Croker Islander Charlie Wardaga puts it, is still easy to comprehend.[19] The reason the seabed is so important to him is because the Rainbow Serpent, a very sacred being, lies on the sea floor. But those brought up to believe that as a 'wandering thing' water is a gift to the public as a whole, may find it hard to grasp the idea of indigenous claims to the water itself.

The ownership patterns of saltwater country are varied: as others have noted, the resulting picture may be like a checker-board pattern of ownership by alternating groups as in coastal northeast Arnhem Land.[20] For Croker Island clans, their marine territories may extend 'as far as my eyes can see', as Mary Yarmirr explained in the Federal Court in 1997. Sea rights among the Yolŋu may extend 'over to where the clouds stand'. Meriam people's reefs and home waters — 'the sea that belongs to the land' — belong to each of eight clans holding sea territory in joint ownership or common property. Among the Torres Strait Islanders and the Cape York seafarers, sea estates extend far beyond the horizon: the Sandbeach People of Cape York Peninsula say their territories reach the outer reefs of the Great Barrier Reef. Distant cays like Ker Ged or East Cay, nearly 68 kilometres northeast of Mer, belong to particular Meriam clans whose nameholder bears the responsibility to share it with other members of his clan. For Bardi and Jawi peoples of the southwest Kimberley, very distant waters may belong to an association of clans — sea territories that they call expressively 'together-owning country'.

These customary marine tenures are the foundational structures out of which saltwater people's lives and cultural traditions are fashioned — their 'blood and body'. Among the Yolŋu, sacred designs in bodies of sea are bequeathed to their people by ancestral creator beings, and they are duty-bound to uphold, live out and, in turn, hand on these bequests to new generations. Yolŋu people say that their bodies of water 'talk to each other just like people'. Important ties like marriage and other reciprocities between clans create relationships between previously unrelated groups. A clan that provides wives for members of another clan may act as caretaker for a body of beach country or a body of sea belonging to their in-laws. Yolŋu Law man and artist Dula Ŋurruwuthun has likened this act of reciprocity by the caretaking clan to the lighting of a fire for the owning clan: it sparks and spreads creating new fires. An endless series of gifts and return gifts ensures the future life of the joined clans. Pathways between the owning and the caretaking clan are established and nurtured by intermarriage between the two. The Torres Strait Creole word *rod* or 'road' is useful here. It refers to two kinds of pathways: those joining places on land and sea, and to reciprocal or two-way associations between people.[21]

A fourth feature common to saltwater peoples is that although they pride themselves on their own traditions, they are also living and adaptive peoples, with long-standing relationships with other peoples, across sea and land. Many of their customs have changed, or have disappeared for a time as a consequence of invasion and colonisation, but some have been renewed. Take the example of the ancient fish-traps built by two widely divergent peoples. In Bardi and Jawi saltwater country in the southwest Kimberley and in the territories of the Meriam of eastern Torres Strait, ancestors built large stone fish-traps on the fringing reefs, an ingenious way of getting the fish to come to them.[22] The fish swim into these three-walled traps that extend out into the sea from the foreshore and are caught inside their stone walls at low water. The saltwater peoples of the Torres Strait and those of the southern Kimberley became involved in the pearling industry or, in the case of the Bardi and Jawi, were compelled to move to institutions and camps away from their own sea country. Many of the fish-traps fell into disuse for decades. Since the 1970s, the fish-traps have been repaired by the owners and their relatives. Today, people fish once more in the fish-trap owned by their clan from times before living memory, using fish spears similar to those of their forebears, but with metal rather than bone prongs.

In everyday life, these four features of the tropical saltwater peoples are often intertwined like the mesh of fishing nets, and may act as cues for one another. An example of the interweaving of the spiritual and the practical, and of the adaptability of saltwater peoples, is the sharing of the first turtle caught for the season. During the southeast season, a time of turtle scarcity, a collective rite involves blessings for the sea and the returning of the turtle bones to it. The Meriam say that their sea god Malo, who came to them in the form of an octopus, brought this custom, uniting their eight clans. After the missionaries arrived in 1872, the Meriam adapted this ceremony to new conditions and beliefs, moving the ceremonial site for this 'everyone together' turtle feast from the old site to the foot of the Cross beside the church. Prayers and blessings replace the old chants.

In the past, the Torres Strait Islanders and the seafaring Aborigines of northern Cape York Peninsula developed complex exchange and trading patterns which took them on sea voyages. Along the tropical coasts, Macassans and saltwater Aboriginal groups traded and learnt new ways. Now, at the beginning of the twenty-first century, senior people with responsibilities for sea country still look to their long-standing law and custom to help guide their future. Saltwater peoples live not only in face-to-face communities; they also live in a world defined and dictated to by globally-shaped market economics and electronic media. Many people see 'following in the paths of tradition' — an expression used by Bardi and Jawi people — as consistent with seeking new forms of economic independence.

In 1997 young Meriam people on Mer Island produced a broadsheet called *Maber* to advance both the struggle for the recognition of their sea rights and the community's commercial fishing project. Named after the sacred trumpet shell, its masthead featured a half *dari*: the other half of the well-known feathered headdress and 'national' symbol of the Torres Strait Islanders was absent. The missing half points to unrecognised sea rights. The central and upstanding feather of the *dari* comes from the frigate bird, a soaring bird of prey which arrives at the Murray Islands in the season of the southwest winds. On the headdress the feather is topped with a tassel of small white feathers. The straight feather signifies the strength of the sea — 'a tower of strength'. George Kaddy, a senior Meriam, explained to me the meaning of *dari* and the sea: 'When the dancer wearing *dari* does the dance he is already a part of the sea.' The white tassel at the very top is the foam formed by currents and winds on wind-torn waves.

EACH SALTWATER GROUP IS REMARKABLE FOR ITS ingenuity in meeting the demands of a particular environment. Salt waters and fresh waters — sea and land — and the creatures that belong to each are different in nature. Inshore salt waters and open seas have their own distinctive characters, as do different peoples. The two major Yolŋu groups known as moieties have their own distinctive 'natures' and so do the clans. To bring disparate bodies of water, of land, and of peoples together may seem a daunting task. But Yolŋu are keen observers of their world: they see salt waters and fresh waters swirling at the river mouths, spreading forth as two separate streams that never fully merge into one another, yet travel together. The movements of such duos are a metaphor for their life's design. In his life story published in 1987, the late Wandjuk Marika, a Yolŋu leader and a custodian of the sacred beach known as Yalaŋbara, explains how people along the coast tell 'exactly the same story' as he tells. Through the creation story, the sacred matters of each, they travel together.[23] In Marika's scheme of things they are like kinfolk.

3
Seascape and Memory

Remembering the sea

The following recollection comes from a Larrakia man of the Darwin area in the course of a land claim first made in 1979. An elder had accompanied a young boy to his home island where the elder and other senior men instructed him on matters of spiritual significance and hunting practice. The pupil later recalled the words of the elder: 'You get to keep that [knowledge] in your mind and in your heart, to keep on remembering it you draw it in the sand,' so he could pass on the knowledge to the coming generation.[1] The Larrakia people of the Darwin area and the Kenbi chain of islands nearby are seaboard people. In 1936 the Acting Chief Protector, W. B. Kirkland, described them as 'naturally salt-water people'.[2] Perhaps more than any other of the saltwater peoples described in this book the Larrakia were dispossessed. They were pushed to the fringes of their country as the city of Darwin grew.

Populations declined, they were moved from camp to camp, some of the children became inmates of institutions. Yet they kept returning to their islands and seafront country.

Today the Larrakia cling to generations-old traditions, to the narratives of the creator figures who swam or walked the paths that came to define their territories and themselves. Their 1970 claim to a section of waterfront known as Kulaluk in the Darwin suburbs may well be the first claim to sea country made along the tropical coast of Australia.[3] Larrakia memories of seascape carry intense feeling and emotion. They are about living connections with the sea and with one another, connections which are often changing. The past is continually being transformed as it becomes their present.

In his book *Arctic Dreams*, Barry Lopez evokes the vibrancy of Inuit–Eskimo attachments to their landscapes and seascapes. What it is to be an Inuit does not finish at the skin; it extends out into the landscape and seascape. It seemed to Lopez that they were attached to their country as if by luminous fibres. To cut them, he says, would cause physical pain and a sense of dislocation. This also rings true for the saltwater peoples of the tropical coasts. The way Larrakia people's traditions and sense of identity have survived their tragic circumstances is a poignant testimony to the enduring strength of those bonds.

From the 1970s onwards the coastal and island peoples of Australia began to affirm their feelings for the sea in public settings. What the poet Samuel Coleridge called 'reliques of sensation' may be helpful in understanding the strength of memories that carry intense feeling. These, Coleridge says, 'may exist for an indefinite time in a latent state, in the very same order in which they were originally impressed'.[4] Is the Larrakia elder's injunction to the younger man to keep the knowledge he gave him and live by it drawn from memory of this kind? Have memories of place and identity endured because these attachments carry intense feeling and lie close to the skin, as Lopez says about the Inuit?

'Seascapes of memory', as I call them, are dynamic; they relate to often hidden tradition which is brought to the surface at times of testing or of cultural renaissance. Memories may lie close to the surface and be easily accessible. Or, as Irish writer John Banville has written in *The Untouchable*, 'pieces of lost time [may] surface suddenly in the murky sea of memory, bright and clear and fantastically detailed'. Memory, Inga Clendinnen wrote in her memoir *Tiger's Eye*, may have the elusiveness of an eel. However, during moments of a serious illness, Clendinnen had the experience of living pieces of memory breaking forth like volcanic fragments.

In the era of *terra nullius*, people were often pressured to forget. Relaxation of that pressure may release fragments of lost time; suppressed memories may gather together like bubbles rising to the surface of a glass in a surging foam. In the final quarter of the twentieth century, knowledge of places, kinfolk, stories, language about which people had been silent, often came to the surface clear and bright. Since the 1992 *Mabo* decision recognising native title to land, native title claims have begun to tap rich stores of knowledge, belief and experience. What came to light in the 1999 land–sea native title claim by Bardi and Jawi people of the southwest Kimberley was the finely grained detail of the memories of cultural leaders and land–sea owners, especially of creation sites.[5]

There are some memories people would like to forget and with others, only persistent effort will bring them to consciousness. The narrator in John Banville's novel *Eclipse* speaks of the peculiarity of memory in fixing insignificant-seeming scenes in a fierce hold, so they resonate in a way 'rife with significance'. While the subject of lost or latent memory in the colonial situation has been little explored, I feel that these various aspects of memory have a place in any full understanding of repressed memory.

Terra Nullius *and the denial of memory*

SOME 6,000 YEARS AGO THE FLOODED NORTHERN reaches of present-day Australia stabilised. Around 3,000 years ago reef flats were formed in the southern reaches of the Buccaneer Archipelago in the far northwest of Australia and at the islands of Mer, Dauar and Waier close to the Great Barrier Reef in the northeast. Many beliefs and practices were passed on through the period of colonisation, to the beginnings of a cultural renaissance in the 1970s and the native title era. The sea frontiers became places of special conflict and change in the nineteenth and twentieth centuries. The ravages of the pearling and trepanging industries for several decades before 1871, when missionaries arrived in Torres Strait, left the northern seaboard peoples desolate and dwindling in number.[6]

All the saltwater peoples have experienced colonisation. As 'remote Aborigines and Islanders' many of them managed to go on fishing and many of them continued to live on their homelands by the sea. However, they were not 'let be'. The sea peoples were brought together by government and missionary authorities at places along the coast, some of which belonged to other clans; some groups were placed on 'reserves' with other saltwater people, others with inland groupings, often with their traditional enemies. Some of them were drawn into towns and centres because their existence outside them had become uncertain and the centres offered hope of government rations. 'Coming in', this process came to be called. Others were moved away from the sea to cattle stations, inland missions and reserves. Some people were corralled within their homelands in the name of 'Protection' and 'Welfare'. Many people were forbidden to perform their religious ceremonies or sing their sacred chants and were sent to church and to school; yet, as the records show and people recall today, at least in the half century following federation of the Australian states in 1901, the schooling process was restricted to imparting the '3Rs'. For example, the state school at Mer–Murray Island was equal to any other state school in Queensland in the late 1890s; but on 30 January 1903 it was deregistered and soon replaced by an 'Aboriginal school' with only a very elementary syllabus.[7] Saltwater peoples were not to escape cultural colonisation; even in the 1980s Yanyuwa children at the township of Borroloola were punished for speaking their mother tongue in the school grounds.[8] Children of some coastal people were taken from their families by welfare bodies. I remember poignantly the story of Nicholas Wymarra, a light-skinned boy from a coastal site near the tip of Cape York. Nicholas escaped being taken away by government officers because his Aboriginal family blackened his skin with charcoal. His children's recollections hold a note of triumph.

In December 1979 I was sitting in the community canteen at Injinoo in northwestern Cape York sipping beer with landowner Snowy Woosup and his wife, Sepi. Injinoo people had suffered terribly — not only in the past. Even when I first met people at Injinoo it seemed as though hope had been extinguished. They told me the inside story of how their parents and grandparents had gathered together at Injinoo before the 1920s. Since that time they had become forgotten people. Now in the late 1970s a cultural renaissance was beginning. Elders, community leaders and families were enlisting the help of 'trackers' of lost names, lost places, lost language. Morale had begun to rise. Fresh footprints could be seen now along the beaches as people returned to Injinoo. People were recounting their memories of tragedies, of spiritual strength, of unwritten conflict with pastoralists. I felt impelled to write their story and that of the

Kaurareg, their neighbours across Endeavour Strait; in 1992 these stories appeared in *Footprints along the Cape York Sandbeaches*.

Before colonisers arrived the saltwater peoples had battles with 'hostile' clans. In the wake of those battles they forged trading and marriage links with their neighbours. The British invaders came with imperial aims and with the firepower to enforce self-proclaimed rights to Aboriginal lands and seas; this brought change of a qualitatively different kind to any experienced previously: the authority of the state over land, sea and peoples. The colonisers reinscribed the land and sea of Australia with their own names and memorials; they were generally unmindful of the inscriptions of the first peoples. *Terra nullius*, 'empty land' belonging to no one, was expanded: the inhabitants were nobodies with a barbaric past. This denial of their social existence meant the denial of their memory. Traditional ways of owning the seas and beaches along the coasts were rarely acknowledged, even less were they the subject of negotiation. However, with faint regard for consistency, the colonial authority sometimes bought or leased land adjoining the sandbeaches. For example, in September 1913, the Queensland government paid 60 shillings to the traditional owners for three portions of land at Mer–Murray Island, Torres Strait.[9]

For up to 120 years, a new calendar intruded upon the traditional one, and timetables with alien rhythms came to predominate. In parts of the Torres Strait, well before the end of the nineteenth century, new calendars relating to school, church and work on pearling luggers competed with the old seasonal and tidal calendars of life. Within three generations the beautifully crafted canoes like Manu's *Kie Marina* were gone. The sea people of that area worked on pearling cutters and luggers, some as independent producers, most of them as divers. The vast customary exchange networks — the cone-shell voyages to the New Guinea coast — were compulsorily ended by Customs rules soon after federation of the Australian states in 1901.[10]

Along the coasts the seacraft changed. Today people travel in metal dinghies with outboard motors. Many people, in the Torres Strait especially, own crayfish and other fishing boats equipped with modern instruments and fishing gear. In one sense the metal boats are symbols of a change so radical that saltwater people appear quite different from their forebears. Yet unbroken threads join the present with the past. Ceremony did not die, it altered; new songs were composed; dances about the sea were choreographed afresh; children learnt to fish with nylon lines and metal hooks; dugong spears remained supreme.

While the colonisation of the saltwater peoples followed the same basic pattern as the process inland, there were two main differences in respect to the colonisation of land and sea with enduring effects. First was that in the eye of the coloniser, the marine domain was, unlike land, unownable space. The freedom to fish, enshrined in the English common law, brought saltwater industries to the tropical coasts. And it did so in the belief that the territorial seas are open to everyone.

The second difference was that, while initial encounters at the sea frontier were often tempestuous, large stretches of northern coasts and islands became backwaters, little valued by the settlers. In 1959 one anthropologist wrote of how the Yolŋu, who inhabited country in northeast Arnhem Land considered inaccessible by the settlers, still retained 'much of their traditional culture'.[11] A similar situation appeared to exist along the coasts and islands of western Arnhem Land, perhaps surprisingly because it was country with regular and appreciable rainfall. Although this lack of interest by European settlers allowed the local inhabitants to follow many of their traditions, they were pressured to change in several ways. In the Torres

Strait region and on the northwest coast of Western Australia, men and women became labourers in the pearling industry. Nonetheless, for the first couple of decades of the twentieth century the Torres Strait Islander pearlers retained considerable independence, purchasing their own boats and making their own decisions. Islander leader George Mye recalled this era to me, in 1979, as 'the good times'. He explained: 'In those days we were free. We took our [pearl] shell to Thursday Island and sold it to whoever we pleased.'

In cases where the pastoral industry pushed the land frontiers to the back doors of the sea people's territories — for example, in the Somerset region near Endeavour Strait — 'dispersal' and disease took their toll of the clans of the sea frontier. Older people I spoke to at Lockhart River community on the northeast of Cape York Peninsula called up their childhood memories of men being brought in from cattle stations in chains. The women and children had followed them. Urbanisation — in the Darwin area especially — led to the displacement and dispossession of the saltwater Larrakia people, who moved from camp to camp as the town expanded. After 1900 the saltwater peoples' lives came to be regulated and curtailed by racially discriminatory laws and practices known as 'Protection'. In its name, light-skinned children were removed from their families and placed in missions and foster homes, some of them to become part of 'the stolen generation'. In the Torres Strait, which became the focus of a pearling industry, the 'pearly gateway' to the Australian mainland was firmly barred to Islanders and other non-white people. In the worst times, however, during the 1930s, Torres Strait Islanders became virtual prisoners in their home islands, being required to obtain permission from the government representative to visit other islands or the coasts. Even in the 1950s and early 1960s the Torres Strait Islanders were subjected to 'dossier-rule', where the Director of the Department of Aboriginals and Islanders Advancement (DAIA) kept life-to-death cards recording wide-ranging details on each person in the manner of totalitarian regimes.[12] Finally, from the 1970s onwards, mining, tourism, recreational and commercial fishing began to create new economic priorities. Perhaps ironically, the bauxite-rich lands at Weipa in northwestern Cape York Peninsula and Gove in northeast Arnhem Land provided the context for claims to land, and, eventually for rights to sea territories.

However, for most of the period of colonisation the saltwater peoples of the Australian tropics managed to sustain themselves from seafood and land food. They eat 'just about as well as we do', visiting anthropologist Baldwin Spencer wrote of the island Yanyuwa people of the Gulf of Carpentaria at the turn of the century.[13] In the 1990s, the sea peoples of Torres Strait were eating at least half a kilogram of home-caught fish per day. Overall, the tropical coasts of north Australia are perhaps unsurpassed as rich habitats where terrestrial and marine environments meet. The coastal country of the seafaring Aborigines of eastern Cape York Peninsula is less subject to drought-induced good years and bad years than inland areas, as it is formed by a mountain range which runs for more than 300 kilometres almost to Cape York. Anthropologist Athol Chase and linguist–anthropologist Peter Sutton concluded that 'the complex patterns of plant communities, marine environments and animal life' of the tropical coastline offer unique opportunities for a varied range of foods 'which can hardly be exceeded elsewhere on the Australian continent'.[14]

The saltwater peoples had prodigious knowledge of their sea-lands. They lived within ever-present dangers — human, spiritual, elemental — but to outsiders they appeared well fed and healthy.[15] Whatever may have been the case in the past, in the period of invasion their spiritual and their physical survival depended upon their continued observance of rights and responsibilities to one another, to ancestral beings, and to their land–sea worlds. Colonial rule did not extinguish people's attachments to ancestral place, but among some saltwater peoples their knowledge of clan territories is lost and they have come to see themselves as a single landowning group or 'tribe'.[16]

As I mentioned, the Larrakia of the area near Darwin were among the most dispossessed of the tropical saltwater peoples. Yet their recent claims to native title to land have shown how their networks — many of them partially broken — were invisible to authorities and settlers. Meanwhile others, like the Yolŋu people, have found the strength and confidence to educate *balanda*, as they call non-indigenous people.

What kind of remembering?

THIS STORY COMES FROM THE MID-1970S: A SENIOR Yolŋu landowner of northeast Arnhem Land, Daymbalipu Munuŋgurr, was teaching *balanda* newcomers to the staff of the school at Yirrkala the principles of ownership and succession followed by his people. On a blackboard he drew first the course of a river, the mouth being the foundation of clans that are related to one another. Beside the river Munuŋgurr chalked in a tree. He explained: 'The roots of the tree are its foundation. People may be likened to trees. As the trunk of the tree grows and branches extend out and leaves grow from them, so groups of people grow.'[17]

The 'original foundation site' and the 'founding group' always remain the source and site of groups of people — both those who grew from this tree and those who attach themselves to it in the course of life through marriage. Munuŋgurr is speaking a foundational truth about his people's tie to place. In conveying a sense of relationship between people who spring from the tree and those whom he says attach themselves 'like the leaves' by marriage, he is speaking in a Yolŋu way of creating interrelationships. Because they bring together separate and often inimical groups, the power of these interrelationships is like a live coal of fire — a glowing ember. The key idea is of acting on behalf of a group or an association of groupings. The critical word is 'our'; even when a person says 'I am the owner of this land', he or she usually means 'I am the nameholder speaking for others who are joint members of our landholding group'. This ethos is quite different to that of individually based private land ownership, known as severalty in European law, where 'I alone own this land, and I may keep or sell it as I wish'.

The tree, with its roots, branches, leaves and clusters of neighbouring trees, is a felicitous metaphor because it points to mutually interdependent sets of rights and responsibilities anchored in particular locations and relating to defined others. The tree fosters a type of remembering that seeks to conserve and respect the structure — in other words, the institutions of the culture and the associated customs, traditions and meanings. As Meriam people say, if each person remembers his or her own business, the whole community is happy. People draw strength from the roots and branches of the tree, often in unspoken ways, and this becomes part of their personal make-up and memory. Remembering *on behalf of* a family, a clan, a cluster of associated clans living together as a community, ties individual well-being directly and indivisibly to particular other people and to particular named locales.

This brings us to a second metaphor used by Yolŋu — at the river mouth by the tree described by Daymbalipu Munuŋgurr, the swirling waters of fresh and salt streams meet. Here is the feature that marks the sea off from the land: movement. The seasons and the sun follow cyclical patterns, but only the sea has tides that flow and ebb. Movement of tides and currents, and the sounds they produce, are central to the life of the sea. For Yolŋu and for other sea people the patterning of these sea movements has special significance. In her study of Yolŋu sea cosmology, anthropologist Fiona Magowan observed that the patterning of movements derived from sounds, shapes and colours of the seascape and its rhythm are matched with one another and related to particular groups. These marks of particular groups may be represented in song through the names for the sounds of their waters.[18]

People live through events and experiences, but do not always fully take hold of those experiences at the time, creating what contemporary Irish writer Colm Tóibin has identified in his own life as 'frozen memory'. The combination of strong association to seascapes, to ancestors and to other humans may, under conditions that stir memory, be an explosive mix, emotionally charged, combative: 'These are not any white men's names. They are the names of my ancestors. I say Bazmet — my grandma's name.' These are the words James Rice, plaintiff and land–sea owner, uses to describe matters of the utmost importance to him, as he sits in one of his yam and banana gardens on the island of Mer, remembering. He is playing a traditional pan-pipe he has just made out of the bamboo he has grown. It is 1989 and he has recently given evidence in the *Mabo* case in the Supreme Court of Queensland. He explains to me how the strength of his totem was with him in court as he faced the Queen's Council for the state of Queensland, the main defendant in the *Mabo* case. He was claiming land and sea his father bestowed upon him, on behalf of his family and sub-clan. In calling on memories of his family tree, his sense of place is validated by the emotionally charged recollection that this garden land was given to his grandmother as a wedding present. He claimed these and other inherited land–sea territories against the state's claim that they are part of the waste lands of the

Crown. His eyes are round and glaring as he recalls to me how the strength of his totem, a warrior fish with sharp teeth, was with him during his cross-examination in court.

This form of remembering remains attached to the root and base of the tree of ancestors — the *giz*, as they call it in the language of the Meriam people. Remembering on behalf of others has become more vigorous because it has been suppressed or placed in shadow. In contrasting the 'us' and 'them' of the colonised versus the coloniser, the 'I' of personal conviction becomes the vehicle through which to act on behalf of a structure — the tree, its roots or branches. This is cultural memory.

The Reverend Dave Passi told me in 1980: 'It came to me very strongly in 1976. I'd become more proud of my culture.' We were sitting at his home village of Zomared, Mer, as he recollected how this new awareness came to him while giving a sermon in Cairns Anglican Cathedral. He compared the values he had inherited and those brought by Christians in the light of Christ's teaching and distinguished between the thief who comes to steal and destroy and the true representatives of Christ. A few years later these memories would bring him as a Meriam land–sea owner, along with his eldest brother, to make claims on behalf of their family in the *Mabo* case.

Seascapes of memory

THE LIVING CONNECTIONS OF THE SALTWATER indigenous peoples to the sea is imprinted upon them. This imprinting is rich and many-layered, and I can only begin to illustrate it. It is there, for example, in the way they configure their seascape through performance and song; that is, their songs 'speak' the seascape. Memories are condensed in story, in performance, in iconography, so that to sing or dance or paint or carve is to remember. The sea is esteemed in memory as living shapes and figures which often stand for humans. I say the name of a sea bird to a Murray Island woman and she begins to cry. I ask: 'Why are you crying?' She replies: 'Because the frigate bird makes me think of my father; this bird was one of his totems.' Her sister sitting beside her breaks into a song about the south-west wind blowing strongly from the sea, bringing the frigate bird to her home island, Dauar: *'I looked and saw clouds on the big hill of Dauar / But they blow* waumer [frigate birds].'

'Seascapes of memory' may bear the imprints of ancestral actions, but these are not quite the same as historical or personal memories in a Western sense. They evoke beliefs, emotions and images which themselves signify relations between people and their lands and seas. Elements of the seascape — sea creatures, sea birds, winds, tides, currents, waves — act as metaphors for ancestors and relatives. Where the frigate bird itself, or its name, calls up the memory of the father, a train of associations is set going which refer to a larger cultural seascape. As one student of musical forms has understood it, Yolŋu women's ritual 'crying songs' 'call up' kin through the names of the seascape.[19] We may understand seascapes of memory as the patterns in bodies of water etched by the journeys and actions of hero figures and ancestral beings who brought the Law. When traditions have been suppressed, along with memory itself, the creation of a new performance, song or painting becomes a way of remembering, of cultural survival and regeneration. Here are the words of a song of living memory composed by one Meriam cultural leader, the late George Passi:

> *Standing in my garden on the hill of Mer*
> *I thought someone was whispering*
> *But it was* maiso mir,
> *the murmuring of the Great Barrier Reef.*

IT IS JULY 1999 AND I AM IN THURSDAY ISLAND. I HAD explained to George Mye, a very senior Torres Strait Islander leader, what my book was to be about. 'Ah yes, "spiritual inheritance",' he repeated. His face lit up and he began to sing a Meriam song about a place they call Ker Ged (East Cay), which belongs to the Meuram clan of Mer: a place where the waves crackle with laughter as they break on the beaches. The song about Ker Ged is about rugged sea identity and its calmer opposite, but it is also a statement about ownership. In 1998 I had asked George Kaddy, another senior Meriam, how they weathered the bad times of his youth and manhood, and he said, 'by dancing and songs about the sea and winds and birds and fishing. That spirit in you allows you to disregard the pressure.' Another senior man rolled up his hands and unrolled them like waves unfurling as he sang about the sea. The energy of the sea people and the waves is repeatedly relived. In performance and song their repetition signifies a reaffirmation of important truths. Remembering is not random.

Historian Simon Schama, in his influential 1995 book *Landscape and Memory*, writes that memory may assume the form of the landscape itself. So it may. But landscapes and seascapes are shaped in different ways in different cultures. Seascape in Western thought is associated with a visual image of the sea and its representation in sea paintings. The word seascape often evokes the marine scapes of the Dutch painters of the seventeenth century, who in turn provided inspiration for the seascape paintings of English artist W. M. H. Turner in the nineteenth century. Turner was, above all, a visual artist who sought to reproduce the scene he saw. Some of his critics have attempted to reduce one of his masterpieces, *Snowstorm — Steam Boat off a Harbour's Mouth* of 1842, to 'soap-suds and whitewash'.[20] Yet his devotion to representational art was strong. Turner claims he had himself lashed to the mast in a stormy sea, not because mythical Sirens might weaken his seafaring resolve, but in order to convey authentically a sea scene of vortex and void, of non-location in the midst of wonder and terror.

Nevertheless, for all their aesthetic appeal, Turner's paintings can only represent one way of imagining seascape. Cross-cultural explorations of seascapes are only beginning. There is a need to reshape and expand our understanding of seascape, and to locate the traditions of peoples whose lives speak the movement, the sounds, the vibrancy and strength, the cross-currents of the sea. The shapings of the sea that Yolŋu artist Dula ŋurruwuthun depicts are very different to a seascape visualised by Turner or Cezanne. 'The landscape thinks itself in me,' Cezanne wrote.[21] He saw his task as one of grasping the landscape in its totality, of recapturing its structure through widened eyes — 'caught alive in a net' from which nothing could escape. I think of Turner strapped to the mast taking in the snowstorm at sea, missing nothing; he is seeing *his* seascape caught whole at a critical moment.

Yet there are two important differences in the way the seascape 'speaks itself' for Turner and the way it does so for the classical Yolŋu artist. The Yolŋu's creation is not the seascape 'thinking itself' in a purely individual sense, the way Cezanne described it. The artist as 'Law-man' or ritual leader is more like a 'vessel' whose creative powers are shaped, given inspiration and content by his Dreaming within bodies of sea in which he holds ancestral rights. Landscape and seascape are themselves living things and their topography and geography are shaped and given life by ever-present beings. Seeing and sight are merely 'moments' within a vast tapestry which bring all the senses into play; webs of associations of birds, grandfathers, stars or winds stand as metaphors for one another, and may act as signals for each other, so evoking a family of memories.

Seascape does not only activate personal memory. We are speaking not of the memory of a landscape 'out there', but the 'remembering' of a landscape which bears the imprints of ancestral actions. What Yanyuwa people call 'the road' is not something straight or narrow, but a neighbourhood; not a fixed boundary but a 'performance path'; not a single ancestor but a galaxy of travellers. Graphic depictions of seascapes and landscapes rely on metaphor, but in indigenous art the use of metaphor does not amount to free expression. Metaphors carry particular relationships of the culture: to land, to sea, to other people, to ancestors. The more serious the painting or the dance the heavier the load of meaning carried by these symbols. They act mnemonically, that is, as aids to memory, calling up layer upon layer of relationships to land and ancestors.

Seascapes which move, which have an animate nature, which speak to those who can listen, are one with human actors. Simon Schama praises the aim of recreating a living, active and creative nature from 'inanimate topography', but he withdraws from pursuing this aim himself as being too difficult to achieve. Yet the sea worlds of the indigenous peoples of tropical Australia have always remained animated. One large reef in the Sir Edward Pellew Islands is named Kaluwangarra by the Yanyuwa people. Anthropologist John Bradley told me it means 'they coiled the rope there'; he was alluding to a group of Spirit Ancestor Dugong Hunters who 'left a rope there of considerable power which is now a reef with dreadful currents'.[22] Coiled rope denotes strength and spiritual power; the dugong hunters are the human epitome of that strength, exemplars for others to follow. In colonial times, when Yanyuwa people's self-respect as sea people was placed in question, the traditions of their great sea hunters acted as a beacon to them.

Gateways to lost memories

In *Landscape and Memory* Simon Schama brings to life a shadowed world, marking out a track of new memories of things past. He takes the reader along a path of rediscovery of lost traditions where, as a 'curious excavator of traditions', the reader discovers a clue which leads him or her beyond the commonplaces of everyday contemporary life into the realms of a hidden heritage.

Indigenous sea people, like their bush compatriots, were not recognised or respected by the colonising culture as peoples in their own right with worthwhile traditions. But the last quarter of a century in Australia has seen the stirrings of a cultural renaissance: memories of suppressed selves have found expression in statements of commitment which have gone on to inspire action. In turn, this has prepared the ground for further cross-cultural understanding: 'They really care about the land. A gentleness comes into their voices when they speak of it.' This is Bill Kehoe, an experienced commercial fisherman in far north Queensland, reflecting on his experiences in working with members of the Aboriginal community at Kowanyama over the last twenty years. He recalls a community of people who have drawn upon their remembered traditions in caring for their ancestral waterways and land.

In identifying cultural differences, memory can uncover clues to a lost past. In European tradition the search for lost histories is often laced with a nostalgia for the more directly face-to-face existence of local community. Today, non-indigenous people's sense of a loss of tradition and their attempts to remake distinctively local community provide fertile ground for their re-education about Aboriginal people.

Anthropologist Howard Morphy suggested recently that even though indigenous and European people lived side by side and interacted for quite a long time and influenced one another in particular contexts, 'it can almost seem as if they occupied different conceptual space/times'.[23] The premises of their lives, as well as their conceptions, are constructed differently. Identifying cross-cultural difference in ways of being human, Canadian anthropologist Sylvie Poirier writes of an Australian Western Desert people for whom land is both sentient and personified; it was shaped and went on unfolding and revealing its own being through ancestral actions and human experiences. Her perceptions of Kukatja desert people, for whom the ancestral order is a continuing presence, is quite foreign to the dominant Western way of thinking and acting and, in turn, to Western territorial jurisdictions.[24]

Western thought about nature privileges detachment, not encounter; in this perspective, the sea is emptied of its sentient and spiritual character. Such detachment and objectivity produce a sea space 'freed' of story and memory; base lines and limits measure in a linear manner. In the history of European expansionism, this objective stance was intrinsic to a market-based view of the sea in which possessive individualism became the central cultural value. A senior Yolŋu points to a stark contrast: for non-indigenous people, he says, the sea is just for enjoyment and the dollar.[25]

Fortunately, there are mariners from the Old World who stand at a gateway between two outlooks: the developing nineteenth century European attitude of detachment, precision and measurement, and the vision of the romantic poets who evoked the magical–religious memories of the European past. William Wales, the poet Coleridge's mathematics teacher, was also astronomer and meteorologist on the *Resolution* during Captain Cook's second voyage. Wales' work was to keep an hourly account of weather and wind conditions and a detailed astronomical log. His special interest was the refraction of light from celestial bodies under conditions of mist, haze and cloud, a subject with major implications for bearings of latitude. In his seminal work, *Imagining the Pacific*, art historian Bernard Smith concludes that Wales' own sense of wonder at the creation of haze through winds and weather in the tropics was able 'to awaken or strengthen in his pupils an awareness of the wonder and beauty of the heavens'.[26]

Coleridge's great sea poem, *The Rime of the Ancient Mariner*, was composed soon after Cook's second voyage. Bernard Smith has explored the debt owed by the poet to the voyage of the *Resolution*. He concludes that it was Wales who provided Coleridge with the theme and story of *The Ancient Mariner*, although it was Wordsworth who suggested the theme of the dead albatross to him. Albatrosses were shot during Cook's second voyage and perhaps Wales transmitted his sense of revulsion about this to Coleridge the pupil. Smith suggests that the source of the poem's magnificence may be found in the stirring of 'unconscious memory' in the poet, calling up an ancient belief that to shoot the 'good luck' sea bird is to invite retaliation from the sea.[27] The world of the saltwater peoples of the Australian coasts can be better understood by a mind sensible to the strange, the supernatural. The ancient navigator enters a world of wonder and mystery: whirling pillars, waterspouts and whirlpools, darkness, are called up by the spirits of the dead. Are ill-omens attendant upon the wanton destruction of the great sea bird?

In important ways, Matthew Flinders stands at the same gateway as William Wales. A detached observer, recorder and charter of sea, heavenly bodies and winds, Flinders also displayed the capacity to wonder and marvel at the elegance, the skill and attunement to the sea of the sailors of the Torres Strait, who skimmed dangerous, reef-strewn waters in their slender, lightly built seacraft. He charted the coasts of the land he named *Terra Australis* in a manner which left little to do for those who followed him. Flinders meticulously recorded altitudes, azimuths and angular distances of celestial bodies, compass bearings and time-keeper distances. This work was indispensable to the imperial project which brought invaders to the tropical coasts.

Flinders' own expressions of wonder at underwater tropical life were matched by his appreciation of the local inhabitants' responsiveness to the dress, the movements and the music played by the marines; and his sense of the local people's own prowess as maritime peoples is counterpoint to his work on the charts. The work of both Wales and Flinders was integral to the evolution of the detached, objective approach essential to the ascendance of trade and commerce which shook off the magical–religious stance and pushed the poetic to the sidelines. Flinders' introduction to his *A Voyage to Terra Australis* gives a reminder of the ascendancy of the conquering and colonising perspective: the British Admiralty, he says, had instructed him as Commander of the *Investigator* to open up 'fresh sources to commerce'.[28]

It is this objective stance too that leads people of the modern West to see those whose sensibilities 'speak' their sea environments as more lowly forms of life than themselves. The silence created by this view needs to be broken through. This does not mean we should romanticise people who themselves are anything but romantic, trouble-free, detached or harmonious. The everyday lives of the Australian saltwater peoples are intensely practical and their knowledge is applied; they are sea hunters for whom the violence of death is commonplace.

As the history of post-invasion Australia illustrates so poignantly, the European gaze, as it evolved in the last three centuries, is necessarily unreceptive to indigenous people's ways of accommodating the land and sea. It is the same attitude which placed in shadow those facets of non-indigenous people that historically bear similarities with the sensibilities of indigenous peoples of the Australian tropics. In the process of coming to understand indigenous cultures one may come to recognise what has been suppressed in dominant European attitudes.

PART III

SALTWATER WAYS

4
Living Connections

Inheritances

Saturday 18 September 1999, Casuarina. A clear Darwin night with the trace of a southeast wind. It is Darwin Festival time. Actors from Macassar, Indonesia, are performing the operetta *Trepang*, side by side with Yolŋu from Galiwin'ku–Elcho Island in northeast Arnhem Land. From the late seventeenth or early eighteenth centuries until 1907, Macassan seafarers from the island of Sulawesi set sail in their praus as the winds turned northwesterly, their course heading towards the coasts and islands of Arnhem Land and the western side of the Gulf of Carpentaria.

The operetta *Trepang* evokes the tempestuous voyage of a Macassan prau to the island homeland of the Yolŋu-speaking people of Galiwin'ku. The Macassans brought gifts of food, cloth, tobacco, knives; in return the Yolŋu collected trepang, the sea-slug known also as *bêche-de-mer*, for the visitors, allowing them to cook these sea creatures on Yolŋu sandbeaches. *Trepang* draws upon a Yolŋu song-cycle depicting Macassan times; in particular, an event tinged with melancholy: the taking of a Yolŋu bride by the captain of the prau to the island of Sulawesi, a thousand miles away.

Ties of kinship, language and custom are the legacy of those times which were brought to a sudden end in 1907 when Australian taxes were imposed on Macassan praus. This dramatic performance of *Trepang* is given intensity through existing kinship ties. The man who plays the captain of the prau and a senior Yolŋu performer, Matjuwi, are brothers; the captain's grandfather married Matjuwi's great grandmother, the Yolŋu bride whom he had taken to Sulawesi.

The older meanings being played out in *Trepang* in the grounds of the Northern Territory University are heightened as a new historical 'play' begins to unfold. In September 1999 Darwin became a shelter for victims of the wilful devastation of East Timor by Indonesian militias, as well as the point of exodus of a modern peace-keeping force from Australia and the United Nations. As the Saturday performance proceeds, the sun sets in a peak of redness and a fleet of warships sails northward from Darwin harbour to Dili, the capital of East Timor. This performance of *Trepang* is dedicated to the people of East Timor.[1]

The old Macassan voyages were timed carefully. They would sail out southeast from Sulawesi with the northwest winds to the northern coasts of Australia the Macassans called Marege', and return several months later with the trade winds from the southeast driving the praus homewards. The Macassans visited regularly and left important marks on the coastal landscape of Arnhem Land; groves of tamarinds, stone fireplaces and wells remain. Their visits wrought changes in the social relations and material culture of the coastal peoples of Australia's present-day Northern Territory. They also left indelible memories and

A scene from the operetta Trepang, *Darwin, 1999: the Yolŋu warrior is seeking to find out whether the Macassan captain is a ghost or a human being*

changed practices among saltwater and many inland peoples. The widening world of coastal Aboriginal people is registered in art forms. They built models of the Macassans' stone fireplaces; pictures of praus appear in the rock art galleries of Groote Eylandt and western Arnhem Land; and in Groote the sails of praus denote wind totems.[2]

Bodies and surfaces that shine and glisten speak powerfully to Yolŋu people. An example of the elevation of a shining object cast up by the sea — a glass bottle — to the level of a ceremonial clan totem can be found in an effigy of a square-faced bottle carved from solid ironwood and painted with a sacred totemic design. The bottle, seen by Yolŋu as coming from Macassan seafarers and thus part of the Yolŋu heritage, gives a particular clan the rights to this sacred design. A cross-hatched design represents clouds as reflected on the glistening wet surface of the bottle. Around the centre are small trepang, as seen through clear water, an emblem of Macassan times.[3]

The Macassan voyages to northern Australia strengthened the ceremonial exchange cycle among Yolŋu peoples, creating pathways between previously separate and opposed groups, an example of the power of religious rite to overcome enmity. Each Macassan prau carried eight to ten wooden canoes for use in inshore waters. The iron tools used for cutting the 'canoe trees', as the Yolŋu call them, came to occupy a very special place in the cultures of Arnhem Land and the Gulf islands. As items of ritual power and everyday use they created goodwill and lasting friendships with their neighbours. It was not until the Macassan times were over, a decade into the twentieth century, that coastal saltwater people began making their own canoes, some as long as eight metres. The preparation, making and launching of a new canoe became occasions of gift exchanges and ceremonial rites between different groups of neighbouring peoples.[4]

Dugout canoes have become emblematic of Macassan times, the iron tools they brought, and the new relations of cooperation between opposed clans that resulted from those associations. During a long foot patrol across Arnhem Land in 1935, anthropologist Donald Thomson saw on the wall of a rock shelter far inland the drawing of an iron axe of the kind which had been brought by Macassans to coastal Aboriginal peoples. As he remarks, these iron axes were valuable to the coastal peoples, and in ordinary life were parted with reluctantly.[5]

Today Yolŋu people seek again the economic and cultural independence they see their forebears as having enjoyed in the past. They remember 'the Macassan period' as a time of cooperation and trading relationships; a period which brought new ceremonial song-cycles and performance into Yolŋu religious rites and created a new identity. Even though the song-cycles of *Trepang* include songs about the abduction of Yolŋu women, Yolŋu today tend to recall the exhilaration of these 'Macassan times' when they had control over their own lives and their land–sea domains. Important here is the role of memory in self-definition — how Yolŋu see themselves or wish themselves to be. Looking back through the eyes of kinfolk from another culture is like looking into a mirror that reflects light rather than shade: because these men consider themselves brothers, the brutality of capture and retribution in which those relations were born may fall away in memory.

The connections between Macassans and Yolŋu are living connections denoted by kinship ties, shared words, living memories of renewal and enlargement of identity, of cooperative working and exchange relationships. Memories of these times feed a sense of honour and self respect, of an age of satisfaction and of cultural strength and renewal. Memories of the good old days are a little like the memories of diggers who 'forget' the horrors of life in the trenches and remember the mateship. Yolŋu look back wistfully to times in which they believe they were in control of their lives, trading and recreating themselves according to principles of reciprocity. This remembering, albeit selective, is not merely nostalgia. It expresses hope for the future.

The hopes for recognition of native title rights kindled by the *Mabo* case in 1992 have brought to light memories that had lain in shadow. The process of remembering 'lost' traditions was set in train in the 1960s and 1970s and has gathered increasing momentum. But remembering is not a static process. The way indigenous people remember is influenced by, even contingent upon, the needs they see in the present. Irish writer, Seamus Deane, sees both continuity and fracture in the way Ireland's history is remembered. In Ireland we are speaking not of 200 years of foreign rule, as in the case of indigenous Australia, but of nearly nine centuries. Deane believes that in Ireland the certainty 'that there had once been a traditional civilization which had been destroyed by foreign interference soon came to replace the memory of the actual past'. Belief in a continuous, repressed tradition was elevated to a hallowed, authentic and romantic level. However, the belief in a tradition is more important than the factual reality of its character, its continuity or its demise. Deane explains how their belief in a repressed tradition is a felt need among Irish people; it is real and powerful because it is activated by the present. Yolŋu memories of Macassan times also exert a powerful influence today, and whatever the differences, among Yolŋu as among Irish people, remembering tradition 'is an enabling idea and of its nature involves a degree of idealization'.[6]

Yolŋu memories are grounded in the extended range of their lives and influence that Macassan times brought about. As I mentioned, the scale of Yolŋu reciprocities with other Arnhem Landers widened. After 1907, when the Macassans came no more, the local people had to cooperate more widely than before in order to cut, craft and launch the dugout canoes they now made themselves and which had become integral to their way of life. Some men had to take on more hunting during the canoe makers' canoe labouring time. The range of sewn bark canoes is between 6.5 and 13 kilometres. The greater range of the dugout canoe may have increased the territorial base of saltwater peoples. For example, dugout canoes made permanent occupation of Groote Eylandt possible; they also made the far distant islands of the Sir Edward Pellew Islands in the Gulf of Carpentaria more accessible to the Yanyuwa.[7]

In the post-Macassan period the indigenous saltwater peoples lived their lives within new cross-currents: their associations widened on the one hand, and were restricted by the impositions of the *terra nullius* era on the other. The widened canvas of their lives included much more than glimpses into European culture. Their cross-cultural experiences with the Macassans helped them to interpret their memories and to situate themselves reflectively within this widening world. In due course, and in varying degrees, they became equipped to confront the colonising forces on their own terms. But while their ways of living and their sense of themselves were bombarded and fragmented by the processes of colonisation, they managed to a significant degree to live by the principles and knowledge they had inherited. Memories that foster pride in custom and local law are two-fold. They reflect and refract those webs of association with the sea that carry with them beliefs, knowledge and emotions. And they allow people to take hold of tradition in ways which give them the confidence and strength to meet current challenges: to stand on their own and make their future.

It is equality that makes possible the creation of friendships and exchanges within indigenous cultures. The Yolŋu remember the new 'valuables' brought by Macassans, but oral accounts tend to emphasise how Yolŋu ancestors were treated with respect by the Macassans — as equals. They believe the Macassans 'levelled' with them, a quality fundamental to their well-being, yet absent from the colonising process. Again and again, people along the coast decry the absence of this quality in their relations with authorities. 'All the [boat] crews don't want to work under someone. They want men to come up level. Everyone come up equal.' This was the late Iopelli Punuel, a Badu Islander of the Torres Strait, reflecting in 1979 upon his life in the pearling industry.

In 1983, at Lockhart River Aboriginal community on the east coast of Cape York Peninsula, the late Michael Sandy, a Kuuku Ya'u man, told me of the important changes which the hero of his culture Iwayi, Old Man Crocodile, wrought among his own people long before missionaries or colonial authorities arrived in his area. The very powerful Iwayi religious ceremony turned profane danger into sacred power. In bringing together the six groupings of the Sandbeach People of eastern Cape York

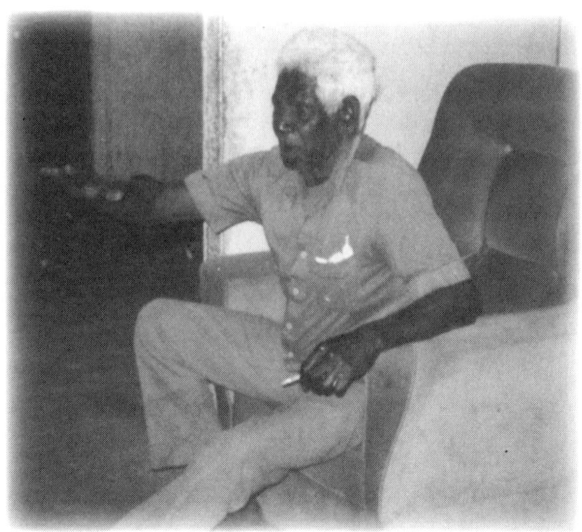

'They all come up level now': Michael Sandy, Lockhart River Aboriginal Community, 1983

Peninsula in a regional association, the Iwayi 'Hero Cult' extended the range of their lives, so making for cultural change.[8] They made voyages along the coast in locally made dugout canoes equipped with double-outriggers, resembling those of the Torres Strait Islanders. The transformation that these new exchanges with their neighbours brought about were described to me in 1983 by Michael Sandy, who had the inherited right to tell the Iwayi narrative. 'They all come up level now,' he explained, with a levelling sweep of his hands; in other words, the Sandbeach People and their neighbouring clans are like kinfolk.

'Not like Bush People'

THE YANYUWA PEOPLE OF ISLANDS IN THE GULF OF Carpentaria describe themselves as 'those people whose spiritual and cultural heritage comes from the sea'.[9] They relish the abundance and variety of seafoods available to them, they revel in the sense of freedom offered by the sea winds, and they identify themselves by making contrasts with inland or mainland people. 'Yes, I tell you this, these [are] people of the sea not that scrub country,' a Yanyuwa woman says of her people.[10]

Saltwater people's country consists of dry land, the marine territories of islands and the coastal fringe of the continent and islands off-shore. Their country may follow watercourses and tidal rivers to the point where they cease being tidal and salty. These ancestral land–sea estates, or territories, were owned mainly by clans, and to varying degrees today groups of associated clans and families continue to live their inheritance as sea peoples.

More than half a century ago, anthropologist Donald Thomson commented on the sea Aborigines of eastern Cape York Peninsula and their unsurpassed skill as dugong hunters, a dangerous occupation and one befitting 'a warrior people'.[11] Like the Torres Strait Islanders to the north with whom they fought and exchanged gifts, the Cape York seafarers sailed out to 'show the flag'. They carved sea-going canoes with double outriggers from local cotton trees; they also made bark canoes for river travel like those of the various peoples of coastal Arnhem Land.

Across the tropical north, life swings on the axis of the two opposed times of the year, the dry and the wet. Life is dominated by two main seasons: the time of the cool southeast trade winds from about April until August, and the northwest hot and rainy season from December through to about March, or even later in some areas. In between those two seasons are the 'pausing times' of the northeast and southwest winds. The seasons were decisive in determining the activities and the camp sites of Aboriginal peoples.[12] Thus, for example, the Sandbeach People of the eastern Cape York seaboard divided their times between sites at the mouths of river estuaries where they moored their canoes during the southeast season and the open beachfront where they resided in the northwest season.

Saltwater people's view of themselves is confirmed in the way they are designated by inland river peoples. For example, the 'fresh-water people' living inland from Yanyuwa country, known as Garrwa and Gudanji, see the Yanyuwa's saltwater country as very distinct and travel to it only in the more pleasant times of the year and in the company of Yanyuwa people.

Aboriginal people designate country in several ways; in its widest sense, by ecological zone. Yarralin people, a fresh-water people whose country in its manifold senses lies in the Victoria River district, classify country into three ecological zones: they call these zones saltwater country, riverine country and desert country. The saltwater country is located in the coastal fringe; it also follows the big rivers ending at the places where they cease being tidal and salty. Yarralin people also recognise the saltwater–riverine divide by various distinctive markers such as plants and soils. Among plants, for example, there is one particular edible tuber that distinctively marks saltwater country from fresh-water country and which, according to tradition, was deposited there by the black-headed python.[13]

In making these ecologically informed distinctions, Yarralin people are also making statements about where groups of people belong: because people 'go with' country, they are able to distinguish themselves from saltwater people on the one hand and desert people on the other. According to this understanding of country the Yarralin people's distinguishing feature is the abundance of fresh water.

Indigenous people also make a variety of distinctions between themselves which have no parallels in European classification. Older Yanyuwa see themselves first and foremost as island people: 'these islands are our real homelands,' they say.

They define the mainland as land which begins at the limit of the coastal saltpans and mudflats. These latter are still part of their saltwater coastal country and they feel at home there. They may hunt in the fresh-water margins of their country, yet, paradoxically, they call those fresh-water margins 'dry country'. For them this expression has the connotation not of absence of water, for this is non-tidal riverine country, but of unpleasantness and unpalatability.[14] In the southwest Pacific people of the Solomon Islands and Vanuatu make a similar distinction between bush people and saltwater people.[15]

The sea is most commonly used as a metaphor for the existence of saltwater people; but the sea culture of saltwater peoples is hard to express in ordinary prose — song and dance are its usual mediums. One observer recently wrote of the fishing and saltwater identity of the southern Kimberley peoples: 'There is a high moral value, a sense of righteousness in being a fishing person.' She noted too how, on every daylight trip she had made into Broome from the top of the Peninsula, saltwater Bardi people, on seeing the sea again after an hour or two of inland driving, would exclaim 'Aaah. Salt water!'[16] Marine foods are both highly prized and the preferred food of many coastal people; indeed, they feel their well-being depends both physically and psychologically on eating fish and other marine foods.

However, saltwater and inland peoples are by no means exclusive categories in Australia or elsewhere. Some people are, one might say, 'more saltwater' than others. The Torres Strait Island cultures exemplify this nicely. The largely non-horticultural Central Islanders are overwhelmingly saltwater people; the Meriam, however, are horticulturalists as well as saltwater people. The Sandbeach People of northern Cape York Peninsula are land as well as sea hunters. Even among the Meriam, where nearly all the inhabitants collect shell-fish and hunt fish and turtle, there are groups who are either predominantly gardeners or fishers.

The Torres Strait Islanders made regular maritime voyages for warfare, gift exchange and trading with the peoples of Papua New Guinea and the Australian mainland, while in pre-Macassan times the people of the Arnhem Land coasts and islands sailed bark watercraft for short visits and fishing.[17] When scholars speak of 'truly maritime people', that is, seafarers in contrast to 'intensive users of near-shore waters',[18] they often locate the 'truly maritime' societies of the region as those of the western Pacific.[19]

Many of these complexities have not yet been discussed in ethnographic literature; and scholars have noted a 'general lack of archaeological evidence for the genesis and nature of the bush-saltwater divide'.[20] A useful three-way classification with relevance to north Australia is: saltwater people with a mainly maritime economy based on pelagic fish — that is, fish living near the surface of the open sea; coastal people with mixed economies; and bush or inland people.

'Mixed economies' are very common along the north coasts. Saltwater estuaries may continue inland for 100 or even 160 kilometres, and this may be a contributing reason for a tendency within all disciplines, and in coastal management strategies, to blur the distinctions between saltwater and inland–riverine peoples. Moreover, the word 'bush' is used in two ways by indigenous people and others: to distinguish saltwater from inland country and people, and as a contrast with town in the sense of 'the area away from the town'.[21] It is also used in a derogatory sense to mean 'uncivilised', as in 'the boy from the bush' epithet. In making a contrast between food obtained from land or sea and manufactured food from shops, even dugong are sometimes referred to as prized 'bush' or wild food. One saltwater Yanyuwa man recalls how his grandfather remained a 'bush man', sometimes walking to Borroloola with a 'big mob of dugong on his head' to exchange with his relations for trade goods.[22]

Yet, as much as saltwater peoples continued to 'live their inheritance', they were also adaptable, as Yolŋu's relationships with Macassan traders indicated. Saltwater technologies have been modified over time and metal and manufactured fishing line have mainly replaced local materials. People added manufactured food to their diets and became more sedentary. They became wage earners; they learned to buy and sell within the market economy; their dress changed; their dwellings came to be made of manufactured materials; they came to worship in Christian churches; and some of them lost their long-standing language.

Yet the sea has remained their life-line. The Torres Strait people are a leading example: today their daily diet is partly supplied from land sources and food stores, but their consumption of seafood, obtained themselves, is still among the highest in the world. Two decades ago each person in Mabuiag Island in western Torres Strait was eating on average more than one pound, or half a kilogram of fish per day, a figure maintained for the Torres Strait area in the late 1990s. A three-month survey of the Meriam in 1998 found an average daily consumption rate of seafood as high as two-thirds of a kilogram per person.[23] In 2001, they still supply much of their daily diet from fishing. Currently in the Torres Strait nearly 1,000 dugongs and 2,000 turtles are caught annually by Islanders for their subsistence and ceremonial needs. In the same area more than 500 fishing boats of three to six metres with outboard motors owned and operated by Islanders are used to catch fish and crayfish for sale.[24] Children are taught to fish and by five years of age they know where to collect shellfish and the names of different varieties.[25] By the age of ten children have much adult knowledge of fish; for instance, they know that trevally is a landward fish and that Spanish mackerel feeds at different reefs on different tides. In fact, so important is fishing to Torres Strait Islanders that a child's first catch is honoured by a small personal feast.

Sea power and the power of the sea

ARCHAEOLOGICAL EVIDENCE SUGGESTS THAT THE SEA cultures of parts of north Australia reach back as far as 6,000 to 8,500 years. In that period melting glaciers flooded a major land bridge that joined the Australian mainland to present-day New Guinea, shaping and reshaping the contours of islands and coastlines. Between 17,000 and 8,000 years ago some 25 to 45 metres of land may have been lost each year to rising seas, and Aboriginal people today relate narratives of islands being 'cut out' by the rising seas.[26] The people of the Wellesley islands in the southern Gulf of Carpentaria tell of ancestral Dreamings which 'cut through the land to make channels for the sea'.[27] At least 60,000 years ago, in the era of Greater Australia, which included present-day West Papua–Irian Jaya and parts of Papua New Guinea, early immigrants made maritime journeys from Southeast Asia to the Greater Australian coast of up to 120 kilometres. However, on their arrival they did not develop a maritime economy or culture. While these first mariners appear to have settled inland, in places like North West Cape, which correspond roughly with their position before the sea level rose, there is evidence of occupation beginning there up to 34,000 years ago.[28]

It was not until 20,000 to 30,000 years after the initial water-crossing and settlement took place that coastal resources began to be used and then only fleetingly. A supposed route southwards from the northwest coast of Australia is suggested by current evidence, 'the inland water systems of the savannah interior regions' being 'the main drawcard'.[29] While the archaeological evidence is ambiguous, one line of thinking is that significant coastal settlement began as Greater Australia became more arid approximately 30,000 years after first settlement. Some archaeologists suggest that around most of Australia the islands were not incorporated into the coastal economy until a few thousand years ago, although this may have happened much earlier on the northern coasts.[30]

A little over 3,500 years ago — in the period known among archaeologists as the late Holocene — reef-flat systems were developing. Evidence is accumulating that the stone fish-traps which exist today both in the far northeast at the islands of Mer and Dauar in the Torres Strait, and in the Kimberley region in southern Dampier Land, may have been built in the period just following the reef-flat formation. While the exact dating of their building remains elusive, the Kimberley traps may have been built 1,000 to 3,500 years ago.[31] These fish-traps, made from local stone, make fishing wonderfully simple: three-sided stone walls are built on sandy, muddy or rocky inter-tidal surfaces and fish which swim into these enclosures become stranded there at low tide. Bardi people of One Arm Point near Cape Leveque say today that at low tide you can just pick up the fish.

In 1997, thirty-nine stone-walled fish-traps, in southern Dampier Land from Broome to One Arm Point, were noted and described.[32] Made from stones of 10–60 centimetres in diameter, their construction varied in form, from linear loops, semi-circles and right-angled structures to wiggly lines. Some of them link natural rocky outcrops, others serve as 'weirs' across natural drainage channels. They vary in formation from one trap at each site to complex patterns of up to ten traps adjacent or in proximity to one another. The traps at Mer and Dauar belonging to different clans are built on the reef flats around parts of the islands, forming a lacework pattern. In 1802, Matthew Flinders, observing poles upon the reefs, guessed they were somehow connected with fishing.[33] In fact, they are a novel device developed by the Meriam to stop fish congregating on one or other side of a side wall. Instead the fish distributed themselves in more or less equal numbers in the corners of traps 'owned by different people'.[34] In this way the Meriam contributed to maintaining peace among neighbouring fishing clans.

The fish-traps at Mer and Dauar are, it seems, integral to a maritime economy that may have existed for some 3,000 years. In 1999, an inter-university archaeological team found middens, or shell mounds, at Mer and Dauar containing shell-fish and vertebrate remains, including fish, turtle, dugong, dog and rodent. They indicate a long-standing sea culture. A pottery fragment dating to about 1,000 years ago and an elaborately carved bone pipe dating to about 2,000 years ago indicate extensive trading activities. The existence of the long double-outriggered canoe (described in detail by Flinders in 1802), along with the narratives of Meriam people today, and the considerable evidence of a customary maritime exchange system in the Torres Strait, are consistent with the preliminary conclusion of the Murray Islands' archaeological project in 1999 of a long-standing maritime culture with Mer as a centre of exchange and trade.[35] This is how the Meriam people see themselves: the late Sam Passi, a senior Meriam, told me with pride in 1982 how the Islanders of the central islands 'used to come here during the northwest season to trade fish, turtle, dugong, and go back with some land produce to take home to their families'.

ON MANY PARTS OF THE COAST, FROM CAPE YORK Peninsula to the far west Kimberley coasts, the Rainbow Serpent is a sacred being who united various local peoples. Some archaeologists suggest that the supernatural and sacred qualities of the Rainbow Serpent may have been born out of the turbulent land–seascapes being shaped and reshaped by tempestuous seas.[36] Whether or not this is so, the Rainbow Serpent took on a fully developed form in the rock art and oral history of Arnhem Land about 6,000 years ago, when the sea levels stabilised at the end of the Ice Age.[37]

The Rainbow Serpent is also a symbol of that season of the year when the monsoonal northwest winds blow. Among the Yanyuwa people of the southern islands of the Gulf of Carpentaria, the Rainbow Serpent is taken to be responsible for cyclones, waterspouts and rainbows. It is also seen as influential in regard to human health and is capable of inflicting a particular form of sickness. The Serpent may be harboured beneath the waves, themselves often depicted as snake-like formations.[38] It has dual qualities: danger to the profane and the power of transcendence. The Yanyuwa people sing special power songs to stop the Rainbow Serpent coming out on to the land. At Croker Island northeast of Darwin, the ancestral sea being, Ambij, identified with the Rainbow Serpent, lies on the seabed between two islands; local people all know this and are fearful that outsiders fishing in their waters may disturb Ambij by throwing meat or bone or other ritually dangerous substances in the area.[39]

The Rainbow Serpent is an important sacred figure in Cape York Peninsula but not in the Torres Strait. However, in both these regions the Dreamings — or Stories, as the Sandbeach People of Cape York Peninsula call their creator beings — travelled the sea, swimming, paddling, sailing (even transforming from a sea creature into a canoe during one epic voyage in the Torres Strait). They created features of the landscape and seascape, named them and established the Law. Some Stories or Sea Heroes brought together groups previously unfriendly to one another. The myth of Malo-Bomai united the eight clans of the Meriam people of the Murray Islands, who spoke a common language. The journeys of Malo across Torres Strait also created joining points across linguistic groups. The dugong Gelam who swam from Mua, one of the western islands of the Strait, eventually lying down in the east to become the island of Mer, is also known hundreds of kilometres away at a place on the eastern seaboard of Cape York Peninsula near Lockhart River Aboriginal community. Sam Passi at Mer and Michael Sandy at Lockhart River each explained to me how the story of Malo-Bomai is knit together with those of the Rainbow Serpent (Pai'yamo) and the culture hero Iwayi–Old Man Crocodile, at the Sandbeach People's country in northeast Cape York Peninsula.

Across the continent of Australia 'Dreaming "strings" connect regions', cutting across linguistic and ecological breaks.[40] This also holds true for the sea peoples, but while the same principles apply, the areas and the size of groupings so associated are often much larger; perhaps as a consequence of the extensive range of some seacraft. According to Michael Sandy, the chants of the sacred ceremonies associated with Iwayi, in the region of Lockhart River, have the same tune as those of the Malo ceremonies of the Meriam people of eastern Torres Strait.

These powerful sea figures have brought together many groups of people and forged friendships which are passed on from one generation to another. The Rainbow Serpent, Iwayi–Old Man Crocodile, Malo the Octopus god, and the Djan'kawu Sisters of northeast Arnhem Land who travelled across seas to neighbouring islands in their canoe and arrived on beaches to create fresh-water sacred wells — all are carriers of the power of the sea. The strong tides and whirlpools of the sea of the Bardi and Jawi islander and coastal people of the southwest Kimberley are present in the special songs and dances brought to individual song-men in dreams by their spirit doubles or other beings of supernatural origin. The late Billy Ah Choo repeats the words he was given in a dream-visit to a place in Bardi country: 'I cut across the tide which is full of whirlpools. A whirlpool catches me and pulls me down.'[41]

For the saltwater peoples, the sea is a living being, giving and returning, or refusing to give, implacable and retaliatory. People do not live simply in harmony with the sea, because cross-currents accompany its rhythms. At times the sea rages. Its movements, rhythms and patterns vary with winds and tides and the movements of celestial bodies. Those who live by the sea know it for its changing 'moods' as well as for its eternal repetitions. It has a subterranean life of its own: beneath the waves live sea creatures among sea trees, grasses, hills and vales. Like the terrestrial world it has a visible and an invisible side. As my first lesson from Flo and Fred taught me back in 1978, you must show the sea respect. You give to the spirits of the sea; they return your gifts of kinship and placation by protecting you from hostile spirits — the sea never takes you if you treat it respectfully.

Islanders Flo Kennedy and the late Fred Ware were recollecting the cyclone of 1934 near Cape Tribulation during this lesson. As a pearler at that time, Fred experienced the cyclone personally.

> FRED: Two places we put anchor down and 'e can't come up. Cruel sea (*very softly*). Very, ver-ry careful.
>
> FLO: That's why we Islanders never growl sea or anything. Not say anything bad about the sea when you're on it. Wind's like a person too. Even cyclone, we never call name belong them feller. We just refer to it as *Em* (*Him*). So. We never say because it might bring it when it's strong or when it threatens us.

FRED: We call it *zogo* [spiritual power], that's the one (*softly*). Like an eye. We only believe it's danger (*lowers voice*).

FLO: He said we treat it like *zogo*. We don't say, 'Cyclone, cyclone come!' We never talk about it. We don't call *Em*.

Among Aboriginal sea people a waterspout may 'tell' of some coming event of significance. As the Croker Islanders explained to an anthropologist, after the death of a senior land–sea owner in the mid-1990s, turtle hunting and fishing gear were placed at his grave: the first waterspout to occur after his burial would signify that he had captured his first turtle in his new life.[42]

AS A SOURCE OF HOPE AND OF SORROW THE SEA IS DEEPLY etched in the minds of all sea peoples from ancient times. *The Seafarer*, one of the earliest English poems, depicts the sea as a source of both sadness and hope. '*Sitting day-long at an oar's end clenched against clinging sorrow*,' creates an image of desolation and despair. Yet it is balanced by a hope born of the sea and sea life: '*Cuckoo's dirge drags out my heart, whets will to the whale's beat across wastes of water*.'[43] Nearly a millennium later the seafarer–writer Joseph Conrad looked into the mirror of the sea and found a hidden, capricious and not always governable power there, which 'seems to draw its strength from the very soul of the world'. That power, he wrote in his beautiful book *The Mirror of the Sea*, is held 'to obedience by the frailest bonds, like a fierce ghost captured in a snare of something even finer than spun silk'. Where those frail bonds are broken, the sea can be cruel and merciless.

The local sea people along the north coast of Australia hold the sea in high regard, although they conceive its powers in a rather different way to Conrad. You must show respect towards the sea, never 'growl it', that is, speak of its perils when you are sailing on it. Conrad saw the sea's caprices as a revelation of 'the mighty breath of the infinite'. The saltwater peoples of tropical Australia see them as the unassuaged actions of spirit figures with personal identities. The Rainbow Serpent must be sung back to stop it encroaching on the land. At the height of its power during the wet season, the Rainbow Serpent symbolises danger, especially danger created by rain and water.

Among the Yanyuwa the two words for cyclone are the same as those used to describe the Rainbow Serpent at the zenith of its power. As anthropologist and linguist John Bradley concludes from his long work with the Yanyuwa, 'power songs' are sung to transcend the Serpent's destructive power, to send it back out to sea. 'I sing your head, change direction. You who spins around and around, Away, away.'[44] The Serpent may be coiled up like the whirlpool, stretched out like the waterspout, or arched like the rainbow across the sky. Without its power 'turned around' and tamed, the Rainbow Serpent will destroy: tow boats out to sea, drag you down in the coil of the whirlpool, crush your boat by creating big waves. Putting yourself in its hands by negligence, insult or hubris spells danger and death. In Joseph Conrad's mirror the singular power of the sea is not located in a creature like the Rainbow Serpent. For him that mighty power is neither of a sea creature, a totemic being, or even a god; it is the infinite. Pitted against it are the unequal powers of humankind and their creations, where even the full array of the strongest ropes and tallest spars are 'but thistle stalks, cobwebs and gossamer'.

Yet as for the saltwater peoples in their seacraft, to Conrad the sailing ship is a living, sentient being, 'a sensible creature'. She 'will sail, stay, run for you as long as she is able, or, like a sea-bird going to rest upon the angry waves, she will layout the heaviest gale'.[45] The idea of a boat itself having the qualities of a living thing has ancient origins: according to the Great Babylonian Inscription known as the Hammurabi Code, it is grouped with animals.[46] In north Australia boats were imbued by saltwater people with spiritual power through song and chant; today in Torres Strait and the waters off Cape York, when a dinghy is being taken out to sea for the first time it is always blessed by a priest. A senior Yanyuwa man in 1991 said of the bark canoes and the canoeists of the recent past: 'Truly they were brave men and they knew many kinds of power songs. They would sing these power songs to calm down the sea and stop the wind. The body of the canoe it would be imbued with power songs.'[47]

The sea is the dwelling place of ancestral spirits and untamed, singular spirit beings who must be propitiated with power chants or 'spirit talk'. Some people have the power to listen to that 'language of the sea' and turn danger around. Others have the power to stir up those powers, to make waves form, to cause shipwrecks. These traditions within the sea cultures of northern Australia find points of contact in sea cultures of Europe: in the sea traditions of Ireland and arctic Norway, for example. I explained earlier how Shetland fishermen used certain old Norse words for their fishing gear, for celestial bodies, and for the fish when they fished in their deep sea fishing grounds.

Living connections

In 1978 I was invited to a wedding at Mer Island. It was my first visit to the Torres Strait Islands and I felt rather honoured. Three years later I was told that a 'cone-shell (*wauri*) friend' from coastal Papua New Guinea had been present at that wedding. I listened to the sacred sea myth which had, long ago, bestowed upon this visitor's forebears on the New Guinea coast the right which allowed him to be at this wedding. This myth tells of the journey of the sea gods of the Meriam people, known as Malo-Bomai, a narrative that symbolises their unity as one people. The Malo-Bomai sea myth is remarkable for its range and its strength. It brought former enemies across the seas together, closer than brothers; it brought together the eight clans of the Meriam; it gave them a law forbidding trespass, exhorting them to sow seeds everywhere, and giving sacred authority to inherited rights to lands, reefs and named seas.

Even more remarkable to me at that time was the assured, clear way in which Sam Passi, a senior Meriam man, told me the Malo-Bomai narrative and identified the 'shell friend' at the wedding. Sam's grandfather, the last of the priests of Malo-Bomai, and the first to be married in a Christian ceremony, had written down in English and in his own language 59 pages of Meriam myths, customs and gardening lore for Professor Haddon, leader of an anthropological team from Cambridge University in 1898. By the time the team arrived at Mer, the Malo-Bomai religion had been destroyed as an institution, the sacred houses had been burned, the long voyages they made to New Guinea and to Cape York had ended, and the people were reluctant to speak of their old sea gods or the cone-shell partnerships with men across the Torres Strait. While the evidence was contradictory, the old culture was presumed to be passing away.[48]

Yet here was the grandson with clear memory of knowledge handed down to him. In 1982, Sam Passi and Mrs Passi were sitting outside their home at Zomared village, Mer. Sam spoke classical Meriam language and excellent English. 'I read nature as my book,' he said, and this his father taught him when he was nine or ten years old: 'My father was very clever. "Come here. See this cloud here. This is the sign of first rain." It's written in my brain. Indelible pencil.' The first rain augurs the northwest season, a time to prepare the garden land for planting. So, too, Sam Passi's father held the old knowledge in memory. Sam also shares the white man's knowledge of evaporation by the sun drawing up moisture from the soil. As he says, he has 'plussed' the new with the old.

The passing on of the old traditions did not stop there. When Sam Passi was a young man, his grandfather said, 'Go through the laws of Malo-Bomai and you will know how to go about this world.' Sam went out about 1930, aged 19 or 20, to teach in schools; soon after, his grandfather died. Here is the narrative of the sea gods Malo and Bomai as Sam told it to me, as he understood it from his grandfather.

Bomai, Malo's maternal uncle, began his journey in the far northwest of Torres Strait in the shape of a whale, after leaving from mainland New Guinea, transforming himself into many sea creatures and also a canoe along the way. On arriving at Mer, he took the form of an octopus whose eyes shone like stars, and became the god of the eight clans of the Meriam people. Bomai combined into one the power of the sea creatures he had transformed himself into; in doing so he became the pinnacle of the sacred power known as *zogo*, the ultimate spiritual power of the Meriam. At the village of Las the pipe of peace was passed around the people in the presence of the god Bomai, so prefiguring a way of living together in accord. Dances were performed and chants sung at the sacred ground at Las. Malo — or Bomai, which is his secret and more sacred name — established a Law for all the clans to follow: it is usually called Malo's Law. The last chant for the very sacred star-headed club of Malo was sung as it was passed from one dancer to the next, symbolising the belief that the authority of Malo must continue.[49] Bomai's name, the Meriam say today, must not be taken 'in vain': if you spoke that name in pre-Christian Mer 'you wouldn't see the sun go down'. They didn't tell all this to the expedition from Cambridge. Nor did they say where they had buried the sacred mask of Malo, worn by a priest of Malo in religious ceremonies.

During the 1980s Meriam people began putting together fragments of their partly shattered culture into newer patterns; like a kaleidoscope shaken slightly, basic patterns can be transformed into newer designs. Malo had recreated their identity as one people by placing smaller entities under a shared umbrella. In making people friendlier across the seas, they 'closed ranks' within the island, creating what the visiting Professor Haddon called 'a new feeling of nationality'.[50] Through the Malo sacred rites the warriors were prepared for battle and for cone-shell voyages for gift exchanges and trade with neighbours. Through its message of universalism Christianity extended this relationship. 'Look at my hands, the hands of love,' the old priest of Malo is said to have told his grandson in 1930. 'You will find friends from Saibai to Boigu [the far western Torres Strait Islands] because of these hands of love.'

The Meriam are a sharing people. They recognise that quality as being at the heart of their culture. 'It is something deep within us that sharing,' Gobedar Noah, landowner, elder and religious leader said to me in 1997. They take sharing seriously. Share most in times of scarcity: this is the opposite ethic to the 'me first' imperative of individual rights. It is the triumph of sharing over immediate personal gratification. The *kopat* ceremony, which means 'Everyone Together', is the public sharing of the first turtle to arrive in the shallows or on the beach. It is a public display of generosity performed in the time of turtle scarcity, as early as May, so that more turtles will come in the turtle season which begins about October. There is a deep religious significance in everyone having a taste of this *kopat* turtle.

Senior Meriam people today say that *kopat* is the centre of sharing, that Malo made this sharing possible and that

Christianity strengthened the custom by making the clans more friendly to one another. After the first Christian church was built, the location of the *kopat* rite moved to the foot of the Cross next to the church. As Gobedar Noah explained to me in Townsville in 1997, the word itself stems from *kòp*, 'a sacred or spiritual site where people come together in a ceremony'. This ceremony survived the difficult times of cultural loss; its ongoing history has much to do with very fundamental cultural beliefs and values which Meriam feel are part of their human make-up.

In the current era, a wider awareness has come to play a large part in assisting cultural continuity. At first sight this may appear paradoxical. Reverend Dave Passi told me how for him Malo's message is universal; it expresses a need to be with the whole community, not just his own clan or family. In contemporary life remembering the Malo era suggests a capacity to compare and contrast. One outcome is that people come to see the Malo past as unique. Harry Captain of Erub Island explained the cone-shell friends of the Malo era to me in this way as we sat together in Thursday Island in 1979: 'If I give you that *wauri* [cone-shell] . . . you're my blood family. When *wauri* becomes known others will see it as one part the Gospel has left behind: "Be kind to one another".' This way of sharing — gift exchange — also throws light on the ways in which people confronted and resolved the paradox of Christian love and colonial containment.

As I mentioned earlier, Reverend Dave Passi, a plaintiff in the *Mabo* case, had compared Christian teaching and colonial appropriation years before the court case. In a sermon at Mer in 1989 at the peak of the court hearings, he drew again on the Malo tradition and Law: 'Malo says to you and he says to me and he says to the rest of the world: "Don't let your feet take you to steal what is other people's".' In these words Reverend Passi was telling the world that these were stolen lands. He was asking the

High Court to act in a moral way. And this is what the Court did in its famous judgment recognising native title to land on 3 June 1992.

Like the Yolŋu people's recollections of Macassan times, the Meriam people's memory of the Malo era is not primarily nostalgic. They are saying: We came from and continue to be a certain kind of people. We have a tradition and a religious law rather like the Law of Moses — Malo's Law. Witnesses explained this again and again to the court during the *Mabo* case. The Meriam freely tell people how their parents didn't teach them 'the bad side of Malo' — that part of the tradition where wrongdoers were threatened with death. However, like the Yanyuwa today who say likewise that their parents did not pass on the power chants, the subject remains a talking point. This 'other side' of the Malo era has become shadowed in memory, and the enabling side of the Malo tradition is to the fore. The sea god Malo, who appeared in the shapes of many sea creatures, told the Meriam to be kind to one another, and to share in times of scarcity. This rendering of tradition is enabling because it defines a strong people and gives them strength to win back their lands 'against the whole world'. On a practical level, it gives them strength to begin a money-earning community fishing project in inherited waters and to win recognition of their right to and responsibility for these waters.

5
Sea Dreamings and Seamarks

Echoes

You people stay at your place
At the land where you carry bow and arrow and club
I'm going back to Ker Ged
I'll put a collection of driftwood
I'll put them together, burn them
And listen to the crackling of laughter
Coming away from the waves
It's coming from the waves as they break and crack . . .

These are the words of a song about the cay known to the Meriam people as Ker Ged and belonging to the Meuram clan. The song was sung to me in the Meriam language by George Mye in July 1999 at Thursday Island. The song acts as a way of remembering, triggered in the singer's mind by mention of a spiritual inheritance from the sea. Songs of different groups mark the boundaries of belonging; where people break into song or dance they reveal the identity of 'us' and 'not us' — in this case 'us the Ker Ged type of people', who don't carry bows, unlike the people of Mer, who do. Song and dance and visual art about the seascape is not about the seascape as detached natural environment 'out there'; aspects of seascape become metaphors for 'us', for 'the ancestors', for the interrelation of kin and country. The Meriam song about Ker Ged tells what sort of people these clan members are by saying what they are not. Through the act of singing the singer is joining his people to the ancestral spirits at Ker Ged.

Sound and movement are woven tightly together in oral tradition. Seascapes are marked by sites and tracks of sound as much as sight. I think of Ker Ged as a mark on a map; the Meriam know it as a living force where the waves crackle and break as they spend themselves in order to rise again. The sea not only moves, but its movements create sounds and the saltwater peoples have names for distinctive sea sounds and patterns of sound. In the opening to this book, Yolŋu Law man Dula Ŋurruwuthun explains that 'the tail of waves' of a named body of open water is called Wulamba. Sounds thus named remain in memory, resembling and often becoming the names of places. The sounds of movement conjure up memories. In song and movement the Ker Ged people perform the shapes, the flow, the cross-currents, the breaking and crackling of the waves. In doing so their memories are taking the form of the seascape — its movements, its distinctive, regular sounds and the patterns that movement and sound create.

SOME SEVEN KILOMETRES TO THE NORTH OF THE GREAT Barrier Reef lie the three islands of Mer, Dauar and Waier, named Murray's Islands by the captain of the *Pandora* in 1791.

These three islands of the Meriam maritime people are no more than six square kilometres altogether, but the coral reefs that are part of their sea–lands cover an area some thirty times the combined islands' land mass.

The Meriam describe the sound of the sea breaking on the Great Barrier Reef in the language of Mer, Meriam Mir. The words for the sea's distant murmur heard from the islands echo the sound itself. *Maiso*, pronounced 'my-so', means 'murmur' and *mir* means 'words' or 'talk'. 'Whoo . . . like a drum. This is the sea speaking to you.' *Maiso* is very distinctive to Meriam ears and tells them lots of things: 'It's going to be calm weather. If the Reef makes a louder noise a big wind is coming. A bad time for voyaging.' Like the word 'murmur', *maiso* recreates the sound it describes. 'You murmur,' the poet Francis Webb says in a 'conversation' with the sea in his sequence of poems on the explorer Edward John Eyre.[1] The sea murmuring, the flight of sea gulls, birds screeching, the wind in the waves, foam and white caps, bubbles along the shore: these evoke the poetic and religious imagination perhaps universally. Among the Meriam these emotions and aesthetic experiences are placed within a framework of meanings in which the sea does not just speak: it speaks to *them*. Linguist and anthropologist John Bradley gives a beautiful example of Yanyuwa people's reliance on onomatopeia, where the word echoes the sound it describes. The word *karnkarn* describes the call of the white-bellied sea eagle and is similar to their name for that bird. Furthermore, it is the same word they use to describe the calls and movements of Dreamings in sacred songs and rituals associated with this bird. They call out these words: '*Crying out*, "Karnkarn, karnkarn!"/*White Chest feathers shining*.'[2]

When a Meriam person listens to the sea it may tell him or her something. George Kaddy, a senior Meriam man who explained to me about the Great Barrier Reef 'murmuring', said you can understand what the sea is saying 'when you're in the ancient path, where you walk'. He is talking about *his* patch of sea: 'That's where I roam. It's my stamping ground in white men's terms. Yes, my piece of turf.' When he 'stands' in his own 'ancient path', 'the sea is me and I am part of the sea'. His words may sound romanticised to Westerners; but this 'voice' of the sea is both practical — telling a person whether to go out or not — and sacred. The 'voice of the sea' is echoed in the sound of the trumpet or triton shell blown by the Meriam and other Torres Strait Islanders to make important announcements. This trumpet shell is known as *maber* (with a rolled 'r').

The seasonal round: Moving like the waves

AMONG THE YANYUWA PEOPLE THE RISING OF THE constellation named the Pleiades by the ancient Greeks is a sign of regeneration. '*Regenerating, Pleiades rocking in the eastern sky, Shining brightly, Regenerating*': these are Yanyuwa words of a song which people remember, according to John Bradley, although they do not sing it today. The rising of the Pleiades in the eastern sky in the coldest time of the year is a sign of seasonal change, a star signal that the dugong will be nearest to the shore, seeking the warmest shallow waters very close to the mangroves.[3]

The appearance of the Pleiades is also a special time of renewal among other saltwater peoples. Although the example I will give relates to the Meriam of eastern Torres Strait, similar seasonal calendars of four to six seasons are followed by other land–sea peoples in the tropical north.[4] The Meriam call the rising of Pleiades 'Usiam time', their name for this constellation. When Usiam (the Pleiades) appears on the horizon this is the time for yam planting, and in the past it was the time for the famous cone-shell voyages to the shores of New Guinea and Cape York mentioned earlier. In islands all over the Torres Strait, the Pleiades and Orion are part of the vast constellation of the seafarer Tagai. Tagai is seen in the sky by the Meriam and other Torres Strait Islanders as a man standing in a canoe; his left hand, the Southern Cross, holds a fishing spear; in his right hand is *sorbi*, a red-skinned apple-like fruit (*Eugenia*). The Meriam have a narrative of profound significance relating to Tagai. Tagai had a twelve-man crew, consisting of six Usiam (the Pleiades) and six Sèg (Orion), who ate the food and drink prepared for a journey. So Tagai strung the Usiam together and threw them into the sea; to the Sèg he did likewise and their images came to be set in a pattern of stars known as the Tagai constellation.[5]

Each of the seasons and changes of the winds give signs to the Meriam of coming events. Everyone knows at least some of them. Every Meriam child knows, for instance, that the Torres Strait pigeon will arrive from the northwest towards the end of the southeast season to eat the rich red plum known among Islanders as the *wongai* (*Mimusops browniana*) on its way to the northeastern side of Cape York Peninsula. From Mer to Boigu in the northwest of the Torres Strait, the Islanders share the legend: if you eat a *wongai* plum you will become like a bird and always fly back to the Islands.

The pattern of activities of all the saltwater peoples is framed by those seasonal movements, by tidal movements and the paths of celestial bodies. Meriam life swings upon the axis of the two great seasons of the tropical year. Their lives today are lived in part according to the following calendar.

About September, the winds turn in a northeasterly direction. New star marks appear. The constellation Tagai begins to rise. First Sèg, whom the Greek seafarers called Orion — he who makes water — appears on the northeast horizon at sunset. Then Usiam (the Pleiades) starts to rise. This is 'Usiam time' when the weather is good for voyaging and preparing plots of garden land ready for the main planting after the first rains. The sea becomes smooth, like a blue-green skin. 'Like grease', the Meriam describe its shiny flatness. The white caps have largely disappeared from the waves. Until the 1870s when a missionary burned it, a divinatory shrine on the northwest side of Mer would be consulted. Garden produce from the July harvest was prepared. Yams, bananas, sweet potatoes, were mixed with sea turtle fat, and then roasted, dried, placed in bamboo tubes and sealed. Water was carried in bamboo tubes. Power songs were chanted by the departing voyagers. Certain plants were carried in the bows of the canoes to ward off hostile spirits. Women and children were not present at the departure and did not sight the fishing gear. In earlier times it was not customary to say 'good luck'. Although a respectful attitude to the sea continues today, younger people will say 'Good fishing' to family members pushing off their metal dinghies.

Around October the wind moves round to the southwest. This is turtle-mating time. In November, turtles begin to lay their eggs on the beaches. The first rains arrive. The Meriam say: 'Have you planted the wild yam? Have you planted the shallow-rooted yam that spreads out "like an octopus"?'

The northwest season may be heralded by a rainbow-like sunset. The voyagers returned with new canoes and other gifts for Malo at the ceremonial site at the village of Las. The season opens about December, often with a stillness in the air. Thunderstorms follow. After the heavy rains men may plant up to 30 varieties of yam. There are champion yam growers amongst the Meriam and yam growing is surrounded by secrecy, ecological and magical knowledge, and garden lore. To be a champion yam grower is the height of honour among 'masters of gardening'. Its prestige rivals strongly the title of champion turtle hunter. Turtles are plentiful; people fish in their ancient stone fish-traps. The winds turn to the southwest again about March. Early vegetable foods are harvested.

The southeast season from about April until September is cool and dry. About May, when the shark constellation rises, the first turtle arrives in waters of the home reef area. An 'everyone together' feasting ceremony continues in contemporary times to mark the arrival of the much-prized turtle. Word of its arrival was traditionally sent around by blowing *maber*, the trumpet shell. Harvest time begins for yams, bananas and other garden produce. The peak of the Meriam religious calendar was reached towards the end of this season. One phase of the three-yearly rites of the Meriam gods Malo-Bomai was performed to prepare men for battle or for gift exchange in 'cone-shell' voyages to neighbours. The ritual dances were performed on ceremonial ground in front of sacred round houses made of grass at the village of Las. The dancers drew their strength from the movements of the currents and the winds in the waves, most of all from the epic journeys of the sea gods Malo and Bomai.

Seascapes and Ancestors

THE SALTWATER PEOPLE'S DANCES EVOKE THE movements of the sea creatures, the waves, the shimmering of the sun on the water. The movements of 'natural' beings and 'things' speak through them. Humans and other creatures occupy the same space — ultimately because through spirit ancestors they share the same Law. The Dugong Hunter Spirit Ancestors of the Yanyuwa illustrate graphically how creator beings walked (or swam) the path which human beings can follow. Ancestral beings may be transformed into humans, so non-human beings may share space with humans.[6] In his lucid book,

Aboriginal Artists of the Nineteenth Century, published in 1994, Stuart Sayers shows us how the work of Aboriginal artists in the southern part of the continent highlights this form of sharing in their depiction of ceremony. In his drawings, the famous Aboriginal artist, Barak of Coranderrk, often incorporated animals not as part of bush surroundings or landscape, as in European artistic representations of corroboree, but *inside* the dance with the human figures.

Aboriginal and Islander people are keen observers of their living world; as anthropologist William Stanner has written, they are people who miss little of the world around them, 'particularly the presence of shapely visual form or pattern'. Life's design is 'written' or patterned in the 'natural' scene: spirals on shells, their radial whorls and honeycomb divisions, the networks on spider-webs, crystalline patterns on rock minerals, bird colour markings, patternings of reptile skins. They are *intentional* for humans in the sense that they are 'a kind of command' for humankind to act upon; they provide a template for the patterns of human life. The patterns arrange themselves in spatial relationships of symmetry and asymmetry within the idiom of the visual patterns that occur in their surrounding world.[7] These patterns are given to each group as ancestral bequests. They find expression in visual art and in ceremony: in the former, the artist seeks to produce a correct clan design and, most importantly, in doing so to create or recreate ancestral power. Thus the design of a snake or a turtle is 'right' for it in the same way that certain designs belong to particular clans.[8]

The patterns of movement given in sacred designs passed down from ancestors are those of cosmic cycles and these continue to find artistic expression today as sacred political geographies. These geographies encompass sites, people, their languages and the sea Dreaming figures who speak 'to and through' local people. This may be close to what artist and ritual

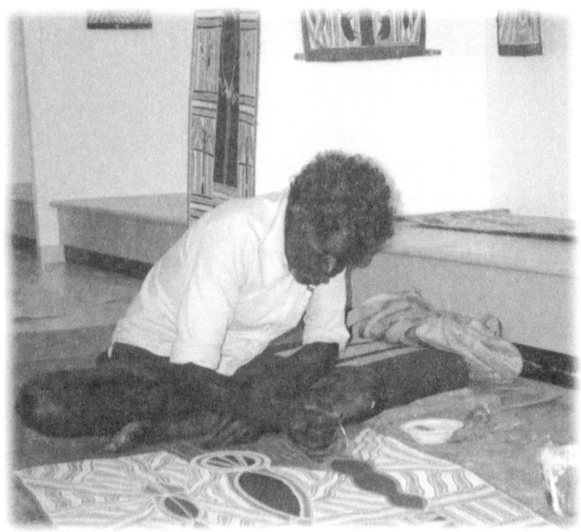

Yolŋu artist and ritual leader, Dula Ŋurruwuthun, painting at Buku-Larrŋgay Mulka Centre, Yirrkala, 1997

leader, Dula Ŋurruwuthun, means when he says 'We are sacred design' in the Yolŋu book *Saltwater*. At the same time the sacred geographies may represent cyclical time in the daily cycle of the sun and its tidal counterparts.

As linguist and anthropologist Peter Sutton has shown, a 1972 painting on bark by Liwukang Bukurlatjpi, an artist from Galiwin'ku–Elcho Island in northeast Arnhem Land, maps cyclical time onto space, while at the same time giving artistic form to the sacred topography of the chain of the Wessell Islands which run northeastwards from Galiwin'ku. The female squid pictured on the left-hand side of his painting is the ancestral creator of all the families and places along the chain. And the male squid on the right-hand side, in his journey southward, allocated these sacred places to estates owned by the eleven different clans. The site names are said to mean 'squid' in the various clan languages. The female squid transformed herself

'Squid and Turtle Dreamings', ochres on bark, painting by Liwukang Bukurlatjpi, Galiwin'ku–Elcho Island, 1972

into a turtle which 'speaks' to the local people: in her annual journey northward along the chain of islands her breath turns into clouds, which are a sign that the sea will be calm for canoe fishing.[9] The cross-hatching beside the male squid and on the carapace of the turtle are in the order black, red, yellow and white, representing the diurnal cycle of night, sunset, sunrise, and still water at midday.

William Stanner has written that in Aboriginal life there is symmetry between the social and the cosmic world. Their human quest is for ancestral spiritual power that can transform and ultimately transport a person's undying soul, his bones and ashes into his 'bone and soul country'. In this way he or she holds a place within cosmic space or cycle, one in which the Dreaming 'is represented as a continuing highway between ancestral superman and living man, between the life-givers and the life . . .'[10]

In the lives of the land–sea people of the tropics, assuming different forms is not the preserve of ancestral beings only. In the Torres Strait Islands and among Yolŋu people, for example, a dying person performs the movements of his or her totem; this may be a sea creature like shark or dugong, or one of many fish or seabirds. Among Yolŋu people, as the song-cycle being sung by a dying person's relatives arrives at each totem, the dying person imitates the movements of that creature.[11] Where people view themselves as 'multiple, simultaneous entities encompassing and encompassed by the landscape and seascape', these movements may signify their becoming one with their ancestral selves.[12] At that moment they may be saying 'I am dugong', or 'I am shark'.

Yolŋu people believe the souls of the dead of a particular moiety — one of two complementary groups into which their society is divided — ascend a length of possum-fur string which stretches up to the sky. When they reach the Milky Way, the spirits can be seen from the earth as shining stars, while a part of them also rejoins the clan's ancestors. Thus they become part of a more generalised ancestral power which manifests itself in various ways, the most tangible of which are sacred objects.[13] In such traditions ancestral power is not 'up there', or 'out there', but immanent. People may become directly involved with the ancestral past through rite, song, dance or visual art.

Shimmering waters

In some cultures brilliance or shimmering radiance may operate with an aesthetic intensity as if in its own right. Refractions of light, the sun's rays, the sun setting on the sea, light sparkling in bubbling fresh water create an emotional response. In the hands of poets such sparkling beauty is often recreated in words that convey joy and happiness. In her novel, *The Waves*, Virginia Woolf draws upon such sea pictures to evoke the uplifting of the human spirit:

> The surface of the sea slowly became transparent and lay rippling and sparkling until the dark stripes were almost rubbed out. Slowly the arm that held the lamp raised it higher and then higher until a broad flame became visible; an arc of fire burnt on the rim of the horizon, and all round it the sea blazed gold.

Shining light and shimmering, as I have said, speak in a special way to Yolŋu people. They have the word *bir'yun* for this kind of brilliance as an aesthetic property, to which anthropologist Donald Thomson drew attention in field notes he made in 1937.[14] As conveyed in works of art, the emotional effect of *bir'yun* may be interpreted as pure aesthetic experience, although the Yolŋu artist's creation of beauty is inseparable from a more profound quest.[15] Thomson noted how a shimmering effect created by Yolŋu artists by fine cross-hatched lines is seen by Yolŋu as 'a likeness to the *wangarr*', the ancestral past.

Anthropologist Howard Morphy deepened Thomson's insights through his work with Yolŋu artists in the 1970s. In reproducing shimmering light by the technique of cross-hatching Yolŋu artists are creating 'that intense flash of light that is ancestral power'.[16] This visual effect seeks to create an emotional response in the viewer. Yolŋu say it makes people happy. The 'canvas', characteristically the bark of a particular tree, begins dull and moves to a state of brilliance, less through the sheer intensity of shining light and more through the creation of variations in intensity over hatched areas. These variations are embedded in a rhythmic structure with complex tensions, bearing comparison with Western Desert dotted paintings.[17]

While recreating shimmering light is seen by Yolŋu artists as an expression of ancestral power, that power may be recaptured by turning people themselves into sacred objects — by making them shine. The bodies of initiates are rubbed with ochre and fat, decorated with feathers and ancestral designs. This makes them like the ancestral beings themselves. On bodies or barks the shimmering effect created is dangerous to the uninitiated person; in the past, perhaps until the 1960s or 1970s, the artistic representation of shimmering was the restricted province of a circle of men. Men themselves looked at these paintings through the corners of their eyes. The paintings had to be returned to their dull state by smudging or smearing before women and children might look at them; what Yolŋu would call their 'inside meaning', the meaning associated with their likeness to the ancestral past, was thereby rendered invisible.

This transformation from dull to brilliant recreated through fine cross-hatched lines in visual art is also created in songs, stories, song-cycles and performance. A good example is found in one of the central songs of the Djan'kawu Sisters, ancestral beings belonging to the Dhuwa moiety. The image is of a bird known as the rainbow lorikeet. *Drying its feathers in the rays of the sun/Children of the Djan'kawu . . . shining.*[18] Where the sisters laid down their dilly bags at a beach called Yalaŋbara, the rocks into which they transformed began to radiate red and blue colours of the sunlight reflected in the waters of the swamps.[19]

In other land–sea traditions too, shiny and shimmering features are embedded in sacred song and performance. In their sacred ceremonies, the Torres Strait Islanders wore pendants and armlets of shiny, polished cone-shell. The Yanyuwa sacred song for the white-bellied sea eagle, which I mentioned earlier, tells of its chest feathers shining as the movements of its Dreaming are recreated. A Maori chant recalling the invocation to calm the pathway of the legendary hero, Kupe, who voyaged to Aotea Roa, the Land of the Long White Cloud, is a song about shimmering water. It is reproduced by David Lewis in his book *The Voyaging Stars:*

> *Let the calm be widespread*
> *Let the sea glisten*
> *Like the* po-enamu *[greenstone]*
> *Let the shimmering warmth of summer*
> *Ever dance across your pathway.*

Salt and fresh

YOLŊU PEOPLE OF NORTHEAST ARNHEM LAND SEE special meaning in the way the saltwater and fresh-water streams come together at the river mouth: in meeting, the streams never dissolve one into the other but retain something of their own diversity or 'natures'. Yolŋu people have a special word — *ganma* — that expresses this brackish mixing of fresh water and salt water. It is particularly significant that *ganma* does not dissolve one inside the other — salt and fresh waters are overlapping streams that do not meld or homogenise.[20] *Ganma* is also used as a metaphor for marriage, and is a common motif in Yolŋu life. The mouth of the river is a symbol of new life. It is a turbulent place where salt and fresh waters meet, collide and mix; the tide races into the river mouth and then recedes. Yolŋu clan leader, Daymbalipu Munuŋgurr, who likened his people's land ownership to a tree grounded at a point of origin, also drew the mouth of a river. He was showing how the creation of life, the beginnings, occur characteristically at the river mouth, the 'space' between land and sea. As a place of tidal change where waters flow out to the sea and where, in turn, the tide comes flooding back into the river, the river mouth is a place of ending and of re-creation — like the cradle of a land-and-sea people.

In joining land and sea the spirit ancestors were not eliminating the distinctions between the two — the existence of fresh-water or land clans and saltwater or sea clans demonstrates this. In the song-cycles that are sung to transport the spirit of a dead person to a safe place, people sing only their own parts of the cycle, handing over the singing to the next clan whose members then sing their segment. These cycles cross fresh-water and saltwater country, and they respect different saltwater territories belonging to different clans. Clan cooperation is based on a recognition of distinctiveness which has also a combative aspect: among Yanyuwa people tradition has it that the saltwater dugong hunters and the mullet hunters fought and the former were the victors giving them the reputation for unsurpassed strength.[21]

Nor are salt waters themselves homogeneous; they are divisible into different salt waters. The waves of the inshore waters that lap upon the sandbeaches are distinguished from those of more distant open waters. Moreover, inshore waters themselves consist of two local Yolŋu groups belonging to the same ancestral being and jointly owning the same song-cycle. The following words, given with language names, help a non-Yolŋu person understand how highly potent sea metaphors are used to depict these interrelationships between place and people.

> *[We are] Gulalay and Mandjikay, we are both Walamaŋu. [Our] rough waves heap beach shells in the Milingimbi area and the Bunbuwa area, where my [i.e., the Bunbuwa area] waters terminate, breaking onto the shore.*[22]

The sea in this perspective is not just waves of water but an assemblage of parts in which appearance, movement and sound are expressive of the creative power of the groups to which they belong. Creative power is manifest in the sound and movement of the waters which includes changes of form.[23] The two salt waters express their creative power differently; saltwater people say the waters 'speak differently'.

Among Yolŋu people these two salt waters have their human resemblances in the Dhuwa and Yirritja moieties — two independent groups which are made complementary with one another through marriage ties. In saying that the two groups 'speak differently' Yolŋu mean they have different social characters. Importantly, marriage ties and other reciprocities between clans also create links between bodies of water. As Dula Ŋurruwuthun explains, Yolŋu say that 'different parts of country talk to each other' in the same manner in which people identify themselves to one another through kinship ties.[24] So these two moieties not only refer to human groups: everything on the land and sea territories of the Yolŋu belongs to one group or the other.

The regular crashing of the inshore waters on the sandbeaches in 'lines of foam bubbles' is salt water 'habitually speaking'.[25] The more distant waters do not speak like crashing thunder: they 'rumble' and 'growl'. They may murmur like the sea on the distant Great Barrier Reef in Meriam waters. Both kinds of waters show forth visual signs, both move, both change their form; sound as much as sight is part of their character. Yet in a sense the two are parts of the one. For the Burarra and Yannhaŋu peoples, Yolŋu groups of the Blyth River–Crocodile Islands region of northeast Arnhem Land, parts of the sea (divided according to various criteria) form one whole which they liken to a body. Thus the waves may be 'knees', the shoreline edge 'teeth' or 'mouth', moderately distant waters, 'abdomen', with distant seas 'chest' and far distant waters 'lower back'. They view the Arafura Sea in their immediate area as consisting of two distinct bodies of salt water: *gapu dhulway*, a body of shallow inshore water belonging to the Yirritja moiety, and *gapu maramba*, a separate body of open sea water belonging exclusively to the Dhuwa moiety.[26] At Galiwin'ku–Elcho Island the Arafura Sea is seen as two salt waters, known to people in northeast Arnhem Land by their moiety names of Manbuyŋa and Rulyapa, which 'play' with one another as they join, separate and come together afresh. Within these waters are the pathways of ancestral creator beings, their sea totems and song-cycles.[27]

The idea that the sea is made up of salt waters with different characters is part of a greater complexity which includes the seabed. As we have seen, Croker Island people refer to this seabed as being 'inside' the sea. This is the homeland of ancestral beings, notably the Rainbow Serpent, which as land–sea owner Charlie Wardaga explained in court hearings of the *Croker Island Seas* case may be called 'barracuda' in everyday speech.[28]

Saltwater people differentiate expanses of salt waters through the way these waters 'speak'. They use the same criteria to differentiate their own social 'salt waters' and then go on to weave themselves together as 'people of the sea' in a very sophisticated and ingenious way. When the Yanyuwa of the Gulf islands say they are 'those people whose spiritual and cultural heritage comes from the sea', or 'we originated in the sea', they mean that their ancestral spirit beings come from the sea.[29] The sea itself is also a Spirit Ancestor which the Yanyuwa share. This belief is in accord with that of the saltwater people in northeast Arnhem Land: that salt water itself is an ancestral being. This inheritance is given in sacred narratives, in the sacred design of bodies of water, in song-cycles, in ceremony that re-enacts the journeys of Dreamings. They mean something 'everyday' as well, but it is very different to the everyday realm of scientific and secular knowledge of European tradition. It is everyday because spirit beings authenticate their place in the scheme of things whose everyday reference point is situated within cosmic or cyclical time.

The story of the ancestral spirit women known as the Djan'kawu Sisters who travelled westward in canoes from a faraway island across to the northeast Arnhem Land coast, to a place called Yalaŋbara, speaks powerfully of the joining of saltwater and fresh-water territories. This narrative, which belongs to the Rirratjiŋu clan, tells of the creation of the clan, its territories, sea and land and resources. In saltwater country the Djan'kawu create fresh-water wells with their digging sticks. As the sisters travel the sea, the waves rise and fall, the foaming spray surrounds them, the waves crash against their canoe, the water bubbles up, the waves break on the shore. As they arrive at Yalaŋbara, the sisters sing a sea–land part of their song-cycle:

Waves rising
Waves breaking
Hitting together with [the] spray
Pushing the canoe into shore.

The white ochre smeared on the children's bodies and the white ochre on the arms of the men dancing in ceremonial performance represents the sea foam of the turbulent waves as the Djan'kawu party paddled their canoes to northeast Arnhem Land; the feathers of their sacred emblems are the waves themselves. The waves are hitting together, 'Pushing the canoe into shore' at a safe place on land, Yalaŋbara. The Djan'kawu arrive at the beach safely and hang up their dillybags on a sacred tree. These are stolen by the men of their party and in that moment the men take the ritual power and knowledge for themselves. The epic journey now continues on land as the Sisters create the sacred fresh-water wells. The children of the Djan'kawu are painted in the ceremony with symbols of the land: the kingfisher and the bands of the plains turkey are land creatures and symbols of the fresh-water, land clans. Most importantly, the Djan'kawu's epic journey joins together the land and the sea.[30]

Knowing the dugong

THE DUGONG IS A LARGE SEA MAMMAL WHICH LIVES in most of the waters of the northern Australian coasts; they are found rarely in waters of eastern Torres Strait where the sea-grass meadows upon which they feed are virtually absent. The people of western Torres Strait recognise 27 varieties of dugong. Right across the tropical coasts there are also sea turtles of different varieties, and hunting dugong and turtle is a much-favoured activity of all the saltwater peoples.

Dugong, the Yanyuwa people say, are human-like. When they feed, often in a herd, you can hear them breathing, coughing, whistling, hiccuping. A dugong will sometimes bring its whole head out of the water and look around. The locals believe the dugong are watching them, the hunters. Local people know the dugong's habits such as the 'last quick meal' it has just before it travels out to sea as the tide turns. At times sea grass floats in thickish swathes on the surface of the sea.

A dugong will rise to the surface, head out of the water, snout pulled back, eat the sea grass as it swims through it, having a last snack before swimming off to deep water.[31]

Traditional knowledge about dugong includes their life cycles as well as feeding patterns at different stages of seasonal and tidal cycles. Though this knowledge is very practical, it is closely tied to esoteric or spiritual knowledge. Local people know when and where dugongs will mate and where they will give birth — 'the nursery', Yanyuwa people call this area. They also know the sea grass on which the dugong feeds and its habitual growth at different times of the seasonal and other 'natural' cycles. 'Dugong people' know so much about dugong and their habitats that it is difficult to convey the detail and sophistication of this knowledge to a person unaccustomed to acquiring his or her own food and who may never have seen a dugong. Even more difficult perhaps is the problem of transmitting a sense of just how much the dugong meant and still means to the sea people. John Bradley, who has a deep appreciation of Yanyuwa people's relationship with the sea, conveys superbly a sense of the dugong's significance to the Yanyuwa people of islands of the Gulf of Carpentaria. His study in the 1980s and 1990s ranks alongside Donald Thomson's important work on the dugong hunters of eastern Cape York Peninsula in the late 1920s. Their work informs the following discussion on the cultural significance of the dugong on two different parts of the tropical coasts.

Dugong hunters are men of very high status in coastal and island cultures even today. In the old days it took a man at the height of his powers to become a Dugong Man. In 1934 Thomson described dugong hunting among the Sandbeach People of eastern Cape York who crafted small dugout canoes as 'undoubtedly the most dangerous and spectacular occupation practised by an Australian aboriginal', requiring the utmost skill and presence of mind.[32] The title of Dugong Man — 'belonging to the dugong' — accorded certain hunters, is a title of the highest esteem. Yanyuwa people call such men 'dugong hunters of excellence'. Their excellence helps define the uniqueness of a whole people. Being dugong hunters of excellence, desiring to harpoon the dugong, even speaking Yanyuwa language, signify a bond between the people, the sea and the dugong.

Words alone cannot convey the esteem, almost veneration in which an expert harpooner was held by his community and, while this relates to the traditionally perilous nature of dugong hunting and to the tremendous skill and knowledge of the accomplished hunter, it has deeper roots. Dugong are taken to be like people not just for perceived similarities in their behaviour. They are like people because they too have Dreamings or ancestral figures, and these figures made definitive sea voyages. The Dugong Hunter Spirit Ancestors travelled between the islands of the Yanyuwa and they and other hunting spirit ancestors 'infuse the entire geography of the islands and the sea with hunting'.[33] They gave the Yanyuwa the gift of hunting the sea and therefore the Yanyuwa's first responsibility is to safeguard these sea creatures and the rights of the invisible hunting spirits who continue to frequent these waters. Without this gift and without the practices required of the sea people which keep them in good standing with their invisible 'companions', skill with the harpoon counts for nothing. This dual attachment and respect for the Law of each was, and to a certain degree still is, the condition for living with the sea.

The Sandbeach People of Cape York Peninsula also illustrate this in their tradition of what earlier observers called a 'magical bundle'.[34] This was made from beeswax obtained from inland 'bush' neighbours, heated by the hunters and then rubbed on their stomachs. This practice, they believed, made the dugong sluggish and hence easier to catch. The ritual also prepared the hunter psychologically. Donald Thomson recalls the words of the most expert harpooner he had ever met, a man at the camp of the people he called the Yintjiŋga on the Stewart River estuary in 1928: his 'magical bundle' preparation made sure 'that dugong *must* die!'[35] The harpooner's expression of certainty signifies how the hunter feels in himself, and how he believes his thoughts affect the outcome. The Cape York Sandbeach People, like the Torres Strait Islanders to their north, also 'sang' the dugong; that is, they chanted power words to make the dugong tame. Meriam land–sea owner James Rice recalled to me in June 1997: 'When grandfather uttered *zogo mir* [magical or power words], the turtle became tame.'

What does all this mean in the thinking of today? It has been suggested recently that the dugong and the harpooner are 'co-dependent' or 'matched' and that power chants and substances strengthen that co-dependence.[36] Another way of saying this perhaps is that the hunter must feel 'right' and be thinking positively in order to succeed; together this means 'being the dugong', that is, putting oneself in its place. Today the people may not carry talismans or 'magical bundles' or chant power words; they are more likely to say a prayer, but they continue to make food offerings to the sea.

The Islanders of western Torres Strait developed a technique to capture dugong which called upon their knowledge of its habits without always having to go out in their boats. On moonlit nights towards the end of the southeast season the reefs are covered at high tide and dugong come in to feed on patches of 'dugong grass'. The late Wees Nawia, a Kaurareg man and Islander leader in the Torres Strait, was a great dugong hunter. He explained to me that 'The dugong leaves a mark on the sand where it has been feeding on sea grass.' After observing these marks he knew the dugong was likely to return on the evening tide to eat again. He and his sons built a dugong platform over the sea-grass bed, a structure unique to the Torres Strait. It is made of six bamboo poles lashed together on top of which rests a canoe centreboard. As a harpooner finds his mark — the dugong's head — he leaps down upon the dugong and removes the hardwood spear shaft while someone throws a rope. The harpooner flings himself backwards away from the rope so as not to become entangled. Silence is golden throughout the procedure as dugong have keen hearing. Hence the dugong hunter places the long axis of the platform in the direction of the wind; if it was built across the wind it would make a noise as the wind blew through. But it is also considered disrespectful to the dugong to talk while hunting. The hunter waits at his platform in total silence for the dugong to return to the spot where she left her mark. Notwithstanding the application of all this knowledge of the habits of the dugong and its habitat, a wooden or stone image of a dugong placed on the platform was believed to carry the power to attract it. When all the power and acumen available was given full rein a dugong could be taken 'with ease'.[37]

In the 1970s geographer Bernard Nietschmann made a study of this complex knowledge stored in the minds and practices of certain men at Mabuiag Island, western Torres Strait. He accompanied the hunters on dugong-seeking boat journeys, recording their memories, watching their numerous hand movements which illustrate paths and sea movements — directions that cannot be recorded in words alone. He noted the hunters' condensed knowledge of natural phenomena and their interrelationships, and he noted their special interest in the meanings of exceptions to the regular beat of the waves. In contrast to the Western objective stance, the saltwater people do not push to one side 'voices' of the sea that suddenly stir up a storm. Irregularities may be signs of the life of invisible 'companions' or powers dangerous in ordinary life.

When an Islander in the western Torres Strait today says he is going to the sand and sea-grass basin-like depression in the interior of a particular reef to look for dugong, he is locating a 50-metre-wide hunting ground on a fifteen by eighteen-kilometre reef within a 640-square-kilometre sea territory. That reef is named in its three dimensions from its windward and leeward sides and these include channels, sandbanks, sea-grass areas, bays, various drops, slopes and grooves.

Clearly topographic knowledge and familiarity with the structure of this reef and that reef, as particular instances of the solid structures and surface patterning of all reefs, are indispensable to a dugong hunter who says he is going off to 'such and such a reef' for dugong. This is the type of knowledge on which fishers the world over have always prided themselves. Importantly, the sea is constantly moving and the skilled hunter knows how a dugong will behave, which of the tides is likely to be a dugong-bearing tide, and where she is likely to be on this tide or that tide.

Torres Strait Islanders have a comprehensive knowledge of their water world. In western Torres Strait they track the movements of daily tides by the lunar calendar. Their system (described by Nietschmann as 'elegantly conceptualized'), 'keeps track of the daily tides, changes in height and current speed, time of occurrence and duration, seasonal shift (due to changes in earth, sun and moon orbits), water clarity, surface conditions and associated movements of fish, sea turtles and dugongs'.[38]

The Islanders know for example that one of the four daily tides will be an hour later each day, and will increase in speed and height with new and full moons. They have six terms for a rising or flood tide and five terms for an ebb tide which describe the vertical dimension of their sea world. Complex knowledge can appear easy to Torres Strait Islanders: they see that every living creature has a life cycle of birth, childhood, adolescence, maturity, middle age, old age and death. People's lives follow this course, as do the lives of dugong and other sea creatures. So too do the tides, which are born weak and small with each new moon, move through the life stages, finally dying as the moon travels to the end of its last quarter. Yet the tides and the moon are reborn eternally.

Tidal movements are the essence of sea life and the human life that 'matches' it. The continuous reordering of their sea territories has a *temporal* and a *locational* dimension for the Islanders. Their lives move in step not only with seasons, with lunar and daily cycles, but with the complex rhythmic set of arrangements which are continually reborn in new tides that have their own life stages, each of which varies according to wind or season.

From their observation of the surface of the sea Islanders distinguish and name two major wind-current relationships: when the surface sea is choppy the wind is blowing against the current; rolling waves or smooth seas indicate a wind travelling with the current. Winds that ride with the current are flood tides moving from east to west; northwest winds reverse this relationship so that west-to-east tides move with the wind.

Among the northern sea peoples foam and white caps, waves and lines of bubbles are not just foam, subjects for poetry and art as in Western tradition. These characteristics of the sea are a guide to life in two senses. As roads or boundaries or marks in the sea they are signs that make possible the sea people's survival; they are also signs of an invisible, noncorporeal yet inhabited world.

Seamarks and sailing

IN HIS BOOK *WE, THE NAVIGATORS: THE ANCIENT ART of Land Finding in the Pacific*, a great contemporary navigator, New Zealand-born David Lewis, writes of his experiences navigating and land-finding in long voyages in the Pacific Ocean without compass or other modern equipment. With co-writer Mimi George, he writes too of way-finding in snow-ice in the arctic tundra by Chukchi people of the former USSR and by the Inuit peoples of arctic Canada. This method of direction-finding is often termed 'cognitive mapping', and depends on what are often called 'maps in the mind'.[39]

Lewis mentions an array of sea signs and lore used in navigation by the Pacific Islanders. These systems include star paths from east to west, including the 'zenith star' which gives north–south longitude and may equate with the 'island star' or 'overhead star' which points to an island; these are guiding stars enabling a navigator to follow a star path as it rises in different seasons. Sea signs also include reflected waves or swell patterns off land. They include the mysterious phenomenon of 'underwater lightning' which oceanographers now suggest may be a form of luminescence, perhaps from a backwave. This may be seen at night darting out from the direction in which an island lies. Lewis mentions also 'dead reckoning', which he calls 'informed guesswork', for setting longitude (a technique replaced by Cook's chronometer); 'expanding the target', that is, steering for a whole archipelago and then locating individual islands by land clouds; bird zones (for example, the observation of terns flying off to islands nearby), and altered swell patterns; brightness of the clouds and the greenish hue they take on when appearing over land.

Navigating by means of sea signs is but one means of wayfaring by what Lewis and George identify as 'directionally significant images' — others are wave patterns, animal tracks, wind marks on snow-ice or desert sand. Such sea signs are still well known by Pacific Islanders today; however, their study by scholars from other cultures is limited. Only in the twentieth century did wave reflections and their directional significance become a subject of interest to Western oceanographers.

I first heard the term 'seamarks' from David Lewis. In *The Voyaging Stars: Secrets of the Pacific Island Navigators* he writes of a complex world of sea and sky signs, indicated by all kinds of marine phenomena — clouds, waves, sea birds. Seamarks may also come in the form of certain fish, the 'sinuous lines of drifting seaweed marking current junctions', the loom of far-away land and the flashes of underwater luminescence I have mentioned. Lewis also includes among his sea signs ant, spider, crab and starfish movements.[40] Sir Arthur Grimble, an English anthropologist with the British Colonial Service who had a 60-year association with the Gilbert Islanders, writes of how the Gilbertese used seamarks in much the same way as Europeans used landmarks. He lists eighteen such signposts stored up in Gilbertese cultural memory which relate to particular sea zones around their islands: these include phenomena such as special kinds of waves, the enclosure of sharks, the habitual leaping of flying fish, a submerged reef, a special flying formation of terns.[41]

The saltwater peoples of the Australian tropics have a rich store of seamarks, sky signs, rock positions, headlands, beaches, sandhills, swamps, and other on-land points of reference. The mosaic of signs which guide their lives are of the same order as those discussed by Lewis, and include waters roaring and murmuring and even the smell of the reefs on the evening low tide. Seamarks are one feature that makes saltwater people distinctive; peoples who follow seamarks are hard for the 'land mind' to fathom.

The Bardi and Jawi people of the spectacular and dangerous sea country of the Buccaneer Archipelago live with tides that may rise six to eight metres each day. Within their shared sea country lie many named sites and features; 70 of these include islands, reefs and surrounding water, turtle and/or dugong area, exposed rocks, rocks and reefs, pools, sandbars, passages, tidally covered rock areas, turtle and trochus areas, places where water shoots through at low tide, island and deep-water areas, rocks and sands where pelicans and sea birds sleep. These sites change with the rise and fall of the tides.

Most fascinating to me is people's understanding of tidal currents as seamarks. Through their detailed knowledge of these currents they are able to distinguish what they call 'roads in the sea'. These pathways depend on the movements of named tidal currents, some twenty of which lie between the Dampier Peninsula and Sunday Strait. By setting out on the right tide or 'sea road', the Bardi and Jawi could ride a series of tidal currents on their mangrove rafts, moving from site to site as they wished.[42] A dangerous occupation, it would seem to a land-lubber, but a spectacular example of the imprint of seascape upon the mind and memory.

In the past, Torres Strait Islanders voyaged in long canoes with double outriggers across Torres Strait to the New Guinea coast and down south along the eastern and western coasts of northern Cape York Peninsula. Their seamarks and sky marks were confined mainly but not entirely to waters inside the body of the Barrier Reef, at least before the days of the pearling cutters and luggers, and even before the late 1940s, when these boats were fitted with engines.

Torres Strait Islanders today are aware of the vast constellation Tagai as a guide to seafaring, gardening and land sea ownership, even though they may not know the intricacies of the 'star mark' navigation method followed by their forebears. Star marks certainly guided the men who worked as divers and sailors in the pearling industry which began around 1850, reached its peak by the end of the 1800s, and collapsed in the 1960s. Older Meriam women recalled to me in 1999 how they had rowed out from Mer to the Great Barrier Reef and to Ker Ged to dive for trochus shell in the 1950s. They relied at times on star navigation.

Saltwater people who worked as pearlers recall today the importance in navigating of the currents, the wind direction, bird behaviour; at night, the smell of the reefs at low tide, underwater lightning, star guidance. Always they talk about 'detecting reefs', which is another way to say finding passages through them.

Those Torres Strait Islanders who recall the seamarks and the star marks remember them as part of flowing sea paths. They say that they know the sea as others know the land, that those who don't 'live with the sea' cannot imagine it as they do: signposted with seamarks, guiding paths and sea boundaries that link places together. As Meriam elders Eses Gesa and George Kaddy said to me in 1999, 'A sea person can see all these clearly. If you have never been a sea person you can't.' This seems to me to be true and makes communication between land people and sea people difficult. Fortunately there are substantial bodies of literature about seamarks and sea knowledge among other peoples who follow similar basic principles. To the mind contained by the stillness of the land, seamarks which are subject to the ebbs and flows of waters are hard to imagine. The contrast is greatest with urban people where direction-finding is ruled by straight lines.

The size and depth of reefs vary enormously, and the Islanders in the central islands call the Meriam eastern island people 'Barrier people' or 'heavy water people', that is, deep-water people. In 'greasy-fine weather', the northeast season, the Meriam can see Saper Kes, a passage between the island of Mer and Dauar, very clearly. It is a ring of water stirred up from the centre, resembling boiling currents rising up from underneath — as though a cavern lies below in this sea world studded with ancient craters. There are many bodies of water, passages, cays, reefs which connect, interlace, separate and configure in four-dimensional space in waters moving horizontally and vertically. Sea birds — seagull, tern, frigate bird — tell the sea people important things. Towards evening the direction they fly points to land and shelter; birds carrying fish in their mouths tell of young ones and the proximity of land and rocks.

Torres Strait Islanders today say that smell is very important in their navigating: on low tide at night the smell of drying seaweed tells them a reef is near. They also distinguish a passage through a reef by observing differences in the phosphorescence in the water: in a passage in deep blue water the flash is occasional; on a reef the flashes occur every few seconds, the northwest season being the main time for the emission of these 'signals'.

Even though much of the old navigational knowledge may be lost, some Torres Strait Islanders today can recall image maps and some seamarks. I believe that their accumulated knowledge bears a similarity to that of the Pacific Island navigators. In order to traverse thousands of kilometres of sea, Pacific Islanders developed star compasses and directional wind compasses based upon comprehensive knowledge of the character of local winds. David Lewis writes that the Pacific Islanders' 32-point wind compasses are essentially similar to the wind roses carried by sailing ships of Europe, by the ancient Greeks, or the Indian-Persian seafarers.[43] These wind roses, likened to the lotus flower and to the octopus, are regarded as the symbol of ancient mariners.

The Torres Strait Islanders' sea world is dominated by reefs; one can always sight other land from any island, so these mariners did not need directional wind compasses. They set their courses by landmarks and by seamarks; their lives depended upon detailed knowledge of winds and tides. Even the identities of the clans are distinguished by the wind that 'belongs' to each clan locale. For example, the Meriam clans and sub-clans designate themselves according to the wind direction of their clan locale and with their help I was able to draw up what I have called a twelve-directional 'wind-circle of Meriam identities'.[44]

People of the Caroline Islands of Micronesia have a word for their systematic knowledge of things at sea, animate and inanimate, but all translatable as the 'sea life' associated with the marine environment encountered when sailing in a particular direction from an island. Deriving from the Carolinian word 'to bind', their word may refer to an association of an island and its surrounding environment including the sea and the sky world. Contemporary Japanese ecological anthropologist Tomoya Akimichi reveals with great clarity unique aspects of the image-mapping prowess of Carolinian navigators. Each island has its own 32-point star compass and each segment of the compass is associated with certain things, animate and inanimate: fish, birds, sea mammals, driftwood, sea snakes, whirlpools, foam and waves. Many of these sea creatures (as well as reefs) are used as 'seamarks' in locating other islands and fishing grounds, and for this navigational purpose they may be real or imagined: for example, the 'image' of a large triggerfish or a whale lying on the water, with five different islands and reefs corresponding to its various bodily parts. Thus on the south side of one particular atoll there 'lies' a giant whale with its head pointing north towards the location of a particular island, giving the navigator directions from atoll to island and back. Imaginary or supernatural, these 'seamark creatures' have their counterparts in the stars. A nice example is the constellation known to Westerners as the Crux, or Southern Cross, which is seen by Carolinian navigators as the star equivalent of the 'large triggerfish' image in the sea. Circulating anti-clockwise between the celestial and the marine worlds, this 'image', real or imagined, becomes a star set or constellation as it rises on the eastern horizon at sunrise, being transformed into the shape of the fish when the star sets and sinks down into the sea.[45]

6
Owning and Belonging

Calling loudly: Our right, our fish, our territory

TWO BRIEF SALTWATER DRAMAS IN THE MIDDLE OF 1998 speak strongly of the feelings of indigenous peoples today towards seas adjacent to their lands. The first occurred on 6 May when several Islanders raced out in their dinghies to a place they call Dugong Reef, some 30 kilometres from Mer–Murray Island, their home island. They boarded the boat of several non-indigenous fishermen; they removed the catch and took it home, selling it to the Murray Island Council freezer facility: 'it was our rights, it was our fish and it was in our territory', one of them explained later in court.[1] Meriam sailors have always sailed out to 'show the flag' in their home reef waters and their more distant seas. Years before the *Mabo* case I watched them go out in their dinghies and ask outsiders who have come into their home reef waters what they are doing there.

In boarding the boat and removing the catch as they did, some younger fishermen were acting spontaneously and directly and not necessarily according to the ways of their elders. A claim of robbery with violence was brought against the Meriam fishermen: one of them was said to have threatened the non-indigenous fishermen with a crayfish spear. The Meriam fishermen claimed traditional rights to the fish within a Protected Zone declared under provisions of a Treaty between Australia and Papua New Guinea in 1978 known as 'the Torres Strait Treaty'. The Islanders eventually won the case based on an honest claim of right, in this case their honest belief the fish belonged to them as Murray Islanders. Two-and-a-half years later, a jury in the District Court in Cairns brought down a 'not guilty' verdict and the court acquitted the two men of armed robbery.

Under the rather different circumstances of a 1998 Federal Court judgment in the *Croker Island Seas* case, the Croker Islanders engaged with the same underlying issue: the belief in their exclusive right to the waters surrounding their islands. A community meeting discussed the decision of Justice Olney in the Federal Court on their claims to native title to seas around their islands: he decided that native title rights to sea areas claimed are non-exclusive and non-commercial. In recognising the native title of the Croker Islanders, Justice Olney took the well-established position that public rights to the sea take precedence over any other rights. At the community meeting, chief plaintiff Mary Yarmirr took issue with this judgment: 'Nought out of ten' she said, rather dramatically and decisively. While these events among two sea peoples separated by thousands of kilometres of coast differ in their style, they carry a common theme: as first peoples, the Croker Islanders and the Meriam see themselves as holding a primary right 'against the whole world' to sea territories handed down to them from their ancestors.

The Meriam case rested on the narrow ground of what people 'honestly believe'. Yet in drawing attention to the two fishermen's manner of disposal of the fish it opened up wider questions: in selling them to the community-based freezer facility 'the community gets the benefit' and in emphasising this legal counsel for the Islanders was asking whether it was better for the Meriam to earn a living from fishing than to 'sit back and rely on the Government just giving them money because there's nothing for them to do'.[2] This subject of independence, dear to the hearts of Meriam leaders and many community members, is ongoing.

The High Court of Australia has recently made its decision in the seven-year long *Croker Island Seas* case (*Yarmirr v. Northern Territory* [2001]), the first entirely sea claim to come before an Australian court. This case also expresses a more general trend. Along the northern coasts and islands and elsewhere where sea custom and tradition are strong, indigenous saltwater communities have, as they say, one foot in the dinghy and are now ready to push off their native title sea claims.

As I mentioned briefly in the first chapter, on 18 September 2001 the High Court recognised native title to seas claimed by the Croker Islanders. Anthropologists Nicolas Peterson and Jeannie Devitt had tendered a report to the court on native title. There they identified the sea-owning group among Croker Islanders as the *yuwurrumu* (clan), who trace their descent through the male line. They listed ten native title rights among the clans and these included the right of ownership of sea and seabed, the right to hand on these rights, to make decisions about all aspects of their area or estate and to control use of and access to resources. Importantly, they included the right to exclude or restrict others from entering the area.[3] It was this latter right that divided those five High Court justices who affirmed that native title rights extend out into the sea.

Justice Michael Kirby delineated a question of cultural difference as being of major relevance to this sea case. He said that while the common law inherited in Australia from England drew a relatively clear distinction between the laws applicable to land and sea, 'the intersection between the common law of Australia and the traditional laws and customs of Australia's indigenous peoples' raises the problem that no such distinction is made by the latter.[4] Bodies or areas of *both* land and sea are subject to ownership. Given this cultural perspective, the Croker Islanders had dared to hope that a recognition of native title rights to the seas they claim would give them full responsibility for those areas — that is, exclusive native title rights.

The wish to take primary responsibility for inherited sea territories is now part of a national saltwater agenda: it received strong expression in the declaration of 200 delegates to the first National Indigenous Sea Rights Conference held in Hobart in September 1999. Pressure for sea rights is becoming like an underwater volcano surge causing waves to form, but many Australians do not know what is causing the waves. More than twenty years ago limited recognition of marine rights to the low-water mark in the *Aboriginal Land Rights (Northern Territory) Act* 1976 was followed by the closure of seas to outsiders on two parts of the Arnhem Land coast. Among scholars of marine property, a small body of literature records how estuaries, bays and waters adjacent to their shores are regarded by indigenous coastal people as part of their lands. Yet as we have seen, for saltwater peoples, owning marine territory goes much further than narrowly conceived rights in these seas.

The sea hearings in the Northern Territory before the Aboriginal Land Commissioner in 1980–81 were precipitated by the reported experiences of Yolŋu coastal people of actions of disrespect towards their creation sites and the irresponsibility of some non-Aboriginal fishers towards the marine environment

— old nets and gear left in estuaries, wastage of unwanted fish. Behind the determined stand of sea country owners in northeast Arnhem Land were the broken promises of some barramundi fishermen: 'Already the fishing boats are doing the thing that they said they would not,' one witness said at the sea hearings, to the accompaniment of other community members shouting their agreement.[5]

Today there is at last a limited understanding that saltwater peoples have a concept of sea property that is quite different to the European conception of territorial seas embedded in Anglo-Australian law. There is also a growing awareness that what the Croker Islanders or the Meriam are seeking — the right to have the last and decisive word on who comes into their waters, whether for recreation or for commercial fishing — is finding expression in other countries. A flamboyant example was the so-called 'lobster war' that broke out in December 1999 between licensed non-indigenous Canadians in the waters of New Brunswick, Canada and Mi'kmaq Indian fishers. The dispute followed two decisions made in the Supreme Court of Canada in a case known as *R v. Marshall*. The first upheld an appeal made by Donald Marshall, a Mi'kmaq man charged with an offence of fishing for eels without a licence on the southern shore of Nova Scotia. He claimed that contemporary fishing regulations violated the rights his people had secured through a treaty with Britain in 1760. In response to the furore that ensued, the Supreme Court later qualified its decision, licences were required of indigenous fishers and seasonal rules imposed on them. [6]

While relatively few non-Islander fishermen find their way to Meriam waters, the principle at issue here is the same. One Mi'kmaq chief summed up his people's belief that: 'the fish belong to every Mi'kmaq man, woman and child'. His sentiment was virtually the same as that expressed by Eddie Mabo. In the *Mabo* case the Meriam claimants explained to the court how the clans owned the beaches, reefs, waters, passages and more distant fishing cays like Ker Ged. The first plaintiff, Edward Koiki Mabo, had claimed reefs, lagoons and foreshore; he had also claimed distant fishing grounds, including parts of the Great Barrier Reef. Before he died in January 1992, he reaffirmed those sea rights in words reproduced in the film 'Mabo, Life of an Island Man': 'According to my tradition those fish, the prawns, whatever is in that sea belongs to me and my people. That's important,' Mabo said, and is a right that should be claimed.

Indigenous people's right to take primary responsibility for their marine territories is not limited to the right to decide who comes into these waters. It also concerns the right to determine their whole future and establish their economic independence. The Yolŋu, the Croker Islanders and the Meriam all see themselves as trading as well as fishing people. As we have seen, they call on their traditions of exchanging and trading in envisaging self-run marine enterprises today. Following the High Court's 1992 decision recognising exclusive native title rights to Murray Island land to the high-water mark, the Meriam began to realise an old dream: they took steps to establish a commercial community fishing project within their traditional maritime boundaries. In 1993 they defined a Murray Island 'economic zone' within traditional sea boundaries mapped by a Meriam draughtsman and drawing upon the knowledge of senior Meriam who drew the boundary markers in the sand. They secured a fish freezer, and used family-owned metal dinghies, usually with 40-horse-power motors, to fish the waters. The fishers sold their catches to the Murray Island Council, whose community freezer facility is for the benefit of all the Meriam. They were exercising inherited rights to seas surrounding their islands; and in doing so showed they had by no means given up their claim for sea rights.[7]

Since then, Meriam leaders have drawn public attention to the connection between rights to sea territories and economic independence. Winning native title to their islands was a first and major step. However, dry land is but a tiny speck within vast Meriam sea territories, which comprise perhaps thirty times the dry land mass. 'We are an ageless seafaring culture,' explained Ron Day, the chairman of the Murray Island Council, on the '7.30 Report' on ABC television in May 1999. He was making a public call for sea rights in the context of striking new archaeological findings in 1999. The latter pointed to a maritime culture stretching back to times soon after the reef flats were formed around Mer, Dauar and Waier some 3,000 years ago. The reefs and seas handed down to them, a Meriam fisherman explained on the '7.30 Report', provide the Meriam with an economic base: their economic prospects lie 'wholly and solely with the marine resources' of the seas 'given to us by our forefathers'.

On 21 December 2000 'Small Island, Big Fight', the film the Meriam made about themselves, was shown in Australia on ABC television. In this film they explained how their links to the land and the sea remain unbroken. They also made it clear that the old life where they grew or caught what they needed was no longer adequate today. Many Islanders have left home to find jobs on the mainland and three-quarters of those who remain are living on welfare payments: 'We are desperately trying to find ways to use our sea resources and our sea skills to make a living within the modern market economy,' Ron Day explained. The Meriam people's circumstances are somewhat different to those of Yolŋu or other saltwater peoples, but the sentiments and hopes expressed strike common chords.

A way of owning

As we have seen, groups of people inherit inalienable customary rights to bodies of water often in complex patterns of joint or overlapping ownership. They speak and act for *this* salt water or site not simply as individuals but as nameholders for a group of people united in one body.[8] In classical indigenous social organisation these are usually clans, but among some groupings today knowledge of their clan territories has been lost. So for instance the Wuthati, a Sandbeach People of eastern Cape York Peninsula, describe themselves today 'as a single land-owning tribe'.[9]

In 1969 William Stanner wrote of the Aboriginal way of owning in which people are joined to the land by spiritual and material bonds.[10] 'Owning' and 'belonging to' the sea or the land 'are like two sides of the one coin'.[11] Linguist–anthropologist Bruce Rigsby and anthropologist Athol Chase extend Stanner's thought: because each person's spirit comes from a specific place a 'person incarnates a spirit that indissolubly connects them with a country of origin'.[12]

Musical anthropologist Fiona Magowan deepens this understanding in relation to the sea and saltwater ownership. In her unique ten-year study of Yolŋu cosmology, she shows the way Yolŋu saltwater clans are tied to named bodies of water each with 'its own set of names and ancestral aesthetic'. She conveys too a sense of the unique complexity of the interrelationships between these diverse groups and their ancestral seas. An ancestral water may cross over and carry along those of another group underneath it; but importantly, they are never dissolved one into another. They carry one another as mother and child or child and mother. 'Seas then are skins or wombs, holding objects and encasing them, concealing and revealing their identities.'[13]

Three aspects of inalienable bonds join people with the sea. The first is 'Speaking for *this* Salt Water': when a person 'speaks for' country he identifies the rights and responsibilities of a group of people to particular bodies of salt water, sites and seabed. The second, 'Travelling Together', taken from the Yolŋu people's perception of the interchange and overlap between salt and fresh waters, is an enduring symbol of alliance. The third notion, 'Ancestral Pathways', refers to the 'footprints' or tracks left by creator beings and human ancestors, which both demarcate and join saltwater territories.

Speaking for this *salt water*

MERIAM LAND–SEA OWNER JAMES RICE ADDRESSED the Supreme Court of Queensland as a plaintiff in the *Mabo* case in the following words: 'Father said then at Dauar: "This is our boundaries, this is our land, this is our reef." He used to tell the whole story [of our land and sea property], come back and tell the whole story again.' James Rice's father began teaching him about his land and sea properties when he was six years old in the late 1930s. The court heard other Meriam witnesses explain about their land–sea property in similar ways to Rice and drew the conclusion that the Meriam people owned plots of land in bounded allotments. The idea of blocks or plots being the property of persons was intelligible to the court. The Meriam explained repeatedly how their 'plots', and they themselves, were like branches and sprigs of particular trees which are rooted in named locales. They also explained to the court how their rights to land and saltwater territories carry responsibilities to the joint owners who have inherited these specific and inalienable territories. Groups trace their inheritance to a common male ancestor and inheritance is in joint or common ownership. Speaking on behalf of family or clan groups, the male heads act as nameholders. Their inherited right also endows them with the responsibility to ensure the younger brothers and unmarried sisters are given areas within these land–sea clan properties. In broad outline this form of ownership is characteristic of saltwater property systems of both Aboriginal and Torres Strait Islander peoples. As I noted previously, they are frequently called 'customary marine tenures'.

The land–sea owning groups among two Aboriginal saltwater peoples who have brought native title claims to court are described below very briefly. Each illustrates a common property form of ownership and I believe these two examples are representative of the land–sea ownership patterns along the tropical coast. The first example is the Croker Island people, the second the Bardi and Jawi of coastal Dampier Land and the southern islands of King Sound in the Kimberley region of northwest Australia. The first is drawn from public documents of the *Croker Island Seas* case; the second exclusively from Geoffrey Bagshaw's Anthropologist's Report prepared for the Kimberley Land Council on behalf of the native title claim of the Bardi and Jawi in February 1999.

There are seven land–sea owning groups of Croker Island and adjacent areas, each of which traces or claims descent through the male line. As I mentioned earlier, the Islanders call these seven groupings *yuwurrumu* and they are the right-holding groups to tracts of land and sea known as estates. Each *yuwurrumu* consists of people with joint rights in an estate, often referred to as 'land or sea country', and these membership rights, acquired by birth, are inalienable, that is, they can neither be sold nor bought. All members have free access to their estate and its everyday resources, the senior members having special rights (and responsibilities) in regard to sites of ritual significance and subsistence resources. Sea country boundaries are clearly marked along the shoreline and the distance out to sea is 'as far as the eye can see'. Taken from the shoreline, this may be a distance of about twenty kilometres.[14]

Bardi and Jawi land-and-sea tenure is based primarily on local estates or country known to them as *bur* or *buru*. Today there are twenty Bardi and four Jawi *bur*, and there may have been as many as 40 in the past. Senior men explain their inheritance in a straightforward way: 'you get the country from your father's footsteps'. Everything, as they say, 'comes from our father's side'. In that form of descent, known as 'patrifiliation' in anthropological literature, men are often considered to be incarnations of spirit children who belong to a particular estate. Members of each estate are under an obligation to look after it and not defile the ground in any way. Those not familiar with country who enter it without permission remain 'unrecognized by the country itself' and may get sick. A senior Bardi man explains the seriousness of the obligation: 'we belong the ground . . . ever since time began . . . [if you] break up ground [you] break up family spirit.'[15] Members of a *bur* have rights to speak on behalf of, and exercise responsibility for, the physical and spiritual welfare of their country. These include rights to enter and move within the country, and to exclude unauthorised persons from it; and rights to hunt, fish, reside, burn off and develop residential locations there. Boundaries of near-coastal sea country are defined by such environmental features as beaches, creeks, rocks and marine passages. Distant offshore areas lie mainly outside the boundaries of the *bur* and, like the Bardi and Jawi hinterlands or scrub, the 'deep sea' or 'distant deep sea', as they name it, belong to *bur* adjacent to it. It is what they call graphically 'together possessing country', that is, sea country belonging to an association of neighbouring *bur*.

Individuals making claims are always acting on behalf of a group or an association of groups. Even when people say 'I am the owner', they mean 'I am the nameholder speaking for others', or 'I am a member of that jointness'. This is quite different to ownership in European law, where an individual as sole proprietor of a piece of land may dispose of it as he wishes. I have drawn upon the tree analogy used by the late

Daymbalipu Munuŋgurr to explain the feature that distinguishes indigenous customary land–sea tenure from the individually based property rights of Western systems. Branches, trees, clusters of trees: these are very suitable metaphors because they embody mutually interdependent sets of rights and responsibilities anchored in place or locale. Family, clan, associations of clans, and associations of language groups are identities in which the smaller, more intimate groups are not submerged by larger associations. An analogy is provided by the traditional Russian doll sets, in which ornamental dolls of different sizes fit inside one another. If we imagine them as transparent, then we may see through to the innermost and smallest doll, which represents the primary group and place. 'In my first thought is my real homeland, the village of Zomared; after that Murray Island, the several Meriam-speaking islands, and after that the whole Torres Strait Islands,' the late Sam Passi, a senior Meriam, explained to me in 1982.

When the Torres Strait Islanders decided in 1999 to put forward one unified regional sea territory claim it was based upon a common understanding that the traditional sea territory of each island is recognised and respected by all the other communities. Clearly, the idea of island sea territory does not itself cut across or cancel out people's more primary associations. This is a fundamental principle of ownership of land and sea in which 'each belonging' enfolds itself inside a larger one without losing its identity in that new context. To return to the Russian doll analogy, each group and its territory is present, even where only the largest doll is visible. People's identifications may expand; they may feel they are all one people through intermarriage and other reciprocities and be aware of their links with both their immediate clan locality and the land of their whole community of associated clans. That this coexistence of rights exists today but is not always understood cross-culturally was illustrated in the hearings of *Mabo v. Queensland*.

Reverend Dave Passi and James Rice, both of whom own dry land, foreshore, reefs and waters at Dauar Island, explained to the Supreme Court of Queensland in 1989 how they let other Meriam, but not outsiders, collect turtle eggs and make themselves at home on their sandbeaches and adjoining waters: '[people] can go fishing there but they know this area belongs to me,' James Rice explained. Quite mistakenly, His Honour took this generosity on Rice's part as evidence that the old traditional system had been lost, and 'any erstwhile intruder' might now use the beaches claimed by Reverend Passi.[16] Yet a clash between two landowners — Koiki Mabo and Mawer Depoma — about rights to a particular beach, during the visit of the Supreme Court to Mer Island in 1989, displayed most dramatically that the marine ownership system remains alive.

In native title claims to sea territories, clan or estate groups often cooperate to provide the outline of their boundaries. In 1997 the main emphasis of a meeting at Maningrida in northeast Arnhem Land was to 'make a very strong voice for sea rights'. Maps were on the walls. Clan estate owners spoke with assurance and the keynote was cooperation between the clans, particularly important as their claim joined up on its western side with that of the Croker Islanders. Most of the people were speaking in Yolŋu language and remembering appeared effortless. 'Here is a map,' one man said in English. It seemed however that *balanda* had reversed the positions of two places on the map. Yet this didn't cause contention among the owners. Only a question of detail remained: 'Bring the claimed sea area around the Point or leave it where it is?' The meeting came to agreement about the area of claim: at one point twenty kilometres out to sea to a sacred site in the water along the sea boundaries of the Croker sea-owners' claim and 'back up the river a little bit, not where the fresh water is; but where *balanda* sneak in with their nets and fish'.[17]

Travelling together

IN THE CONCLUSION TO HIS STUDY OF ABORIGINAL classical traditions linguist–anthropologist Peter Sutton makes a point of critical importance for an understanding of indigenous ownership of land and sea. 'Classical Aboriginal culture concentrates on human relationships, *or on how things lie in relation to each other*, rather than on things themselves.'[18] In his study of Aboriginal topographic icons he draws the important conclusion that their icons or 'religious images of topographies' are not direction or distance markers or finders in the way that maps are. They are not accumulations of knowledge within a single plane; they are 'constituted by knowledgeable and emotionally rich *performance*'.[19] Relationships between people, and between people and place, are central to Aboriginal cultural traditions. These relationships permeate notions of ownership; they also define ideas of 'non-belonging' and the rules that non-belonging engenders. They determine which groups 'travel together' as salt and fresh, as salt and salt, today, before and later on.

When James Rice's father showed him his lands and reefs he did so with his hands and voice. As other witnesses in *Mabo* also explained eloquently, in this act of telling the father was recording a cultural design of belonging which his son memorised. He was passing on a responsibility that bound the boy James to a place and to a line of fathers.

'Travelling together', as Yolŋu people say of disparate waters that are *contraposed* to one another, is a central preoccupation of the Yolŋu clans. 'Travelling together' means finding ways of accommodating difference. Through intermarriage or other reciprocities, hostile relations can become friendly, although not necessarily harmonious. Why? Because being brought together entails a measure of civility. Where clans most 'opposed' or different to one another are brought together by the propitiating force of intermarriage, the alliance is powerful.

When senior Yolŋu spokespeople at Yirrkala decided in 1997 to create 80 bark paintings depicting sea rights, they were doing so outside the constrictions of Anglo-Australian legal precepts. They were then in a position to explain their perspectives on sea rights in their own way. These paintings reveal their central preoccupations and priorities. The focus of the artists' written statements, which accompanied the sea paintings in the book *Saltwater*, explain the clan designs and interrelationships represented in their paintings. Senior ritual leader and artist Dula ŋurruwuthun 'speaks' in the lead declaration of 'sea rights'. According to the Law of Yolŋu his sea rights extend out to where the clouds rest at the horizon. But Yolŋu connections to the sea do not end there. The clouds at the horizon stand for the ancestral beings to whom the living are tied. Lots of the children's names come from this place in the sea, so that Yolŋu people living today are, he says, founded 'in the design of this special place'.

Dula ŋurruwuthun explains how three clans of the Dhuwa moiety are caretakers of a particular off-shore sea area on behalf of the ancestral spirit beings who laid down the sacred Law for Yolŋu to follow. Sacred art today and long ago draws upon the visual design etched by this body of water, known to the Yolŋu as Gapu Dhä-yindi. Yet Yolŋu know it not only by its appearance; for the clans who own or act as caretakers, particular bodies of water are distinguishable from one another by sound, by taste and smell.

Ownership or rights to seas bring together the cooperative associations of groups of clans: kinship relations mirror and are mirrored by the relationships of these interrelated groups to a named body of water. Yarrinya is a body of deep salt water in Blue Mud Bay belonging to three closely related clans — the Munyuku, Warramirri and Lamamirri, linked spiritually in the painting by Dula ŋurruwuthun in the book *Saltwater*. The clan that looks after Yarrinya on behalf of these three clans is the Madarrpa clan. Why? Because from ancient times men of the Munyuku clan marry the daughters of Madarrpa mothers. This caretaking Madarrpa clan has an ancient and continuing relationship to the Munyuku clan and to the body of deep salt water called Yarrinya. Their 'power name', 'the long paddlers', refers to their heritage and prowess as deep saltwater people whose long oars reach down low. As ŋurruwuthun explains, the Madarrpa people 'make the shelter that protects the country', 'they feel the caress of Yirrwarrya (the south-east wind) as their paddles stir the water'. They 'ritually welcome the southeast wind that comes from Munyuku sea country'.

Dula ŋurruwuthun is saying something very important. Using the metaphorical language of fire and its power to protect people from the cold southeast wind, he conjures up social ties that bind people together irrevocably. In embracing the southeast wind as it comes across from Munyuku sea country, the maternal grandmothers 'light the fires' for the homes of their daughters' husbands. In making the hearth, ŋurruwuthun explains, the fire 'sparks and spreads to start new fires under the tree shade'. Members of the Madarrpa clan have been continuously lighting the fires of the Munyuku, sea people of the southeast wind, looking after the country by making a shelter. This is the substance and form of a cooperative endeavour, which 'sits alongside' the desire to fight the other clan. There is a necessity for reciprocity, overlapping and intermingling to win out over the trends towards hostility and anarchy. It is the triumph too of the hearth over the elements and chaos; or in

Anglo-Saxon early thinking, between the *cynn*-kin and the *wraecca* — the darkness of sea and moor.

Ancestral pathways

IF YOU THROW A LENGTH OF ROPE IT WILL COIL INTO various shapes. The travels of ancestral figures along 'Dreaming tracks' are rather like this. But the traveller's path is studded with dots; these are the stopping places along the way. Now imagine tying several of these ropes together. Their knotting points, as I shall call them — places where different tracks converge — may become sites of joint responsibility.[20] The Yanyuwa islander people of the Gulf of Carpentaria use the metaphor of a rope to denote Dreaming tracks in the sea. A beautiful story told to linguist–anthropologist John Bradley describes how the travelling dugong rope stretched out behind the canoe of the Dugong Hunter Spirit Ancestors, creating a string of islands and joining them together.[21] These ancestral beings etched the sea tracks and drew the designs for generations of humans to follow. Boundaries between different sea groups made by ancestral journeys separated and constituted distinct sea worlds, at the same time giving rise not to inert space, but to Law and life. 'Footprints' signify journeys of figures, both animal and human.

Song-cycles are performances that follow a road or track or path. The Yanyuwa people refer to the Dreaming figures as the original 'map-makers'. They composed sacred songs in which particular named localities are 'joined together by a road'; this road is the path these ancestral spirit beings originally created. Yanyuwa people refer to their songs as maps, and so they are, just as the paintings of ancestral clan designs may be seen as maps. They are maps in the sense that they tell about localities which have both spiritual and secular qualities, and in which the identities of the travellers or performers remain highly relevant. These paths join places and groups, but they also include some neighbourhood localities along the way.[22]

The Yanyuwa people's story about the Dugong Hunter Spirit Ancestors tells of how they came from the east and travelled northwest, giving names to dugong sites on the way. The symbol of their 'performance path' is the dugong harpoon rope. 'Rope is the symbol par excellence of the dugong hunter,' Bradley says. It is 'a very potent and sacred object', the subject of 'a very high ceremony' in the past. In stretched out position the rope binds islands together; in its coiled state it symbolises the readiness of the 'dugong hunters of excellence'.

Coiling the dugong rope is a sign of preparation. The imagery of the coiled rope occurs twice in the lines of the Yanyuwa song depicting the Dugong Hunters' epic journey and the creation of sea sites and islands: they stood 'with their ropes' in a 'silent and breathless land' at Cape Vanderlin; and at the western tip of Black Craggy Island the coiled dugong ropes were transformed into the kurrajong trees from which they were made.[23]

The dugong rope, for which Yanyuwa have at least six names, coiled or stretched out, personifies the dugong hunters of excellence, who themselves symbolise the identity of the Yanyuwa as a unique sea–island people. Coiled, the rope is a symbol of the land — the kurrajong trees I have mentioned. Stretched out, it defines dugong-hunting sea country and people. These two positions of the rope are the antithesis of each other, like land and sea. Together they express a relationship between the strengths of sea and land. Tangled rope has no place in this conception; in the sea world of the dugong hunters, it signifies death.

Dugong hunters represent the pinnacle of human strength and courage. Even their hair texture is said to be strong.

As Bradley told me in January 1999, among Yanyuwa people the term for the hair of dugong hunters is the same term given to the 'roly poly' seed-head of island spinifex, symbolising determination and strength. Dugong hunters are represented today as having coiled hair, and coiled rope is the pattern used in the ceremonial body design of dugong hunters. Here are words from a song composed by a Yanyuwa song composer, Jack Baju, in the 1920s: '*Our hair is strong, tightly coiled and heavily oiled. For we are the dugong and sea turtle hunters of excellence.*' The symmetry between coiled hair and coiled dugong harpoon rope is suggestive. The oiled hair is also intimative of the highly prized dugong oil. The song is a response to a slur from a neighbouring group, the assertion of a particular kind of strength, a self-acknowledged pride in being a certain kind of people.[24]

As anthropologist Deborah Rose explains, the riverine people of Yarralin in the Victoria River district refer to the tracks that join points on a landscape as 'strings'. Strings 'are webs of connection'.[25] These strings may be shaped and reshaped or, in other words, may shape the landscape in different ways; and this figure and ground relationship may vary depending on the context of the song being sung or the story being told. Strings may delineate language groups or they may delineate ecological zones. The important thing about strings is that they demarcate various comings together of Dreaming figures.

Those islands that the Dugong Hunter Spirit Ancestors created and *joined together* are connected into a web as 'dugong-hunting country'. Dreaming strings also create 'boundaries' between this and that country and etch out the world of a particular people who are joined together as dugong-hunting people. But a language-based string or rope may overlap the world of this group of dugong hunters. The coming together of tracks and stopping points does not occur only within a single dimension. Narrative figures do the travelling along these paths;

they stop at places and turn into natural features, or transform into other species. They may be land beings or saltwater beings, and they bring dances, songs, plants to a stopping place, or a series of places. In other words, they leave their *personal stamp* upon a place like a footprint.

In bringing separate places into association with one another, the qualities — or personalities one might say — of those places are retained. Song-cycles bring into bold relief the variegated features of different places and create a sense of unity between them. They bring them alive in such a way that senior Yanyuwa men and women can identify at any moment the particular locality the words of a song being sung portrays. Because the powers of Dreaming figures pervade any of the areas passed through, the song-cycle tells the singers of everything present at each place along the path, both secular and sacred landmarks or 'seamarks'. The song-cycle gives a 'map' of the localities and their joining points, but it is the reverse of the modern map in its intentions and therefore its idiom. The path represented in the song-cycle is experiential, personal and personified; it associates specific places and people. In modern Western tradition, the map homogenises in the interests of linear space: the distance from A to B is primary. The particularities of A or B or the path between them are at least secondary; they may even be an impediment to mapping.

There is no word in Aboriginal languages that translates as 'map' with the meaning given the word in English. Nor do Aboriginal people represent country as 'pictures of nature' in their classical traditions. Indeed, the expression 'nature' itself has no ready translation into Aboriginal languages.[26] Aboriginal representations of land and sea country are about the characteristics of a locality. Yanyuwa people's delineation of roads or pathways is by no means limited to single features on the path; they may refer to a range of secular and sacred features on and off 'the beaten track'. Peter Sutton has argued most convincingly that in Aboriginal pictorial representation, reproducing the 'correct' physical and directional features of a landscape is quite secondary to following 'certain principles of design'. In fact, what he calls 'analogic mismatch' between one's experience of distance and direction is indispensable to performance-inspired pictorial representation, referred to by scholars as 'iconography'. In these cultures cyclical time may be 'mapped' on to (sacred) space in pictorial representation, as in the example of the painting named 'Squid and Turtle Dreamings' I gave earlier; and within landscape and seascape, patterning and movement are held in people's minds as four-dimensional space and time. In this perspective, totally unfamiliar to many non-indigenous people, ancestral beings watch life on earth from 'a space where the stars join the inside of the earth'.[27]

To say that 'boundaries' are experiential is to suggest that one knows them by moving through them. And these tracks won't look like mapped lines joining dots 'on the ground'. Their pattern is not necessarily straight-lined; it may be 'more like spaghetti' than a symmetrical whole.[28] Whatever their shape, they are made by figures who walk or canoe (swimming or paddling or sailing their journeys), not by stretching tapes or taking bearings or making soundings. However, when saltwater people sail they do take bearings from land; it is land to which they are ultimately navigating, because that is where their homes are.

Whether these pathways are referred to as strings or tracks, or whether the travels of creator beings are Dreamings or Stories, founding figures or heroes, they follow the same logic of creating associations between places and relationships between people through the points they connect on their journeys. I believe that this applies to *all* the sea peoples — Torres Strait Islander and Aboriginal peoples. It is not just that the travels connect up points, making tracks or pathways; founding figures also demarcate different kinds of country by the depositing of plants that characterise different ecological zones.

The Torres Strait peoples are rich in these types of narratives. The Meriam people see Gelam, the young male dugong, as giving them their land identity. Gelam joined the western with the eastern ecological zones; he also created interrelationships between the Sandbeach People of northeast Cape York Peninsula and Mer. Gelam travelled from his home in Mua, an island in the west of Torres Strait, with his mother; as he swam away from her he kept looking back as he came to each island. When he could no longer see her he created new paths and new islands, joining them together. Then he lay down in the sea and became Mer island, spitting out two bean pips that became the islands of Dauar and Waier. The everlasting daisy that grows at Gelam's nose is said by the Islanders to have come from Mua. Gelam's footprints are also found in country belonging to Kuuk'u Ya'u people, one of the seafaring groups of northeastern Cape York Peninsula.

When the sea god Malo travelled he set up a track like a star path.[29] Hence came the Law of Malo: 'Stars follow their own course across the sky,' and 'One cannot follow the course that is Usiam's [the Pleiades] nor the path that is Sèg's [Orion].' These statements condense a range of meanings; one is that when these narrative hero figures — Malo or Tagai — point to the stars and their paths, they are referring to you and me. 'Follow the footprints laid down by your forebears; do as they said and did on land and sea.' Following the footprints is also a statement about land rights and sea rights: 'keep to and guard the place handed down to you.'

PART IV

EUROPEAN SEA TRADITIONS

7
THE FREEDOM OF THE SEAS

North Australia: Fishing in public waters?

THE PEARL-FISHING BOATS SAILING ALONG THE GREAT Barrier Reef from about the mid-nineteenth century sounded a different note to the murmurings of the Reef to which 'the Barrier' people of the far northeastern reaches of Australia were accustomed. By this time the whole of the Australian coastline had been mapped, its bays, islands, headlands, bluffs and reefs largely renamed. Seamus Heaney's poem 'North', about another time and a different ocean, evokes for me the impact of the pearl rush in tropical waters:

> *I returned to a long strand,*
> *the hammered shod of a bay,*
> *and found only the secular*
> *powers of the Atlantic thundering.*

The sound of metal clanging to the beat of ships in pursuit of 'trade and geography' rose loud in the Torres Strait and the neighbouring mainland of Cape York Peninsula. Resources were in demand. Vast quantities of pearl shell lay on the sea floor in tropical waters. Maritime peoples from afar were implanting their economic values and their marine industries in the Australian tropics.

Because they lived at the sea frontier, saltwater peoples bore the first brunt of invasion. In his 1982 book *Invasion and Resistance* historian Noel Loos has documented thoroughly and systematically the effects on people of the Cape York northern sea frontier. In the early days, piracy, shanghai'ing (stealing people to work the marine industries as slaves), and exploitation of sea and land resources were rife. By and large the intruders of this era did not ask the local seaside inhabitants whether they could sail their seas or dive for pearl shell on the seabed. Sometimes intruders were chased away or killed. In 1885 Pacific Islanders who had settled at Murray Island were expelled and the Meriam inhabitants were told by the Government Resident, the Honourable John Douglas, that they could have Murray Island to themselves.[1] No mention was made of the foreshore or reefs or surrounding seas in written documents of this time. However, as we will see, there was a largely tacit assumption that these home reef-marine areas were for the common use of the Meriam people.

Pearl shelling in the Torres Strait region came to occupy an important place in world terms by the end of the century. Pacific Islanders, Torres Strait Islanders and indentured labourers of mainly Malay and Filipino origin worked on the pearling cutters and luggers, although the industry was carried on largely by Japanese.[2] Across the three states or territories with tropical outreaches pearl shell and trochus production accounted for more than half the world's production of unmanufactured shell at least until the 1920s.[3]

In the Northern Territory, marine industries began modestly with trepanging being carried out by Macassans who, as we saw earlier, had established themselves as visiting trepangers along the Arnhem Land and western Gulf coasts and islands for about two centuries by the time the White Australia policy and tax barriers excluded them in 1907. A fishing industry began gradually in the 'Top End' — as coastal Northern Territory became known — its slow growth, it would seem, not due mainly to shortages of fish. The early European settlers were fully aware of the abundance of fish in the region, but there were few people available to engage in commercial production. The overwhelming focus of development projects was on pastoral and mining pursuits inland. In the two decades from 1890, the annual production of fresh fish for export in the Northern Territory, the main emphasis in marine enterprise, was the equivalent of only 21 tonnes, about 14–18 kilograms per head annually.[4] While opinions differ on the importance of the fishing industry in the overall economy of the Northern Territory (and those who emphasise its importance cite dried fish production and prawn production in the 1880s and 1890s), the land-based focus of pastoralism and mining was primary. Until developments in refrigeration techniques took place after the Second World War there was little incentive to increase marine food production.

After the Second World War new developments occurred in the Top End's fishing industry. By 1974 the Chief Inspector of Fisheries for the Northern Territory could report a growing barramundi fishery in which production had multiplied ten times during the 1950s. While the mining and pastoral industries continued to make a far greater contribution to Territory income than fisheries in the period he reviewed, the latter provided six per cent of Territory gross income in 1972; seafood production per capita was more than twice that of Western Australia and 25 times that of Victoria.[5] By 1996–97, according to official statistics, the total value of production in the Northern Territory fishing industry was $118.4 million, just over half of which was contributed by aquaculture, with fish amounting to less than ten per cent and crustaceans (mainly prawns) to just over 40 per cent.

The slow growth of a fishing industry in the Northern Territory — small by the standards of the world's fishing nations — was regulated by various fisheries legislation designed to administer and regulate how fishing enterprise was to proceed within the sea boundaries of the Northern Territory. As I mentioned earlier, in law all Australian citizens had an equal right of access to the sea, the context for this being the common law recognition of the public right to fish. Licensing became the essential component of government legislation after 1872 when trepang and pearl shell industries became the industrial marine focus. Thirty years later, in 1904, fisheries regulation became comprehensive: annual licences were required in order 'to take fish for sale or barter', fish below a certain weight were proscribed, closed seasons were introduced and the Governor of South Australia was also empowered to prohibit certain fishing devices. Subject to these provisions, no geographical restrictions were made except in waters that 'ebb and flow on lands' reserved for Aboriginal people.[6]

Alongside the state regulation of open-access seas were minimum provisions upholding the rights of Aboriginal people to fish in order to feed themselves. *The Fish and Fisheries Act 1979* (NT) provided for the use of waters 'in accordance with Aboriginal tradition'.[7] However, until 1979, the advice delivered by Viscount Haldane in the Privy Council in 1914, which protected the public right to fish in Canada, reigned unchallenged in the coastal waters of the Northern Territory.[8] On 8 July 1998 when Justice Olney delivered his primary judgment in the *Croker Island Seas* case in the Federal Court of Australia, he cited Viscount Haldane: 'the public have the right to fish, and by reason of the provisions of the

Magna Charta no restriction can be put upon that right of the public by an exercise of the prerogative in the form of a grant or otherwise.' In Australia, it took this major native title sea claim in the 1990s to 3,300 square kilometres of sea around Croker Island in western Arnhem Land, to bring to national public attention the fact that commercial fishing boats following common law principles and statutory rules and regulations (licensing, keeping log books of catches in various areas) were contravening the law and customs of the Islanders. 'Your common law says that the sea belongs to the Crown, but my law says that this belongs to my sea country,' Mary Yarmirr explained to the court in *Yarmirr v. Northern Territory*. 'We do not trespass into another clan's estate without asking permission.'[9] Nor may you.

The three respondents in the *Croker Island Seas* case were the Northern Territory of Australia, the Commonwealth of Australia, and the fishing industry of the Northern Territory. The first two argued that the public right of fishing formed the pivot of the case; the fishing industry contended that its fishers were exercising their common law rights in commercial fishing. The leading spokesman for the fishing industry, Nigel Scullion, recounted to the court his own activities in Spanish mackerel fishing, explaining how the numbers of fishers had been reduced by 90 per cent over twelve years; how he caught about 40 fish per day, often fishing within the area claimed by the Islanders. He also reported his belief that 'the stocks are in a very healthy situation'. Pointing to the reductions in numbers of fishermen over a decade, he emphasised 'sustainability of stocks' and the good use to which the Northern Territory fisheries had put the knowledge they had gained from the failure of other fishers in Australia and elsewhere to conserve fish stocks.[10]

In determining on 6 July 1998 that native title rights exist in the seas claimed by the Croker Islanders, Justice Olney — referred to later in the High Court as 'the primary judge'

— concluded that the exercise of these native title rights 'in accordance with and subject to their [the clans'] traditional laws and customs' gives them 'free access to the sea and the sea-bed' within the area claimed — but for subsistence and cultural, not commercial, purposes. While the rights of the Croker Islanders may coexist with licensed commercial fishing with its various rules, any inconsistency between the two sets of rights and interests must be resolved in accordance with state laws.[11] He reiterated that the public right to fish remains the central assumption of state law and practice. This means that the fishermen holding licences to fish commercially in waters controlled and managed by the state have a right to fish in waters claimed by the Islanders. As we saw in the last chapter, Justice Olney's view that native title in the sea exists as a non-exclusive and non-commercial right was upheld by the majority in the High Court in September 2001.

Others, far away on the margins of Europe, with claims to inherited 'first people' marine rights have described this type of reasoning about priorities as 'the tail wagging the dog'.[12] In a dispute in the 1990s, the inhabitants of the Irish fishing village of Teelin, County Donegal claimed primary rights to the Glen River estuary. Their claim was backed by an ancient custom and unwritten law in which the sharing of the salmon by the inhabitants is ensured by a rotation of throws of the net, each row boat having its turn to cast. Distinguishing themselves from the 'far-siders' of the towns, as well as the recreation fishers from further afield, the Teelin salmon fishermen were defending a provenance which defines sharing in terms of inherited rights rather than open access; rights which are not ruled primarily by the needs of the economic market or the exploitation of marine resources.[13]

Here we come close to a fundamental, if shadowed, cultural difference which has had a great bearing on the failure of courts so far to recognise the primary right to exclusive possession of the marine areas claimed by the Croker Islanders. Their inherited right to decide whether outside fishermen shall continue to take lobsters off their reefs or fish from their waters is not legally acknowledged. The assumption remains that Northern Territory waters are available for those who are equipped to exploit marine resources and add to the national income. From the Croker Islanders' standpoint, state law founded on the premise that licensed commercial fishermen have a coexisting right to fish is unacceptable because they have a prior claim.

In other jurisdictions the priorities of local indigenous property right holders have been given far greater recognition. In the Canadian case *Regina v. Sparrow* (1990), brought by the Musqueam people in British Columbia, the Musqueam's fishing needs were put first after conservation needs were met; any fish still available after that could be taken by commercial fishermen and anglers. Even more radical in its protection of the rights of the tribes of northwest Washington State is the 1974 US judgment known as 'the Boldt decision'. The District Court for Washington upheld mid-nineteenth century treaty rights of the tribes of the Pacific seaboard to hunt in all 'usual and accustomed places' on and off reservations, the right to exclude others from certain fishing grounds in rivers and bays, and the right to participate in regional fisheries management.[14]

However, in Australia until now, the public right to fish in tidal and coastal waters has continued to override any other custom or right. This is well illustrated by the judgment of Justice Mansfield in the Federal Court of Australia on 24 February 2000 in the *Intertidal Zone and Tidal Rivers* case in the Northern Territory. According to that decision, commercial fishing may continue in all tidal waters seaward of the high-water mark. Despite the recognition of Aboriginal rights to land to the low-water mark under the *Aboriginal Land Rights (Northern*

Territory) Act 1976, commercial fishing among non-indigenous fishers is permissible, including at the mouth of the river.

The strength of the public right to fish in such saltwater areas leads back to questions I posed in the first chapter. Where did this public right to fish come from? Why is it taken for granted today? And how did it come to be a foundation stone of sovereign states? We know it draws upon an ancient tradition of sharing the sea as a gift to all humankind. But several centuries ago this tradition began to be linked to new goals of sea resource entrepreneurship which carried an individualist ethic. It also became the cornerstone of the concept of the territorial seas of sovereign states. Sharing the sea is a most appealing idea and has immense power. However, not always apparent is the paradox between the ethic of sharing that originally nurtured that tradition and the contrary goals of individual acquisitiveness that came to be pursued in the name of freedom of the seas.

In the name of freedom: A common gift

THE EPIC SEA VOYAGES OF THE LATE EIGHTEENTH and the nineteenth centuries carried the spirit of ancient voyages. They were also the culmination of projects which, since the seventeenth century, had enclosed the lands as private property while declaring that the citizens of sovereign states be given 'open access' to newly defined territorial seas. Tennyson's poem *Ulysses*, reviving the hope of unending voyaging, is a metaphor for Enlightenment-inspired beliefs in the ascent of man and material progress: *For my purpose holds/To sail beyond the sunset, and the baths/Of all the western stars, until I die*. The freedom to sail beyond the sunset is an idea whose magnetic pull is entwined with hope for the freedom of the human spirit. The God-given chance to venture out into the dread and glorious oceans stirred ancient dreams. And by the nineteenth century there was hardly a more noble goal than venturing over the seas to expand the realms of empire and industry.

The right to navigate freely the widest expanses of oceans was the indispensable condition for consolidating the rising imperiums of Europe. This very freedom guaranteed the inexorable and rapid development of property in land as an economic commodity value. In turn, it ensured that rising industrial capitalism would demolish the old structures of agriculture, crofting and fishing, leaving vast numbers of land-less and sea-less people with a freedom to sell only their labour power. Herein lies the tragic paradox of the 'freedom of the seas'. The belief in property as the centre of human values sat back to back with the belief in freedom of the seas as a natural right.

In these centuries the freedom of the seas was essential to the opening up of the oceans of the world to trade and commerce. The Dutch jurist Hugo Grotius, at the beginning of the seventeenth century, chose compelling words to legitimise competitive imperial aims on the high seas. In *Mare Liberum, Freedom of the Seas*, he identifies with indignation the grave matter at issue: the intention of the Portuguese and the Spanish to allocate all the earth's oceans for their exclusive navigation, leaving only 'the narrow bounds of the northern seas' for the maritime activities of 'all the rest of the peoples of the world'.[15] His treatise was short, its impact far-reaching.

Grotius' *Mare Liberum* was published secretly in 1609. It was part of his treatise *De Jure Praedae*, which remained unpublished until 1868. *Mare Liberum* became the classic work on the doctrine of freedom of the seas. Its lasting appeal may be found in the deeply held belief that the surrounding ocean was a gift of God to all peoples 'speaking through the voice of Nature'. A monument to Grotius stands tall between the Old and New churches in the public square in his birthplace, Delft, in the

Netherlands. His ideas were to play a profound cultural-political role in realms he hardly mentioned.

Thirty years after the first Latin edition of *Mare Liberum* was published in 1633, another persuasive book was published on *The Right and Dominion of the Sea*, with the Latin title *Mare Clausum*. Its author, English jurist John Selden, offered it 'most reverentially' to Prince Charles. His treatise was written in the context of Britain's search for the legal means to exclude Dutch fishing vessels from her territorial waters. Selden's two important volumes were remembered almost exclusively as being in opposition to Grotius' thesis. Yet Grotius and Selden came to accept the principle of state sovereignty over territorial waters, a concept already firmly established through the work of the sixteenth-century Italian jurist Albericus Gentilis.[16] The words in Selden's treatise, 'the King of Great Britain is Lord of, the Sea flowing about [Britain]' refer directly to marine sovereignty.[17]

Grotius drew upon the works of classical Roman thinkers — Virgil, Ovid, Cicero and Seneca. According to Virgil, the shore, the sea and the air are open to all people; sun, air, waves 'are public gifts', Ovid wrote; nature herself enjoins common use of the sea. Cicero wrote that seas are not private property but 'seem to have been created by nature for common use'.[18] Yet there is an important difference between Grotius and the ancient jurists. Lucius Seneca, one of the later Stoics of Roman times, lived from 4BC to 65AD. He spoke with passion against those who use this common gift of the sea 'for commercial or other gain'.[19] In contrast, Grotius' preoccupations were commercial. *Mare Liberum* was part of a treatise which he had been asked to prepare in support of the Dutch East India Company, to whom he was legal adviser and advocate. His persuasive writing called upon strongly embedded cultural memories of a common right of fishing, which had arisen in an earlier age. He placed these beliefs in the service of aims opposite to the institutions and purposes that had nurtured them.

In succeeding centuries jurists have called upon this right of the people in upholding the King's or the state's privilege in the name of a natural right — what Grotius called God's gift 'speaking through the voice of Nature'. Thus for example, the nineteenth-century jurist Hall, in his 1875 commentary *Hall on the Sea-Shore*, makes a summary statement that the public right to fish 'by the common law, and custom of the Realm' was a privilege vested in the King or given by him as a grant at a time before living memory.[20]

Hall and jurists before and after him are drawing on a cultural tradition embedded in the common law whose source is often forgotten but which is felt elementally: 'like the air we breathe', the sea 'has ever been free and unquestioned in enjoyment', Hall wrote. Although its origin may be unknown to jurists and others, the public right to fish in tidal waters and, by extension, 'the liberty of fishing' in the sea has, until very recent times, been regarded as sacrosanct.[21]

The public right to fish and the vision of the freedom of the seas continued to have the power to stir the emotions over many centuries. In the context of the First World War The Grotius Society was formed in London in 1915 to encourage discussion of the Laws of War and Peace in accordance with the principles of International Law. As a member of The Grotius Society wrote of *Mare Liberum* in 1919, in appealing to laws 'written in the minds and on the hearts of every individual' Grotius 'appealed to the common sense of mankind for what was fair and right'.[22] Like a biblical text its thesis was not available for discussion, even less for critique.[23]

This liberty or public right has been upheld again and again in legal cases and treatises. In his important *De Jure Maris* published in 1787, Lord Hale wrote 'of that common liberty of the common people of England' to fish in tidal waters held in trust for their use by the King, except where he has granted an exclusive right limiting their 'public common of piscary', that is, their common liberty of fishing.[24] Until very recently, legal authorities have stated — consistently it would seem, in cases cited from at least 1674 — that any restriction on *iuris publici*, the public right to fish, preceded the Magna Carta. This view, unchallenged until recent times, has it that the public right to fish in tidal waters in England was enshrined in the common law in 1215.

In a famous moment in history, King John was compelled by discontented barons, who had been denied access to the King's waters, to sign an agreement that all citizens had an equal right to fish anywhere in England. The view that the public right to fish was enshrined in the document he signed — the Magna Carta — has been upheld in modern legal judgments on various occasions: perhaps most famously by Viscount Haldane in *Attorney-General British Columbia v. Attorney-General for Canada* (1914), and in Australia in *Harper v. Minister for Sea Fisheries* (1989) and, as we have seen, by the High Court in the *Croker Island Seas* case in 2001. The belief that any restriction of this public right must have preceded Magna Carta — that is, that several or private fisheries could not have been granted after 1215 — has been questioned recently, as has the meaning of the clause restraining the King from exercising monopoly powers according to his whim.[25]

Whether a provision of the Magna Carta was simply to restrain the King from monopolising tidal waters, or whether it deprived the Crown of creating private, exclusive fisheries, is largely immaterial to my argument here. In restraining the King from infringing on the common liberty of fishing — which, as I have said, owed much to Roman law, but which may also have existed under the Saxon kings before the Norman invasion — the Magna Carta was upholding this common right. The public responded as though a public right of fishing had been reinstated. If so, two ideas on the changing meanings of 'public rights' suggest themselves. The first is that the liberty of fishing came from and was embedded in customary common property rights that may have pre-existed feudal ownership and law. The second is that over about five centuries following the signing of the Magna Carta, the public right to fish took on a new meaning within the changing context of the rise of the modern state.

Sovereigns and sovereignty

THE DECLINE OF FEUDALISM AND THE RISE OF capitalism began in the seventeenth century, the era of the emergence of monarchical sovereign states. In the eighteenth century, famed English jurist Sir William Blackstone upheld the public right to fish, as I mentioned early on. Blackstone believed the signing of Magna Carta five centuries before his time provided a barrier to the establishment of private fisheries, a view under scrutiny, even challenge, today in legal cases concerned with the limitation of the Crown's sovereign rights by native title.[26] Already in 1674 in *Lord Fitzwalter's* case, Lord Hale had emphasised that the right to fish was 'common to all'; and in his work *De Jure Maris*, his interpretation that the Crown prerogative over fishing is a form of public trust accords with that of Sir William Blackstone. The idea that the King was now 'seized in trust for his subjects' was echoed by Justice Heath in *Kelsey v. Baker* (1803).[27]

However, the Magna Carta alone does not explain how the public right to fish spread throughout Europe. Similar rights emerged in European coastal states without Magna Cartas. Nor does it explain how open access to state territorial waters became enshrined in the statutes of all European coastal states. Answers to these questions depend upon the emergence of the doctrine of sovereignty and the rise of the modern state. Here I shall just point briefly to the nature of this transformation, foreshadowing some of the changes that altered the fabric of social life.

In the thirteenth century when King John signed the Magna Carta, the idea that the sovereign exercised jurisdiction over all adjacent seas had not yet found legal form. Between the thirteenth and sixteenth centuries, the concept of territorial seas was given expression largely through the work of the Italian jurist Albericus Gentilis. In this period, in various parts of coastal Europe, rulers claimed power over waters adjacent to their territories. In this 'pre-sovereignty' period the Venetians owned gulfs and bays adjacent to their lands and claimed jurisdiction over the upper Adriatic by right of ownership.[28] Under the Emperor Justinian, who reigned from 527 to 565 AD, portions of sea were enclosed to form fish-traps and some lords had estates with vast sea frontages. Yet it was not until the ascendance of capitalism from the seventeenth century onwards that the idea of sovereignty — that is, a supreme political power above all other powers — found expression in international law. The existence of state territorial seas was dependent upon the emergence of sovereign states; their recognition was expressive of a law between them. Beaches, estuaries, inlets, reefs, fishing grounds, often held in customary ownership by groups of local inhabitants, were absorbed into territorial state seas organised as anonymous space. (The meaning of 'anonymous space' will become clearer later when I explore some aspects of the shift from logs and journeys to mapping and charting of marine space. These changes are integral to the rise of modern sovereign states and imperial projects.)

Purposes new and old

A RESOURCE AND ECONOMIC PROFIT-BASED RELATIONSHIP with the sea carries certain new cultural values which emphasise possession and individual rights. In other words, the redefinition of cultural values is associated with a remoulding of the individual person; the pursuit of profit, commodities, individual 'betterment' defined in terms of material possessions, replaces or at least pushes the ethic of reciprocity and sharing into the wings. Public rights to fish were integral with the rise of capitalist forms of property in land. The ideology of possessive individualism is a grounding tenet of capitalism. While most visible with respect to property in land, it is also integral with exploitation of sea resources, although this connection only became obvious when 'free riding' — an expression popularised by resource economist Garrett Hardin — took a major toll of sea resources in modern times.

One expression of this change is a silence about systems in which commercial trade was or is secondary to self-sufficiency. Such systems are not only forgotten; it is as though they have never existed. This is a powerful tendency. However, memories passed down from 'immemorial time' carry traces of a tradition born of a different social era; yet the very different social conditions which gave the tradition birth and sustained it are lost to memory. Generally forgotten is the fact that *publici iuris* in Roman law was integral with a social life in which the form of private rights, as we know them in modern times, did not exist. These latter were part of feudal law introduced into England by the Normans.[29] In other words, as new goals and social relations emerged, knowledge of the rather different conditions from which they had arisen was lost.

The idea of a public right of fishing had its origins in more or less ancient common property regimes and found expression in customary laws and rules in situations either pre-dating or developing independently of feudal law. These rights belonged to defined groups of inhabitants of particular locales and, at least informally, were passed on by inheritance. The rights of the

Haleygiums of Trondheim, northern Norway, or the rights of members of a Tuath or Kingdom under the Brehon Law of Ireland, are of this kind. Each of these peoples was 'a public' enjoying fishing rights to the tidal waters of their common property to the exclusion of other inhabitants of Ireland or Norway. The Irish case of *Moore v. Attorney General* (1934) supports this interpretation. It concerned rights that may have existed in 1189 to The Salmon Leap, a tidal portion of the River Erne in present day County Donegal. Justice Fitzgibbon, one appeal judge, stated that the right of members of a Tuath at that time 'would be analogous to a public right of fishing'. As he explained, according to the Brehon Law 'the salmon of the place' belonged 'in equal right to every condition of person', by which he meant 'the public' of a Tuath.[30]

Customary rights of groups of inhabitants along the coasts of Britain and Ireland were eclipsed in the name of a redefined public right to fish. As I have said, carrying on in memory are beliefs about the natural liberty to fish. However, this is no longer the right of a local group of coastal inhabitants; it has been redefined as an *individually based* right to fish freely in territorial waters.

The immense and elemental appeal of this belief has been placed in question over the last 30 years when blame for 'free riding' — pursuing single-mindedly one's own individual interest — in open access situations has often been placed at the door of open access itself. What is not often said is that free riding and over-exploitation of fish stocks may not be a product of an inherently selfish human nature. It may be indicative of the possessive individualist ethic accompanying the market economy, which is neither universal nor an essential feature of human nature.

There are two important consequences of the development of a market economy centred on possessive individualism. The first is the above-mentioned emergence of private rights to land and public rights/open access to state territorial seas. The second concerns a contrast between commoners' rights to land with their rights to marine domains in the last few centuries. Human ecologist Bonnie McCay refers to the tragic effects of the land enclosures that took place in England, especially when individual ownership supplanted common lands in the eighteenth century. Were these events paralleled on the coasts? Or were inhabitants along the coasts of European states able to pursue in some degree 'the liberty of fishing' within the carapace created by the public right of fishing? Since this second area relies on lost memories and meagre records, the answers can only be suggestive and tentative rather than systematic.

Private rights to land, public rights to sea

Historically speaking, the transformation of property relations in Europe after the seventeenth century was accompanied by the belief that this new social construction of landscape and seascape was natural and universal.[31] Land became real estate; seas were supposedly unavailable for ownership. Public rights to territorial seas are legal rights but they are not property rights. The privileging of private property in Western imagination and in law meant the disappearance of customary property relations in land and sea both from social life and the imagination. Property held jointly or in common by an identifiable geographically based corporate group of people united in one body was, generally speaking, simply not recognised by states as being genuinely owned.

Resource economist Garrett Hardin is well known for his 1968 article 'The Tragedy of the Commons'. Published at a time when marine resource depletion had reached serious proportions, the article became very influential indeed. Hardin assumed that people put individual gain first regardless of the consequences; they will always over-exploit resources available within public space. 'Free riding', or the irresponsible use of resources, is, according to Hardin, the expression of the pursuit of each individual's 'own best interest'.[32] Hardin's observation is valid enough, but his interpretation is quite specious. He assumed that individual self-interest is 'natural' and sought solutions in the curbing of individual will by the coercive force of bureaucratic regulation. Yet this ignores evidence that some forms of property and social rules of behaviour 'create' a human nature in which individual greed is actually marginalised. For instance, not to be generous with food is shameful among the Meriam and others. Complementary ties between Yolŋu clans guarantee that one will light the fires for the other. And among Croker Islanders and others there is the Law that says: 'take only what you need and return the turtle bones to the sea'. If these examples seem esoteric they will seem less so in the light of recent research findings which locate systems on the margins of Europe that depend on cooperation rather than the pursuit of goals based on possessive individualism.

From the mid-1970s, scholars in fields ranging from anthropology and economics to human ecology have made ground-breaking insights (often in reply to Hardin) into the character of common-property institutions and their relevance in human ecology and resource conservation and management. I can only refer fleetingly here to the enormous contribution they have made both in clarification of concepts and in practical life.[33] Open access to coastal seas has nothing to do with commons or property in common. It has become associated with a mode of individualised land ownership and a construction of 'human nature' as unrestrained individualism. Common property regimes are integral with a way of being human in which rights bring with them inseparable obligations. As we have seen, 'belonging' does not only confer rights; it means acting with or on behalf of those to whom one has obligations. In common property regimes there is explicit or tacit agreement on a set of rules of behaviour. Behind major terminological confusion lie conceptual inadequacies which have led to the belief that 'the misuse of resources' and the consequent 'tragedy of the commons' are attributable to the institution of common property itself.

The history of various types of rights, tenures and fishing practices in Europe is accompanied by conceptual confusion. Our understanding is hampered both by the compounding of categories and the compartmentalism of studies. For example, legal literature on common law rights is saturated in assumptions about private versus public rights and there is an inherent lack of acknowledgement of common property rights. It ignores the transformation in forms of property ownership, and the changes in meaning that freedom of the seas and the liberty of fishing have undergone from ancient times until today. Fortunately economic and social historians have begun to explore changes in social forms and their expression in property relations and rights. The most promising work I believe comes from that centred on the study of common property.

Firstly there is a fundamental distinction between common property regimes and institutions of private individual ownership, known in legal language as severalty. Secondly, open access is not an institution of common property.[34] A recognition of the mistaken equation of common property and open access, or the latter's inclusion within the generic category of common property regimes, is helpful in the process of identifying fundamental cultural differences in the representation, definition and use of sea space. As economic historian Daniel Bromley has concluded: 'Many of us see situations of open access and improperly regard them as situations of common property.' Yet, he says, 'a critical difference between "open-access resources" and "common property resources" turns on the very concept of property.' There is 'no property' in open access situations, 'only the opportunity to use something'. In contrast, a common property regime is taken to be *'a well-defined group whose membership is restricted'*.[35] A difficulty is that English common law and its offshoots have only two categories of rights: private rights and public rights. Neither describe common property rights, whether these be indigenous property rights in Australia or anywhere else. This dichotomy presented a dilemma for legal counsel in *Mabo*. After careful consideration, the original claim defined the Meriam property rights as private; the final claim, redrafted in response to a High Court request, was made on behalf of the collective rights of the Meriam to the whole island of Mer.[36]

In the same historical period when enclosed land — that is, land held in absolute individual ownership — uprooted common property institutions, the marine territories of the coasts were being 'freed' of any customary joint rights vested in local groups in the name of public rights of all citizens of absolutist states. While land was assigned the status of a commodity which a sole owner might now dispose of as he wished, the foreshore and the adjacent seas were being declared the property of no one. As a means to market ends, freedom of access to the seas could simply appear as a socially neutral backdrop to an overarching goal. Yet, as Bonnie McCay has observed, the declaration and practice of open seas was essential for capitalist development.[37]

Characteristically, ownership by a group — a family, household, clan — carries an obligation to members of that group, both living and yet unborn. As I have said, this form of ownership lies behind the tree analogy used by the late Daymbalipu Munuŋgurr to explain Yolŋu ownership to teachers at Yirrkala. Marriage ties between clans, as senior Yolŋu saltwater man Dula Ŋurruwuthun explained poetically, create extended obligations. A person's 'best interest' is defined socially. In fact it is so built into the situation that not being generous is experienced by a person as shame. By contrast, the modern individual owner is no longer restricted by obligations to other members of an identifiable group or through ties to other groups by reciprocal bonds. Economic historian Alan Macfarlane identifies this historical transformation clearly in his book, *The Origins of English Individualism*. The landowner is now 'not merely the trustee or organizer of a small corporate group who jointly owned the land . . . The land is *his* land.'[38] His descendants by birth or adoption can be disinherited by him, a concept unknown and antithetical to joint ownership. This represents a major and crucial difference between the old and the new mode of ownership. It was this new system which came to predominate in England in the seventeenth and eighteenth centuries.

A classification of land–sea tenures and a delineation of their broader classificatory context is both difficult and urgent. It is difficult because both on land and sea mixed regimes coexist within emergent state forms in history and within modern polities. While state territorial seas may be declared as open access domains through government statute, customary rights may continue to be followed in certain locales; in other situations, and despite authoritative declarations to the contrary, the private rights of landlords or capitalist interests to coastal areas may prevail.

Sociologist John Phyne documents the way in which the Crown Estate, created in 1760 by George II as the owner of the seabed and foreshore around the United Kingdom, has operated in Scotland in contemporary times to promote large-scale capitalist aquaculture and 'the enclosure of the coastal commons'.[39] Moreover, despite the beliefs of crofters in the existence of a long-standing open access to the sea, disputes with landlords occur today. A recent case between a highland estate and crofters was reported in the publication *UK News* on 13 December 1996. It concerned a claim by Macleod Estates of Dunvegan on the island of Skye to a Barony title to the foreshore created in 1611. Crofters involved in salmon farming were being asked to pay yearly rent to the estate for use of a pebble slipway, about four metres wide, for access to the sea.

Despite besetting difficulties — and the dangers of 'terminological shipwreck', a graphic expression of economic historian H. S. A. Fox[40] — it is urgent to untangle the confusion between categories of tenure for reasons which go far beyond questions of classification. Nor is clarification an end in itself. Demonstrating the connection between forms of property relations on the one hand and the construction of cultural values on the other hand may open the way to examining forms of property relations based on the interdependence of rights *and* responsibilities rather than on the pursuit of the individual's 'best interests' and the exploitation of resources.[41] I wish to refute the tenacious belief that there are no alternatives to the use of government regulation and policing to curb over-exploitation. Meriam witnesses provided testimony on such a system in the *Mabo* case but were not always understood by the court. Landowner Gobedar Noah told the court: 'My dad told me, "If I am gone, you have every right and all the responsibility" for the land as the eldest son.' This is a truth that all Meriam take for granted: an owner has no individual right to do whatever he wants to; he acts as the nameholder on behalf of a group of joint clan or family owners. Plaintiff Reverend Dave Passi explained the owner's function this way: he is 'a centre for the clan to hold unity within'.[42]

A basic classification of land and sea tenures is set out below. In fact, 'tenure' may be the wrong word to use in relation to open access regimes which, by definition, exclude the idea of property.

Land and Sea Holding Patterns

	Land	*Coastal marine space*
(1)	Common property (inalienable tenure)	Common property (inalienable tenure)
(2)	Individual private ownership (alienable title)	Open access (state 'tenure')

A major distinction exists between (1) common property in respect to 'plots' of land and sea, and (2) individually based private property in land. As already noted, open access to coastal seas developed in integral connection with private property in land, the latter being expressive of a transition that occurred in Europe, and in a most pronounced form in England, from the seventeenth century onwards. That transition may be seen as one from ownership by petty producers to capitalist ownership, as a change from use values to exchange values, or as an alteration in the balance between reciprocal and commodity exchange relations.

The basic distinctions I have made above require several qualifications. All of these are associated in some way with the disappearance of common property institutions from mainstream models of property systems. As I have said, there are only two categories of rights in Anglo-Australian law: private rights and public rights. Yet in practice there are usually mixed systems of access and ownership, exchange relations and productive systems, in which one system is dominant. Only a few scholars have sought to clarify analytically the coexistence of different systems within a society or to delineate their contrasting principles.[43] Distinctive features of tenures are not always apparent. Marine regimes are often constructed as open-access situations; yet unwritten (customary) rules between those sharing common property may exist unbeknown to those who administer 'official' regimes. As one scholar has noted, 'What appears to the outside observer to be open access may involve tacit cooperation by individual users according to a complex set of rules specifying rights of joint use.'[44] The lack of an agreed definition of respective regimes is itself tied to the more basic question of what criteria are used to distinguish various tenures.

Finally, as I have illustrated in the preceding pages, there has been a failure to question long-standing beliefs about an individualistic competitive human nature prone to break out in cowboy-like 'free riding'. This failure precludes an understanding of the socially created character of the individualist ethic as a primary social value. It ignores the difference between social life based upon gift exchange — a hat for a bowlful of corn — and that where the personality of the producer is dissolved in money market relations.

Tragedies and lingering rights

IN HIS BOOK *WHIGS AND HUNTERS*, HISTORIAN E.P. Thompson explains in a graphic way how the British national state in the eighteenth century 'existed to preserve the property and . . . the lives and liberties of the propertied'.[45] Ancient agrarian common use rights in forests and rivers, especially in England, were extinguished by law through the imposition of new definitions of property rights. As Thompson explains, in eighteenth century England the inexorable thrust of the enclosure of common land was registered in the 'Black Act' of 1723. This restricted 'non-monetary use rights' — fish caught 'for the pot' — by outlawing the forest commons. 'Blacking', the practice of blackening the face to prevent identification, was punishable by death and many a man seeking to feed himself and his family from forests that had long been traditional commons went to the gallows. The practice of 'Blacking' arose from the fear of informers and fear of transportation. In the confrontation between armed and disguised foresters and the gamekeepers between 1720 and 1723 the Blacks or 'armed foresters' sometimes banded together in secret fraternities, achieving what Thompson calls 'a hegemony in the forest'.[46]

Tapping into the core of cultural memory, Thompson examines how force of tradition fuelled the actions of country people in defence of their perceived rights to forest, fish and game. Whenever timber was felled tenants were present in numbers, asserting a claim to a share in the offal wood even 'in the teeth of the law'. Thompson cites the words of an authority in 1729: 'It is very observable that the country people everywhere think they have a sort of right to the wood and timber in the forests.'[47] When, for instance, the day came for the sale of faggots in Frensham forests in 1788, the people 'openly carried off' 6,365 faggots in one day and night beforehand; so complete was their solidarity that in that year no forest official could be found to execute a warrant against any one of them for stealing.

Thompson's study of the land commons and their enclosure may well be unique. I have been able to find only the most meagre information as to what was happening to the sea commons in the same period. Bonnie McCay notes the absence of any 'focused history of fishing laws and rights in the Old World'.[48] *The Atlantic Salmon: A Vanishing Species?*, the 1968 book by Anthony Netboy, provides information on the history of rights to fish in the inland waters of Spain, France, Sweden, Norway, England and Wales, Scotland and Ireland, and to some extent in their coastal waters. Netboy illustrates how rights to the highly prized Atlantic salmon became the preserve of the nobility, although there were also important variations in fishing rules. As I have indicated, in Norway peasant holdings included fishing rights substantial enough to create what Netboy calls 'communal systems of fishing'.[49] However, significantly, Netboy's work does not separate out national, regional and local fishing rights, information vital to an understanding of particular systems of marine tenure and fishing rights, their evolution and social historical transformations.[50] Nor does it make a distinction of vital importance to this study — between fishing in inland rivers and fishing in tidal waters.

McCay argues that 'freedom of the seas' became an ideological justification for destroying the 'natural' rights to 'wild nature' (*ferae naturae*), experienced as the right to a 'fish for the pot' or a 'faggot for the fire'. As she sees it, 'While the freedom of the seas" was developing in international law and expanding throughout the globe, the freedom to fish was being severely eroded in Europe.' Whatever the statutes or the promulgation of the public right to fish, open access 'was abridged and supplemented by claims of the Crown and landowners and the development of complex common-law rights'; in fact, '[o]pen access to the fisheries of England and Wales was gradually whittled away'.[51] Those people with long-standing rights to the *ferae naturae* of forests, rivers and coastal areas were forced to either starve or poach.

Even in contemporary times, 'the keepers of tradition' on the margins of the United Kingdom remember this tragedy through unwritten memories handed down to them. In August 1995 I sought out the Gaelic poet and keeper of tradition, the late Sorley McLean, living then at Sconser on the island of Skye. He told me then that the *cairidhs*, usually semi-circular stone fish-traps set below the high-water mark, were in use on the island within the last half century. Like the stone fish-traps built several thousand years ago by the ancestors of the Bardi and Jawi peoples of the southwest Kimberleys and the Meriam people of the Great Barrier Reef, these fish-traps trapped any fish that were on the shore side as the tide receded. The fisherfolk, male and female, would arrive well in advance of operations, the appearance of a certain rock above the water being the signal to begin. Once the word had been given the entire company would advance into the water, slanting their nets until the fish became trapped. This ancient way of fishing was declared illegal in Scotland in the mid-nineteenth century and the *cairidhs* were broken down by landlords wishing to keep the salmon for their guests.

On the island of Skye I saw one of the four remaining stone fish-traps near the village of Sconser, a solitary monument to the inhabitants of sea communities all around the island. Sorley McLean recalled to me how hundreds of these fish-traps were smashed by landlords during the Clearances of the nineteenth century. Were these few remaining *cairidhs* but monuments to haunting memories? McLean pointed to a resilience in the villagers' adaptation to changed circumstances: 'after the clans had gone, the local community exercised group rights to the foreshore'. He continued: 'I remember a traditional rule about how places were for certain people.' Sea wrack is the name used in Scotland and Ireland for the type of seaweed they used as a fertiliser for their potatoes and other crops. When sea wrack came ashore, word was sent round so that every family knew about it. McLean noted that the share of an absent family was always kept for them.

Rediscovering common property rights

THE DEVASTATION OF MARINE LIFE, ESPECIALLY FISH, which came to crisis point in the 1960s and 1970s, has been a stimulus for two opposing trends. One is the public assertion of lingering common property rights or customary marine tenures as a basis for fishing and the possibilities of cooperation among fishers: cooperative management of fisheries and their habitat among and between groups with common property interests and use rights. A second and very powerful trend, developing on a global scale in the 1990s, is a move towards a form of privatisation known as property rights-based fishing. The latter, considered in the concluding chapter, challenges the once unassailable doctrine of the public right to fish and open access to coastal seas. Some twenty years ago, Individual Transferable Quotas, or ITQs as they are known in the fishing industry, were introduced to prevent free riding. The hope was that even limited property rights in fish — 'owning' a quota — might help to overcome the problem of over-exploitation that government regulation had failed to check. The thinking behind this move was that ownership powers would make fishers accountable. At the end of the twentieth century, property-rights based fishing began to challenge, as well as to qualify, open access or public rights to coastal seas.

The first trend brings to public awareness the coexistence of customary fishing traditions and marine ownership with other regimes in various parts of the world, including outlying parts of contemporary Europe. Examples of this trend range across the globe. The *Croker Island Seas* case, the Meriam community fishing project in customary waters, the combined islands sea claim in the Torres Strait, the Mi'kmaq people's challenge to non-indigenous fishermen in 1999, or the recent call for customary sea rights by the chiefs of the four northern islands of New Caledonia (the Loyalty Islands), exemplify this trend in different ways. In a form without parallel in Australia, the fisheries owned by the associated clans of the *iwi* or tribes of New Zealand provide important examples of indigenous commercial and customary fisheries in the South Pacific region.[52]

About twenty-five years ago attention turned towards the skill with which 'small boat fishermen . . . carve out and claim sea territories'. Writing from the perspective of the small fishing communities off the coasts and off-shore islands of a great variety of national states, marine policy authority and anthropologist John Cordell noted the 'cultural embeddedness' of customary sea tenure which manifests itself in a shared set of rules concerning boundary limits, entry rules and general fishing etiquette.[53]

As John Cordell has noted, the few ethnographic field studies of local ownership of sea territories carried out in the 1970s, mainly among indigenous peoples on the periphery of settler colonies, were seen at first as discoveries of 'unique, rare or isolated systems'.[54] In 1998, anthropologist Nicolas Peterson and linguist–anthropologist Bruce Rigsby drew attention to an 'ethnographic blind spot' on indigenous marine rights. They edited a book of essays — *Customary Marine Tenure in Australia* — to which I referred earlier, which drew attention to the relative absence of a literature on saltwater peoples in Australia. In light of a contestation of rights to sea territories by indigenous owners in the 1990s, the earlier failure to take them seriously is seen as 'extraordinary in retrospect'.[55] According to John Cordell, a pioneer in this area of inquiry, the substantive ethnographic field studies of customary marine tenures began only in 1972.[56]

Towards the end of the 1980s, ongoing threats to the marine environment led some scholars to take an interest in the 'sea commons'. An International Association for the Study of Common Property, formed in 1990, helped to focus research interest in unchartered waters through its international conferences on common property and resulting publications. This interest was by no means purely academic. Common property situations, some of them ancient, others a few generations old, had generated and been guided more by the values and practices of a cooperative than by an individualist ethic. It was that moral force of cooperation which seemed to suggest an alternative to the values of possessive individualism, of the pursuit of rights without exercise of responsibilities which is characteristic of 'free riding'.

During the 1990s especially, research began to reveal that in marine areas where customary inheritances and practices were strong and incursions of outsiders few, local people with land abutting the sea-shore had been following unwritten rules which they took for granted as their inherited fishing rights. Public rights or open access to state territorial seas and beaches acted as a carapace within which common property rights of coastal inhabitants continued to be exercised even into contemporary times. However, public acknowledgement of the right to possession of the foreshore or waters adjoining land property had occurred only occasionally. One such statement of recognition came from English jurist and legal scholar John Lightwood in 1894. Concluding that persons who owned land adjacent to the foreshore 'may probably be entitled to possession' of it, his *A Treatise on Possession of Land* identifies 'acts of ownership'. Among persons whose land abuts the sea-shore, even 'acts of slight importance, such as the gathering of sea-weed, the taking of shell-fish, and the planting of stakes for fishing-nets, are often conclusive in claims founded on the alleged possession of foreshore'.[57]

EARLIER I SAID THAT THE CUSTOMARY RIGHT TO FISH often evolved in ancient times when a 'common right' or a 'public right' meant something different to the meaning given it by the modern sovereign state. Because these early rights were often absorbed into modern state systems their past existence has been largely forgotten. Given this difficulty, I draw upon historical experience in places and amongst peoples outside the feudal situation. Northern Norway appeared to be such an exception.

Before visiting Norway in August 1995 I had read about surviving fishing rights and customs in some Scandinavian countries. Anthony Netboy refers to 'peasant holdings with fishing rights' handed down over 400 years in Sweden. He also recounts how Knut Dahl, whose book on salmon trout was published in 1914, was told by old people in the Trondheim district of a long-standing custom where families clubbed together in the autumn to fish the small river pools, dividing the catches equally among the participants.[58] These people were exercising common property rights based upon 'habitation or ownership within geographically limited areas' that give local citizens the equal right to participate.[59]

Peter Örebech, a social scientist whom I met at the Fisheries Institute of the University of Tromsø, told me the origin of common property rights in northern Norway. A famous Norse saga tells how common property rights to an inner land commons and an outer seas commons exclusive to some 23,000 inhabitants at Trondheim or Haalogaland were recognised through 'a King's Gift' between 1103–07 AD. Each fisherman paid five fish in return for this right to 'all fishing gifts' in the area. In 1800 these fisheries of the outer sea commons were opened to southern Norwegians as public right fisheries, and these rights developed alongside the common property rights of the Haleygiums whose descendants live in Finnmark and Troms today, two northern counties of Norway.[60]

Are common property rights dead there? Or have they survived into modern times? It so happened that events in the fishing industry in those northern counties of Norway in the early 1990s were to demonstrate that people there engaged in fishing as 'an informal system of use rights' deriving from 'attachment to a certain geographical sea space'.[61] Around 1990 a local sea commons, which inhabitants had known for generations, was being closed: a quota system emphasising technical efficiency was being established. Anita Maurstad, a sociologist based at the University of Tromsø in northern Norway and an experienced fisher herself, was witness to this historic transformation.

Maurstad's subsequent study of customary practices found that more than 60 per cent of the Norwegian fishing fleet of boats of more than eight metres was accounted for by small boats. In her own home county of Troms and in Finnmark she observed informal structures operating which the participants had taken for granted until they came under threat. These coastal fishermen were practising fishing according to unwritten rules in a dynamic system which accommodated problems of fishing grounds, fish numbers, gear and recruitment of new fishermen. She refers to this limited access common property right as a system where 'an identifiable group hold the right to fish'.[62] Notwithstanding state definitions of public sea space, these local fishers followed long-standing agreements among themselves on the use of marine space, jointly controlling access to the sea area and inducting newcomers into the rules of the group. Maurstad concluded that among these groups making money was subordinate to the focus on family, friends and other non-commercial relations.

Maurstad's seminal study turned Garret Hardin's influential argument on the tragedy of the commons on its head. By closing the sea commons in parts of northern Norway where cooperation between local fishers had long prevailed, a tragedy was being opened. The new criterion of technical efficiency which accompanied the quota system of fishing meant larger boats. Not only were some smaller-scale fishers pushed out of the industry, but to retain an individual quota a fisher *had* to catch his or her quota of fish. 'Fishing for quotas' rather than fish was geared to maximising money-earning and profit. The tragedy, Maurstad argues, is in this reshaping of people by market forces so the pursuit of profit becomes an end in itself. These reshapings then create a self-fulfilling prophecy about greed.

8
Flinders' Journey into Sea Space

State waters and their origin

In 1997 the Commonwealth of Australia released a set of maps and diagrams as part of an Oceans Policy paper. It distinguishes three maritime zones: the territorial sea, the continental shelf and an Exclusive Economic Zone or EEZ. Australia's territorial sea is given as twelve nautical miles and the EEZ or fishing zone is 200 nautical miles. The latter encompasses an area twice the size of Australia's land mass and includes some twelve thousand islands. The area beyond the EEZ is marked as the 'Common heritage of all mankind'.[1]

Geographers and navigators, as well as fishers, know that spring tides are the lower low tides and higher high tides, and that neap tides are the reverse. They study the effects of coastal shape and seabed configurations, and of winds off-shore. But territorial seas require mapping and the creation of maps is historically integral to the idea of territorial seas. The physical topography of these seas — their starting points in space — had to be known and communicable. These starting points came to be called baselines. In Australia a baseline is the lowest astronomical tide. Baselines are derived from averages, ranges in depth and median points. To arrive at such a line, knowledge of tidal, celestial and seasonal movements is compressed and generalised.

The Australian territorial sea today is twelve nautical miles as measured from a baseline. J. R. V. Prescott, political geographer and world authority on maritime boundaries and the International Law of the Sea, observes that Australia is alone in its selection of the lowest astronomical tide as its baseline.[2] Australia has a further variation: the states and territories have jurisdiction over their respective coastal waters to a distance of three nautical miles. Until 1990 this was the width of the Australian territorial sea.

On 20 November 1990 the Governor-General of Australia made a Proclamation extending the territorial sea from three to twelve nautical miles. He did so under section six of the *Sea and Submerged Lands Act* 1973. This Proclamation concerning the limits and extent of territorial jurisdiction is founded upon, and derives its authority from, the exclusive sovereignty of the Australian state recognised in international law.

The idea of territorial waters took final shape in the second half of the sixteenth century with the work of the Italian jurist Albericus Gentilis. It grew out of ideas developed by a succession of jurists from as early as 1200 AD. In the middle of the fourteenth century it was given clear expression in the work of Saxoferrato Bartolus, leading jurist of that time and teacher of law at Pisa and Perugia. In his view, coastal waters, including islands to a distance of 100 miles, belong to the adjacent land territory and come under the exclusive jurisdiction of the ruler of the adjoining territory. Percy Fenn's seminal paper on the 'Origins of the Theory of Territorial Waters', published in 1926, has been most enlightening to me. He concludes that Gentilis brought together the power of the royal prerogative with the modern theory of sovereignty. According to Fenn, Gentilis concluded that coastal seas are 'a part of the territory of the state whose shores they wash'. In consequence, Fenn writes, 'the territorial rights of sovereignty which exist in the head of state are extended *in toto* over the seas adjacent to his coasts'.[3] This remains true for all coastal states today. A coastal state cannot refuse its territorial sea. As Lord McNair stated in the 1951 *Anglo-Norwegian Fisheries Case*: 'International law does not say to a State: "You are entitled to claim territorial waters if you want them." *No maritime State can refuse them.*'[4]

Importantly, Gentilis used the phrase *mare portio terrae* — 'the sea as part of the land' — and applied the word *territorium* or territory to the sea. The Meriam people also have an expression, 'the sea that belongs to the land'. But Gentilis, of course, was not speaking of sea that belongs in joint ownership to particular local groups with inherited rights. Gentilis saw 'his doctrine as part of the law of nations', and Fenn explains the significance of his insight: with his work 'it is literally correct to speak of territorial waters in international law'.[5] Gentilis was a theorist of the emerging post-feudal state, a thinker with the capacity to analyse its rise as it was happening before his eyes. His understanding was grounded in the social transformation associated with declining feudalism; his work spanned a period in which the idea of sovereignty was unimaginable, to one in which it became urgent and in due course taken for granted.

Gentilis' unique concern was with the jurisdiction of states. The change he was interpreting depended upon the replacement of the medieval idea, grounded in feudalism, that the law is derived from custom, to the radically new idea that the law may be created. Jurisdiction over the sea was not new; it had been exercised to suppress piracy and so create law and order on the seas. What was new was the extension of the power of the sovereign over the adjoining sea. The classic Roman doctrine of seas as common to all was placed within a new framework in the light of sovereign jurisdiction: citizens of the monarchical state have the freedom to fish and to enjoy the sea domain of the sovereign. State territorial waters were new and therefore had to be newly defined.

The width of territorial seas, as determined by international law, is measured in nautical or sea miles. Since early in the seventeenth century fishing nations have vied with imperial mercantile powers in setting the limits of territorial waters: by the middle of that century the width of the Danish fishing zone varied in size from eight to 32 nautical miles.[6] By 1864 the imperial maritime powers — Holland, Britain and France — had established the Three Mile rule which derived from the 'Possible Reach of Cannon Shot from Land', or 'the cannon shot rule' as it became known.[7]

In the period when the ideas to which Gentilis gave written expression were taking shape, especially between the fifteenth and seventeenth centuries, the idea of maps as geography rather than as records of journeys gained currency. The mapping and charting of space became separated from the journeying figures who created stories or made logs of their paths. Joan Blaeu's famous maps in *The Grand Atlas of the Seventeenth Century World*, published in Amsterdam in 1662, register this transition. The pursuit of 'geography and trade' required maps and Blaeu was cartographer to the Dutch East India Company in Amsterdam. His maps picture sailing ships, various sea creatures and, on occasion, hunters contemplating a bear; but these are merely adornments largely irrelevant to the purposes of the maps themselves.

In his 1984 book *The Practice of Everyday Life*, French philosopher Michel de Certeau identifies this transition from actual journeying to the mapping of space. A sailing ship and its voyage path painted on a map may describe a journey. But in colonising space, the map gradually pushes aside and collates the ship and its path in such a way that their 'placeness' — the stories and kinships of a particular river mouth for example — become equated and drawn into the geographical conception of space. De Certeau's contrasts are compelling and poignant. He exemplifies the difference between journeying and mapping by reference to a fifteenth-century Aztec map, the log marked out by the footprints of a journey with regular gaps between them, and pictures of successive events that took place on the way — meals, battles, river and mountain crossings.[8] These are of a similar order to the 'travellers' paths', the footprints and seamarks of the peoples of the coastal tropics, which signify their sea territories and join place with place. Charting and mapping these tropical land sea areas is a project of a different order.

From sea place to sea space

THE CHARTING OF AUSTRALIA'S NORTHERN COASTS, completed by the mid 1840s, made later navigation relatively easy. After Matthew Flinders' voyages between 1801 and 1803, the northern coasts were named and 'anchored' in magnetic space. His earliest biographer, Ernest Scott, places Flinders at the forefront of all European navigators, alongside James Cook: 'the supreme excellence of his charts' place him among the greatest navigators of our time.[9] His contribution is not simply as the architect of a set of measurement charts. The French navigator Nicolas Baudin had been informed by the French Admiralty that everything still remained 'to be done and known' in the area of the Gulf of Carpentaria and the north coast of New Holland 'discovered' by the Dutch as early as 1628. Flinders' work overcame that problem. He took the utmost heed of the 'guiding principle' that his survey would be so complete 'as to leave little for anybody to do after him'.[10]

He was not merely charting the unknown. He also made an effort to explore and get to know the surrounds of the coastline. In his 'General Chart of Terra Australis or Australia', Matthew Flinders used fixed points on hill and cape. His chart gave the situation of the ship at noon from the latitudes observed. His time-keepers measured places of observed longitude, marking the following: the direction of the current, the direction of the tide, the light, whether there was a moderate, fresh or strong breeze, fresh gale or hard or heavy gale. The directions of the ship's head were by compass. He used dotted lines to refer to dry or shallow waters or those too shallow for boats; a single line indicated a depth of three fathoms at low water.

As his biographer observes with pleasure, Flinders' keenness and commitment to record as much as possible 'animated the whole ship's company, stimulated by the example of the commander, who never spared himself in his work and interested himself in that of others'. As Flinders himself reports, the ship sailed as close to the shore as possible so that the water breaking on the shore was kept visible and rivers were noted; where the coast was indented, Flinders stationed himself at the masthead. Rough charts were polished up at night and great care was taken to come upon the coast at the same point next morning. On reaching bays or island groups, he went ashore taking angles, measuring, mapping and making topographical notes. Tide levels were noted, naturalists collected plants, artists made drawings, nets were cast.[11]

Like Captain Bligh, with whom he travelled to the Torres Strait as a midshipman in 1792, Flinders treated the reefs of the Torres Strait with immense respect. In his characteristically meticulous way, he writes of the 'threading the needle' of the lacework of reef-strewn waters, concluding that 'perhaps no space of three-and-a-half degrees in length, presents more dangers than Torres' Strait'.[12]

Flinders' two-volume work, *A Voyage to Terra Australis*, is a log of his amazing journey. It is interspersed with observations of the people and the landscapes he observed. In describing the clanspeople he saw at Blue Mud Bay and their canoes, he moves towards the world of Yolŋu marine people, noting how their six-man bark vessel is sewn 'with creeping vine to preserve the shape, and to strengthen the canoe'.[13] Even those few words convey the idea of a people grappling with ways of living successfully with and from the sea. He sees the inhabitants in their uniqueness and above all he views them with respect — the very quality they seek in outsiders. Flinders was a person in the 'gateway' between cultures: his personal stance was intuitive, but the objective and condensed style of his rigorous charts are necessarily of a different genre. Here was a man finely attuned to the people whose footprints his work mapped over. Looked at in this way Flinders is a living contradiction.

He saw virtues in the people he noted and sometimes met face to face. 'These people,' he wrote of the Meriam people of eastern Torres Strait, 'appeared to be dextrous sailors and formidable warriors . . . as much at ease in the water, as in their canoes'. Here he was reflecting upon his experience of the Islander sailors when he accompanied Captain Bligh on the *Providence* in September 1792.[14] He made friends with local people — 'the Indians' as he called them — and he showed the ability to cross over into their world. He empathised with their joy and their tragedies: at King George's Sound in the southwest of the continent, on Wednesday 30 December 1801, he thrilled to the Aboriginal response to the red-coated soldiers drumming their walk. One old man joined the end of the line imitating these marines' movements. The exercise delighted the local inhabitants and Flinders noted how 'they paid the most earnest and silent attention'. This, he sensed, was something that really interested them, the rig of the marines 'having some resemblance to their own manner of ornamenting themselves'.[15] Who else among the navigators was quite so attuned to the way the local inhabitants were responding?

Flinders was a compassionate as well as a dedicated professional. A decade earlier, he had noted the poignancy of a drifting canoe carrying the body of an Islander, victim of the muskets fired from Bligh's *Providence* near Warrior–Tudu Island in Torres Strait. And he was a keen observer of the footprints left by humans and animals and the story they told of life beside the sea near Blue Mud Bay in Arnhem Land–Gulf country; he deemed the bluish clay to be of such fine quality that he thought it might be useful for the manufacture of earthenware pottery.[16] Ernest Scott refers to 'his integrity of heart', noting how he bought up the whole stock of oranges of a fruiterer, 53 in all, for a French soldier whose arm had been amputated.

Yet it was *his* charts above all others which were to map over the imprints made on the land and sea of the people he engaged with. 'Give them presents not bullets', he believed, even though his men sometimes disobeyed him. Paradoxically, his very commitment, and meticulous surveying of the areas that joined land and sea, was indispensable to the imperial project. Not that he was in a position to become aware of the inhabitants' sense of proprietorship over the seas that belonged to their lands or of the vibrant sea inheritances that gave them life.

The cumulative 'discoveries' of European mariners along the Australian coasts, described as 'astounding' in their extent and accuracy, were significant primarily for the stimulus they gave to later explorers coming overland from southern Australia.[17] While Leichhardt's journey, like those of many other explorers, 'comes out' at the sea, it was the land that became important to settler colonialism. Australia, named by Flinders, was being defined as geographical and social space: it was land, and pursuits on land, that mattered to colonial Australia. On the sea fringes what mattered was keeping other powers out.

Far from making the sea more visible, the detailed mapping of the entire north coast of Australia closed off from the imagination the idea of the sea as a living landscape shaping the lives of peoples who lived by it. Abel Tasman, who travelled the Gulf of Carpentaria and the north coast between 1642 and 1644, had been instructed 'to map out and describe very accurately all the lands, islands, angles, bights, inlets, bays, rivers, shallows, banks, beaches, rivers, crags and rocks' as the ships passed along the coasts, and 'to draw their exact positions and forms'.[18] His charts, rated by scholars as of major importance to the creation of Australia, yielded abundant detailed information. The coast was being named, measured, scaled; fixed points and baselines were the reference points. More than 150 years later, Flinders not only drew charts with conscientiousness, diligence and flair; his enthusiasm inspired his men to supplement his angle taking, measurement, mapping and noting of topographical detail by collecting plants, casting nets, noting tide levels and making drawings. The outline of the island continent had become visible; it remained to know and develop what lay *inside* it. This was the task the maritime work of the navigators delineated.

By surveying the coasts, a binary distinction was drawn between land and sea. As we saw in the last chapter, the old customary associations between land and sea among people who lived along the coasts in Old World countries became subject to a new set of rules in the seventeenth century when monarchical states were forming in redefined and redrawn kingdoms in Europe. By the nineteenth century, land was primarily the domain of buying and selling and sea primarily a site of resources for the developing market economy.

In early Australia, with this as the incontrovertible framework of thought brought by the settlers and given official stamp by Britain, by the colonies and by federated Australia, particular priorities developed. These priorities — or cultural premises — determined definitions of preferred ways of working and living, and they in turn coloured judgments of what was good land and what amounted to poor environment. The Dutch explorers had found much of the northern coastal land dry and barren 'without any fruit tree or anything useful to man',[19] and the British likewise saw 'the better country' as lying further inland.[20]

In the eye of the coloniser, the northern coasts were blanks on the map. Northern lands were empty because they did not lend themselves to the presence of the settlers; northern seas hardly registered because, uncoupled from land, they had only an ephemeral reality. The idea of a land–sea companionship, so central to the lives of saltwater people, was peripheral to the dominant imagination. The notion of Australia became coextensive with the continental land mass. Usable space was taken to be *inside* the continent. Writing about the Tiwi people in 1959, anthropologists C. W. M. Hart and Arnold Pilling referred to Darwin as the capital of the 'empty north' and the Tiwi people as surrounded by 'the emptiness of a great sea'.[21]

The north held little to attract settlers. There seemed little potential for fisheries teaming with fish; pastoralism was given primacy.[22] The bombing of Darwin during the Second World War began to create a reassessment of the importance of the north. The extractive industries and tourism have, over the past twenty years, been instrumental to a re-evaluation of potential in northern Australia. A newly revived plan to build a railway from Alice Springs to Darwin, in the context of the devastation of East Timor in 1999, points to changing priorities whose implications for the peoples of the tropical coasts are as yet largely unassessed.

An end to marine custom?

In Australia, the idea of the rights of all members of the public to fish in coastal waters came as part of the cultural baggage of the settlers. All over the Pacific Islands open access became state law. However, there is a noteworthy difference between the situations in Australia and neighbouring countries: indigenous marine territory owners in New Zealand and Fiji, for example, had the chance to debate the issue with colonial authorities. In Australia there was silence, with few written references made to customary marine territories or rights to fish by indigenous coastal dwellers. Where the foreshore or seas were encroached upon by the settlers it happened by stealth or by gunpower. Occasional eye witnesses tell the tale, as for example at Somerset, Cape York Peninsula, where two Anglican missionaries and a ship's surgeon recorded the shooting of Gudang people fishing in their customary sea territories near Albany Island across from Somerset. The tragic story of the saltwater clans of the Somerset region is mentioned briefly in chapter three.[23]

In Fiji and in New Zealand, indigenous coastal dwellers were articulate and vociferous in the defence of their rights. Fijian chiefs wrote letters protesting the imposition of the public right to fish and drawing attention to their customary marine estates. The right to fish within these marine estates, known in Fijian language as *goligoli*, continues to be vested in the local clans: today their right to fish upholds a right to exclude others from these customary marine territories. However, the chiefs were only partly successful. Clan ownership of these marine areas was not recognised by the British colonial authority, a situation which continues in independent Fiji today,[24] although those coastal villagers whom I visited in 1997 told me that in their heart of hearts they believe the reefs and the waters belong to them.

In New Zealand the Crown maintained from the earliest days of settlement that the foreshore, marine resources and seabed was within its control. From the first fisheries legislation in 1866, all subsequent legislation until 1986 carried the assumption of Crown control of marine resources. Contemporary writers have concluded that Maori fishing rights were cast aside for 120 years as a direct result of European settlement of the land. When freehold land titles were issued, this was the end of the matter in European eyes. Customary rights to the sea were invisible.[25] However, from the earliest days of settlement and the Treaty of Waitangi 'Maori protests were vocal, constant, and specific as to the nature of their rights and the fact that they had not given them away'.[26] Their customary landholdings extended into the sea and the foreshore; reefs and fishing grounds 'were exclusive to a group (normally a *hapu* [clan])'. These home areas and certain more distant fishing grounds out to sea could be used by others only with permission, a situation common to indigenous Australia and to the Pacific region, broadly speaking.

Unlike Fiji and New Zealand, very little is recorded on how customary marine tenures were 'ruled out' of existence or simply disappeared as an extension into the marine domain of *terra nullius* in Australia. In tropical Australia customary marine rights did not disappear: they merely went unnoted, at least in official records. To many indigenous peoples the agenda of the European settlers had little relevance and local people continued to follow custom and rules. Oddly enough a rare micro-example of the 'discovery' of customary proprietorship over foreshore, reefs and waters is provided by the last-minute observation of such a system at the island of Mer by a group of anthropologists from Cambridge University in 1898. I say 'last-minute' because after three months working on Mer recording Islanders' current beliefs, customs and recollections, they had not noticed the Meriam system of saltwater ownership until they were due to leave. Ethnographer Anthony Wilkin described the Meriam people's ownership of foreshore, reef, water itself, as well as distant cays and fishing grounds like Ker Ged in the following four-line footnote:

> I think there is what may be termed a spatial projection of the idea of proprietorship. As foreshore rights of landed property extend not only over the adjacent reef *but to the water over it* — as in the case of fish caught within the area — so the inhabitants of certain areas appear to have a pre-emptial right to certain distant fishing stations which lie off their part of the coast.[27]

These scholars also provide us today with insight into how this system was officially 'eradicated': the Meriam were persuaded to relinquish this custom and end their properties at the high-water mark. Or it seemed they had been persuaded. Evidence collected before and after the *Mabo* case, along with the court proceedings themselves, showed how people were able to retain memories of ancestral law side by side with the rules made by colonial authorities. These recent events also offer vivid illustration of the emotional attachment of Meriam land–sea owners to their traditional and 'eradicated' system.

During the visit of the Supreme Court of Queensland to the Murray Islands in May 1989, a marine territory ownership dispute between two Meriam owners could be heard 'in full cry' by the court inspection party. Mr Mawer Depoma was disputing a claim made by Eddie Mabo to a particular area at the village of Sebeg on the northern side of Mer Island. Depoma confronted members of the court making their way to a section of foreshore adjoining his house, with signs of great emotion, 'whoop whooping' loudly, as Justice Moynihan described his actions. Depoma tightened the belt of his *nesur*, an ankle-length, reddish-coloured cloth, and told them loudly to go away. 'This is my beach,' he shouted angrily. 'It was passed to me by my ancestors.' In calmer circumstances Mr Depoma is a genial man, a person able to make jokes about the pomposity of white officials and to see humour in his own behaviour. But he was totally and, one might say, dangerously serious on this occasion, and this event was seen by the judge as evidence of a 'socially disruptive' side of boundary disputes.[28]

Mr Depoma's actions demonstrate the importance of the possession of family or clan-owned foreshore, reefs and waters to the Meriam 'cultural way'. His statements and those of other senior Meriam also give a picture of how this tradition, deliberately suppressed 80 or 90 years before, may sit side by side in a person's mind with the idea that all Meriam may use the beaches. In cross-examination during the *Mabo* hearings, Mr Depoma showed how the European view sat alongside the 'cultural way' of the Meriam. He explained how the Meriam are free to go anywhere since Mr Bruce (the government teacher on the island for 30 years in his father's time) insisted they could. He also said that the Meriam custom that says, 'Don't interrupt another man's [beach] property', 'Leave the turtle you find for the owner of that family beach', continues to exist today.[29]

The way in which two memories, or the memory of two counterposed systems, came to sit side by side in one person is illustrated by recent Meriam history. When the Queensland government authorities came to Mer in the 1880s, after the annexation of the Torres Strait Islands in 1879, the government schoolteacher Mr Jack Bruce told the Meriam that they should discontinue their system of ownership of 'plots of sea' and family-owned stone fish-traps. With the authority of the Governor of Queensland, Bruce came to preside over, and take as more or less normal, land boundary disputes in the Island court. Yet Bruce had a different view about the sea: he told the Meriam that continuation of the sea boundary system would result in endless disputes, and sought to eradicate this custom.[30]

Meriam people today recall their grandparents' memories of Bruce's plea for them to share their reefs and waters among themselves, a plea made in the name of the Christian ethic of sharing.[31] As I have said, that ethic already found expression in the pre-Christian Malo tradition of all-island sharing at times of seasonal scarcity: the sharing of the first turtle for the season for instance. Jack Bruce's plea to the clans to share the sea may well have struck a chord among the Meriam of the Christian era. The Meriam priest Reverend Passi told the Court in the *Mabo* case that he let other Meriam people collect turtle eggs on his famed turtle nesting beaches because they are 'a source of food for people'. Among people for whom sharing food is its own reward, being requested or told to share with one another was not such a very 'big ask'. Nevertheless, Jack Bruce was not merely asking them to share; he was exercising the authority granted him by the Queensland government to place the exclusive rights to fish-traps of Meriam owners into abeyance and to put an end to their whole customary marine tenure system. By the turn of the century family- and clan-owned territories that fronted the foreshore right around the islands ended officially at the high-water mark. The post-seventeenth century European system was in place — or, so it seemed.

Whatever the reasonableness or otherwise of Mr Bruce's eradication of customary marine boundaries, the Meriam did not have any choice in the matter. In 1879 they, along with the rest of the Torres Strait Islanders, were mustered, counted and informed that they were subject to the laws of the white man as the islands now formed part of the territory of Queensland. The context was several decades of intrusion by pearl shellers and trepangers from many nations into the Torres Strait and northern Cape York Peninsula waters. These intruders were a law unto themselves until the arrival of missionaries in 1871, and a law preventing kidnapping in 1878 began to provide some protection to the indigenous peoples. This had been the era of pirate kings who ruled their own divers with revolvers, using and taking pearl shell and local labour resources as they pleased.

The people on the other side of the frontier of colonisation included not only the indigenous saltwater peoples, but also those 'aliens' who ran the saltwater industries on the northern coasts. A few of these were European, but many of them were from the Pacific Islands, from the Malay archipelago, China, the Philippines, Japan. In Thursday Island, the centre of the northeastern pearling industry, two or more decades after the White Australia policy was proclaimed following federation of the Australian states in 1901, there were some twenty nationalities represented in Thursday Island. But that island, described as the 'pearly gateway' to the Australian mainland, was firmly barred: the 'aliens' who worked in the pearling industry were unwelcome on the mainland. The island continent was the 'real Australia'. The mapping and charting of the coasts was crucial to this division and separation. But reshapings could by no means tear to shreds the old webs of association. In some places the new mappings modified the older traditions; in others they were left relatively unchanged.

Drowning the seamarks?

OUTSIDE THE URBANISED CENTRES AND PASTORAL RUNS of tropical Australia, the very mismatch or incommensurability between European and indigenous systems of living and imagining the sea left open spaces for freedom of action. The forgotten and unknown indigenous saltwater peoples whose homelands lay outside the 'real Australia' could find some leeway to follow the 'seamarks' of their traditions. These traditions are, as I have said, dynamic not fossilised ones.

The era of invasion and colonisation induced important cultural change that widened the geographical and social bases of reciprocity and the development of the sharing ethic. When the Meriam were asked to share their reefs and to put family- and clan-owned fish-trap rules into abeyance, they were being told to act as one people. In the past they had kept the peace by following Malo's law of keeping to their own reef, fish-trap, garden and clan land, which of course they had not always done. As I mentioned in Chapter Four, they placed leafy bamboo poles at the corners of their fish-traps. Robert Johannes, a marine biologist with rich specialist knowledge of Pacific Island maritime cultures, explained their purpose to the Court in the 1989 *Mabo* hearings. He saw the practice as a unique way of 'spooking off' the fish so that they distributed themselves more or less evenly in the adjoining corners of the trap.[32] These poles have been used within living memory, but they are not used in the fish-traps today.

Under colonial instructions the Meriam shared the sea among themselves — but as I said earlier, this was hardly out of keeping with their culture. They were already a sharing as well as a squabbling people — first through the Malo religion, then through Christianity. Keeping to your own 'kind' and your own ways expanded to include wider identifications. The key to understanding these identifications is provided by what I have called 'the Russian doll' metaphor. The most intimate group is represented by the smallest doll and this is the primary identification. In May 1993 some of the witnesses in the *Mabo* case told me they did expect other Meriam people to ask permission to fish in their waters: 'If it's a close relation, I just tell them to go and get it,' said one; and 'I always tell my grandchildren that, before you go out to another man's lagoon, you have to ask. I think this is the best way, the way I've been taught. That's our custom.'[33]

In principle then, the practice of marine customary law continues because tracks and song-cycles that demarcate boundaries operate on a level totally different to that of charts and maps. Superimposing maps may overlay a song-cycle. But in their softer form of influence they may leave the 'suppressed' people's cultural geography substantively untouched. So the people at Maningrida preparing their native title claim with a white man's map on the wall may be able to place their named sites within those mapped places. Yet this should not hide qualitative differences. Because the reciprocities that tie people to places are characteristically committed to memory, the radical difference in quality between the journeys of ancestral beings and European mappings is often invisible.

French philosopher Michel de Certeau explains how 'maps cut up' ties between places; they can make arbitrary breaks anywhere. They do so because ultimately maps have the 'character of a nowhere'. Between the real journeys from place to place and maps, there is a gross mismatch. Breaks in maps cannot take account of 'handover' points between owners of terrain and song-cycles, areas at the water's edge or those between bodies of salt water that belong to different groups. As I mentioned earlier, among Yolŋu people, a dead person's spirit is guided from one clan's territory to another's, the songs sung for that person changing and the responsibility for the person's spirit being handed 'over from one land owning group to the next'.[34]

In the main the mappers were oblivious to the dissolutions they were party to. They did not know about the itineraries of

Dreaming figures in the sea; they mapped and annulled what de Certeau calls 'the narrative figures', as had been done in the European past. Between the fifteenth and seventeenth centuries the map became 'more autonomous', de Certeau says, disengaging from and then taking over from the journeys of the 'narrative figures' that had fed its development.[35] The pictorial figures on early maps were gradually eliminated, or retained largely as visual embellishment as on Blaeu's maps. In colonising the space along the coastlines the colonisers declared the seas vacant. Their powerful beliefs in the universality of their own conceptions of abstracted space prevented them from seeing the imprints of those who made personal journeys to overcome the powerful opposition between land and sea.

The personal sea journeys of ancestral narrative figures and sea heroes imprinted bodies of water, the seabed and sea life with their power and authority. Their imprints etched the sea tracks and created the designs in the sea for humans to follow. I call these personified journeys 'footprints' in contrast to mapping which draws on impersonal, abstract and characteristically linear technique to draw lines on blank spaces.

The distinction between footprints and mapping as conceived in European thought and life encompasses differences that have an important bearing on the ways in which people live and picture the sea and their relations with one another. I see three differences: footprints associate places with their peoples; they are a way of knowing; and the paths created by the journeys can accommodate change by incorporating new narratives.

Footprints and maps are used here as a way of marking the difference between the human or personified as against the impersonal. The distinction is manifest in the contrast between place versus space, personal journeys and tracks versus abstract linear measurement and compass bearings. Sea narratives or performative events in which ancestral figures leave their footprints at named places, themselves become 'frozen' into natural features and are represented in condensed form in dance, rite and visual art. It is as if the seascape embeds itself in dance and song like coiled rope that unwinds when memory is activated, say, by the death of a person, or the spearing of the first sea turtle for the season, or an initiation ceremony. Earlier I referred to how Yanyuwa people describe their sacred songs as being like maps: 'the original map-makers', as John Bradley describes them, are 'the Dreaming Powers'. The words sung unfold the singer's country for the listeners.[36]

When newcomers from Europe reshaped the seas bordering Australia into mapped sea space they did not only 'silence' the song paths. The mapping system erased or smudged the footprints of ancestral figures who had etched out each indigenous sea world. It colonised the seascapes in the same manner it had done 'back home' several centuries earlier.

When de Certeau says 'maps cut up' he means that because the personalised figures associated with place are no longer important, the map can make breaks anywhere. Geographer Susan Jackson provides a graphic example of the implications of this in a cross-cultural setting on the Dampier Peninsula in the southwest Kimberley in the 1990s where a mapping project threatened to impose physical and geographical constraints on a song-cycle. Impediments to the purpose of mapping may well be pushed 'into the wings' by cartographers. In this example they were not because the wishes of the owners of the song-cycle were made known to and respected by the planners, who agreed to abandon plans involving the mapping of the song-cycle.[37]

Colonisation of sea space has a particular twist. On land, mapping replaced footprints with fixed linear boundaries associated with, and indispensable to, real estate. The footprints were seemingly raked over, as in a Japanese pebble garden. In blanking out the seamarks of reef and cay and headland and star positions the map converted heterogeneity into sameness. The idea of open space with fixed linear boundaries came into being and cut up the experiential and personal. This points to some deeper questions of cultural difference. Saltwater people often say they have maps in their heads; they remember where a reef is, or a place within a reef structure, and in so doing indicate 'distance' from home, various seas and seamarks along the way, and knowledge of the topography of the reef in question. However, even today when Aboriginal people create a map it is unlikely to be an all-purpose general map of country. Referring to a map of Gove Peninsula drawn by Wandjuk Marika in response to an unwanted move for a bauxite mine there, Peter Sutton makes the important point that such maps as Marika's 'are unique performances'.[38]

As I suggested in earlier chapters, performance of sea figures or the waves themselves tell people about the 'mood' of the sea. In the sea people's minds no one can gainsay that telling: belonging to a salt water commands respect, obligation, giving. Indigenous sea people are likely to be more at home with the poet's sense of the moral influence of topography. In 'The Prelude' Wordsworth confronts 'a huge peak, black and huge' which rose up and 'Towered between me and the stars' while rowing on the lake. Such experiences may remind the sea people of their obligations to ancestral law-makers, of debts to be paid to kin, of the potential vengeance of enemies.

For indigenous sea people the resilience of memory comes from living connections which create webs of association. These exist not only in the imagination but are reinforced and modified in experience. The reshaping of seas and seascapes in the mapping process does not necessarily touch, or at least does not dissolve, these patterns of association. As we will see, they may find expression in the reassertion of ancestral connections; or in an inexorable wish to return to their land–sea country. Such wishes lie close to the skin and words alone may lack the power to convey their aesthetic-emotional dimension, as John Bradley has said of the Yanyuwa.[39] They may find varied expression: a woman feels the sea-wind on her face; a man sees the sea as part of his blood and body; in preparing his land–sea claim for a court, a man reaffirms to himself that the Law came first and so takes precedence.

Fortunately some scholars are aware of a distinction between mapping and personal journeying. In very recent times the use of the words maps and mapping to describe indigenous art and iconography has been questioned: such descriptions include 'art as a cartographic form', sacred designs on spear throwers as 'schematic maps', bark paintings as both 'highly conventional map[s]' and 'also religious icons'. Yet a painting that derives from and is set by clan design does not follow the principles of design used in European map-making. Mythological events and the representation of a particular topographical area are often intertwined in a painting. Hence the idea that a painting is a map states only a limited truth. Peter Sutton, a world authority on Aboriginal art and iconography, identifies a fundamental difference between the European meaning of maps and the seemingly 'maplike' aspect of indigenous icons of country.[40] Maps and mapping describe space in a way that depersonalises it. Mapping removes the footprints of named creatures — animal, human, ancestral — who belong to this place or that place. A map can be *anywhere*. 'Itineraries', however, are actions and movements within a named and footprinted land.[41] Maps do not inscribe the landscape with the footprints of sentient beings: they inscribe with anonymity even though they may follow topographical features like hills and waterways. The sea is not joined to the land except at the level of the national boundaries of a state — and then as a vast stretch of marine space.

Admittedly, the sea can be considered a map if the sense used is as a complex of seamarks — that is, signposts relating to particular zones of the sea that have become part of cultural memory. These may relate to conditions of the waves or the sky, flocks of sea birds, swarms of fish, underwater luminescence, lines of drifting seaweed. Yet there are very sound reasons, substantial and political, for relinquishing the idea that one may, even with some qualifications and signposting, simply use the words map and mapping when referring to Aboriginal classical tradition without reference to their cultural context. In the historical context of the denigration, suppression or simple ignorance of indigenous cultural principles by the colonising power over several hundred years, the case for a different set of terms is compelling.[42]

At the very heart of the difference lie different ways of being human: in Aboriginal classical tradition the person dwells within a personified landscape which is alive, named, inscribed by spiritual and human agents. It is a 'Thou' not an 'It', and I and Thou belong together. People in small saltwater communities may communicate at a distance — via fire signalling, and according to them, by special powers. But face-to-face interaction lies at the heart of their social life; belonging to this land and this group, tied through each of these to the ancestors. In the language I have used here, one may map without knowing, but to 'footprint' is to know.

PART V

FOLLOWING THE SEAMARKS

9
Waves of Memory

Early in this book I told the story of a Larrakia elder handing on to a young boy knowledge that binds him to the seas and the ways of his ancestors, that 'to keep that in your mind and in your heart . . . you draw it in the sand' so your children may know and live it. The knowledge that the boy must keep in his heart is about belonging — to family, to ancestors, to a saltwater country; memory engages his spiritual and practical heritage. A sense of that inheritance endows the moment with intense feeling and emotion. Years later the young boy, now an adult, recalls the elder's words. The intensity of his emotion is heightened by the effects of dispossession and the fear that his children may forget or may not have the chance to know these places and beliefs.

Memories of belief and custom may, as I have said, be held in a frozen form. Such memories may come to the surface like 'pieces of lost time', often brilliant and detailed. They may be remembered in the same form in which they were originally told or experienced; at other times, new experiences and the passing years may cast them in a different light. Memories are often bitter-sweet, finding expression in combative, even belligerent form. So Meriam elder James Rice, in the context of a claim that his ancestral banana and yam-growing plots are 'waste lands of the Crown', argues vehemently that their names are not just white men's names. They are his ancestors' names.

I have illustrated how memories of contemporary Yolŋu people of the trepanging days and their exchanges with the Macassans give them a sense of themselves as primary agents. In looking back to those times they see reciprocities, respect for custom and ownership: the Macassans paid them tribute for the right to collect trepang in their waters. Yolŋu perceptions and recollections of the trading aspects of trepanging days give strength to their current wish to determine their own future. Memories that foster pride in custom and inherited law assist people in taking hold of tradition in ways that give them the strength and confidence to meet the challenges of today.

Over the last 35 years, saltwater people's 'remembering' has grown from knowledge of particular events, places and relationships known by individuals and families to whole canvasses of shared memories. These are memories of generations, memories of country, cultural sites, language and place names.

The stories that follow are about deliberate acts of remembrance. They are a few among hundreds that illustrate the role of memory in the lives of the saltwater peoples and show how these people struggle to find a way into the future by searching their remembered traditions. Through intensely emotional circumstances, resistance, frustration and spiritual strength are often born.

Power and memory in the Torres Strait

THE DIRECTOR OF THE DEPARTMENT OF ABORIGINAL and Islanders' Advancement, Con O'Leary, was asked at his retirement send-off in 1960 what he remembered most from his years as the government officer responsible for the Torres Strait Islanders. He replied: 'the day when the Murray Islanders jumped through the windows of the school house refusing to sign on the pearling luggers'. That event, when the Islanders struck for the right to home rule, occurred in 1936 on the 'Company boats', as the Islanders called their pearling luggers. Twenty years later a leading Torres Strait Islander, George Mye, told me with a laugh that saying 'no' by decisive action has come to be known as 'Giving someone the O'Leary treatment'.

ON 14 JANUARY 1936 ALL BUT TWO OF THE 400 TORRES Strait Islanders living in thirteen Island communities refused to work the pearling luggers owned by the Islanders but controlled by the Protector. While there were many grievances, these coalesced around one overwhelming wish: freedom from the 'closed box' of Protection. 'We are in a closed box and wait for the lid to be taken off,' a spokesman for the people of Boigu island told Con O'Leary, the Deputy Chief Protector in 1936.[1]

The 'closed box' held a collection of intolerable and often ludicrous restrictions, some of which had been imposed by written amendments to the *Aboriginals Protection Act* in 1934, and others of which were the work of a punishing and zealous local Protector with police powers who was stationed at Thursday Island. In 1897, an *Aboriginals Protection and Restriction of the Sale of Opium Act* had been passed by the Queensland parliament. Under that Act indigenous people were supervised by an increasingly paternalist and disciplinary rule. The Islanders were told what time they must go to bed; they were gaoled for speaking alone to a member of the opposite sex, and at least at one island a wrong-doer had one side of his head shaved as punishment. Along with these restrictions of personal freedom they required a permit to visit even a neighbouring island; their boat skippers were appointed by the Protector; the government representative on the island controlled how much money they could withdraw from their savings accounts; local policemen were drawn from other islands with different language and traditions; and the elected indigenous Councillors on each island were 'paid' in rations and issued with shirts with 'Councillor' emblazened across the back.[2] The recipients found this treatment insulting and humiliating.

In the Torres Strait Islands, except among the Kaurareg people of the islands near the Cape York mainland who were forcibly moved from their homes in 1922, the events of dispossession were somewhat muted in their impact. Following the occasion in 1879 when the Queen's representative 'mustered' each Islander group and told them they were subject to the laws of the white man as the islands now formed part of the Territory of Queensland, they were relatively free to continue fishing and hunting in their waters. After anti-kidnapping laws were passed in the 1870s, some colonial powers delegated to Islander Councils, mission and government schools were established, and Islanders learned to speak and write English. At Murray Island the school that the Islanders had petitioned for, by the end of the century, ranked alongside other state schools in Queensland.[3] Islanders were equipped early with the knowledge and confidence to confront the authorities on their own terms.

The Torres Strait Islanders, by and large, continued to live on their home islands. Some groups of Islanders had been resettled on the isles of their close neighbours; they were often grouped into one or two villages on a home island to make their supervision easier. In the 1880s and 1890s at some islands — Mer–Murray is a leading example, where after 1886 they had their islands more or less to themselves — they elected their own Island Councils, conducted their own courts, chose the skippers and crews of the clan-owned 'Company boats', managed their own boat returns and money they earned, and went to state schools on their islands.

Islanders also say today they were 'born into money times', unlike their ancestors. Under the umbrella of indirect rule, Torres Strait Islander marine enterprise initiative was nurtured on a clan or family basis. In 1904 — the same year in fact that Torres Strait Islanders became subject to the *Aboriginals Protection and Restriction of the Sale of Opium Act* (1897) — F. W. Walker established a Christian trading company, Papuan Industries Limited (PIL), with headquarters at Badu Island in western Torres Strait. Its express purpose was to establish independent Islander participation in the pearling industry as boat owners and crews.[4] Gradually, after Islanders came under the Protection Acts, these limited self-determining rights were whittled away.

In earning cash Islanders were workers on a level with others for a time, although for the same work their wages were much less than those of white workers. In the period before 1904 many Islanders had worked with white workers cutting cane on mainland Queensland. Running their own boats, earning and spending their own money, being on a par with others, was a matter of dignity for Islanders. In 1936 they didn't stop working the boats or rejecting Protection because of low wages: they struck to be shown respect, to be treated as equals, to be on a basis of reciprocity with white people; to be free of the 'closed box'. The norm of 'coming up level' lay at the heart of their culture.

Also at the centre of their sense of dignity lay the right to decide for themselves what they did with their earnings, how they used their boats and what they did in their non-working hours. Protectors complained of their casual ways, the sharing of their produce, their use of their pearling boats for hunting and fishing.[5] Islanders did have their own priorities: sharing the first fruits of land and sea, as well as honouring the dead at tombstone unveilings, a custom that emerged in the 1930s. These events required money as well as time. The underlying theme of being treated as equals, that is, with respect, remains strong in Islanders' memories today. Teachers prepared to share their knowledge despite orders to limit their instruction to third grade level are remembered kindly. Islander school teacher, the late Kitty Ware, told me in 1981: 'Everything good came from [the teacher] McIntosh Murray. He said, "Always stick up for your rights".' Another teacher, the late Sam Passi, said: 'A teacher named Chandler taught me phonic sounds; I thought he was great.' Eddie Mabo recalled to me in 1980 how he exchanged lessons in English with lessons in Meriam with his teacher at Mer, Robert Miles.

In appreciating white people who would share their cultural inheritance with them, Islanders were in a position to compare and contrast. Many of them could remember the times they 'were free' to run their boats, sell their shell and spend the money as they themselves decided. 'How we spent the money was up to us,' Islander leader Wees Nawia reflected in 1979. The 400 strikers who worked on their clan-owned boats sought two things: the right to run their own affairs and citizenship rights equivalent to those of white Australians. They fought to re-establish their limited right to take responsibility in their working lives and at home in their Island affairs. At Mer they sought control of the 'Island fund' to which they contributed.[6] So began a struggle which lasted nearly half a century.

Islanders presented a 'log of claims' to the Queensland Minister for Health and Home Affairs who visited the Torres Strait in 1937, with demands for the same welfare provisions available to other Australians — 'baby bonuses' and unemployment benefits. Islanders called these 'citizen rights'. But in no sense were they asking to be 'kept' people. They continued to feed themselves from the sea, from their gardens and through exchange networks among themselves. They worked hard preparing feasts to honour their dead. And they took for granted their participation in the money economy, in the pearling industry and in new ventures such as wolfram mining at Mua Island in Western Torres Strait. There 'a lovely old white man' taught Wees Nawia and others to mine wolfram in family groups. They wished to be citizens on the same level and standing alongside white men, whom they could respect and who respected them.

The post-strike years were by no means plain sailing. 'Remembering' took a quietly confrontational form in the 1960s among one section of the Kaurareg who were threatened with removal from their village at Nurupai–Horn Island to the Cape York mainland. When a representative of 'the Department' arrived at a place named Wasaga village on Nurupai–Horn Island to give them their 'marching orders', he was met by a Kaurareg version of 'we shall not be moved'. The men stood silently each on one leg in the manner of their intrepid culture hero Waubin, a famous warrior figure who lost his right leg in combat but went on to fight many more battles. One of them read out a statement saying they refused to be moved.[7]

Islanders' memories frame Con O'Leary's recollection of the 1936 strike. Why was saying 'no' in this way raised to the status of a custom among them? And why was this memory the most intense one O'Leary retained from his working life with indigenous people? In 1979 Torres Strait Islanders had begun to break free of the powerful hold of the Director of Aboriginal and Islander Advancement (the DAIA), a Queensland government department. Islanders of Badu in western Torres Strait did not speak about this event publicly. It was as though the strike had not happened. If the late Con O'Leary's indelible memory is of the Islanders' surprise defiance and the novel form it took, his secret actions speak differently. In the immediate period of the strike and its aftermath, O'Leary master-minded and implemented a strategy to erase from Islanders' minds the memory that the strike was about freedom from the form of colonial rule called 'Protection'. 'The O'Leary style', as Islanders call it, of quiet manipulation, ran through the whole era from 1936 and was still visible when I first visited the Torres Strait area in 1978. Some memories are held down with heavy anchors. They still arouse strong emotions and are complex, born out of the fear of reprisal, the experience and the threat of humiliation — repressed hatred is often palpable.

When Badu song composer, the late Iopelli Punuel, recollected to me in 1979 his memories of that time, his voice became a whisper even though the only other presence was the sea. He said: 'Okay, we're beginning now.' His voice was soft but it was also deliberate. The weight of his story's anchor coming up was heavy as his voice quickened its pace. I felt myself being transported back to Badu in January 1936 when the pearl divers were defying the Department of Protection. Those who took the school bell are hiding it in the grass; those who joined in the strike on the 'Company boats' are being gaoled. Iopelli's voice becomes louder. 'We are jumping through the window and whistling as we race down to the village shouting, "We will never sign back [on the boats]."' Where did it begin? 'Outside' — at sea. How did it begin? And how was the plan to strike communicated? 'A cargo boat used to come.' It belonged to the Department. The skipper of that boat was a man from Badu Island named Mairu. He 'carried' the closely kept secret plan to strike from island to island: the Department boat *Mulgrave* is 'loading cargo and unloading messages'. Iopelli's memories are as clear as the water above the reef in the northeast season. They had been 'weighted down' by the powerful authoritative move to eradicate the event from memory. Attached to this anchor are other memories: the deliberate destruction of clans, the prize of a Silver Cup to the best diver to help foster the spirit of individualism, the punishment of strong-spirited strikers by discriminatory and humiliating actions. Even after 40 years, Iopelli's voice carries complex emotions: fear, anticipation, exhilaration, a sense of danger — and again, fear, for the ring-leaders, Iopelli's uncles, and the then sixteen-year-old Iopelli himself, were punished and isolated. As he tells the story I can feel him reliving the events.

In his seminal work *The Great War and Modern Memory*, historian Paul Fussell draws attention to the part played by strong emotions — especially fear — 'as an agent of sharp perception and vivid recall'. He draws too on the understanding of another writer, Oliver Lyttelton, who perceives how fear and the milder emotions 'soften the tablets of memory', fixing impressions on the mind 'like the grooves of a gramophone record'.[8] These perceptions fit nicely with Iopelli's vivid recollections. So too does that of John Banville, who writes of fear as an emotion that may stamp indelible memories.

In November 1978, the late Wees Nawia, Chairman of the Kubin Community Council at Mua Island, was the first Islander to recall those days to me. His memories were very clear and he was keen for me to record them. Over the next two years he described the 1930s as a period of total control: how he, as Chief Councillor, was denied the right to control the money he earned as a diver and skipper on the lugger *Manu*, a 'Company boat' belonging to his people; how the Islanders had 'to crawl on our knees' to receive the money they earned. I learned from other Islanders, and later from reading certain Acts of parliament, that in 1911 the school teachers on the islands of Torres Strait were endowed with statutory supervisory powers. 'If she [the school teacher] said "no" that was it; she was the boss over the whole island.' And rations were substituted for money within some Departmental routines: '"Here are two sticks of tobacco, two blankets." That's my pay for [being] Chief Councillor,' Nawia recalled.

'Islanders were schooled to forget about the strike,' Nawia continued. When he invited me out to Kubin to stay with him and Aunty, he delved deep into the history of his people, the Kaurareg, also forgotten by the outside world: 'My great grandfathers before me were here in these Islands before white people came'; and we wish 'to own all these islands ourselves'. Those others who came forward to tell suppressed and sometimes secret stories, like Iopelli Punuel of Badu, made it plain they were speaking out of intense experiences on which they had been forced into silence. Why, I asked myself, had all this been forced back into deep memory?

The answer to this question can be found in a cross-over between O'Leary's memory of the strike at Murray Island and the Islanders' recollection of his retirement speech. Both reveal a hidden history. In 1936, O'Leary, suddenly put in charge of remedying the situation and locating the reasons for the strike, reduced the events in his reports to the actions of 'malcontents' among the Islanders. He stressed the strikers' ties to certain businessmen on Thursday Island and the support of 'do-gooding' and interfering Anglican clerics. In subsequent years he developed a non-punitive form of soft power concerned with 'winning back' the aggrieved men, overcoming their suspicions, and returning some of the latitude which earlier rule had allowed the Islanders. It also meant projecting this event, which he remembered so vividly as having taken the Department by surprise, as just a little trouble among 'the boys' on the luggers. By the end of 1936, the Chief Protector could report the end of the unrest, the allaying of suspicion, a return to work on the boats except at Saibai and the Murray Islands, and plans for an all-island Councillors' conference for 1937. The local Protector, J. D. McLean, whose officiousness had sparked the unrest, had been quietly removed; this was announced as a 'routine transfer'. No public statement was forthcoming on an earlier event at Murray Island in 1935 when McLean punched the Chairman of the elected Murray Island Council, Mimi Marou, and then sacked him. The threat by another prominent Islander to take McLean's 'gills out' and bury him in the local cemetery was recorded in confidential Department letters along with an 83-page report by O'Leary on the causes of the strike. In 1979 I found that most of these records had disappeared from official archives.[9] The 'box' of memory had been almost fully closed.

Islanders' memories of the era were contained. 'They were the dark days. I don't like to think of them,' a Meriam man recalled in 1981. Yet hidden histories are part of a living course that runs like luminous thread linking that period to today. Not 'bending the knee' and pleading for one's own money, not being subject to others, reclaiming rights: these desires keep finding expression. Even in 1982 the Meriam people caught the Queensland government by surprise when they lodged their statement of claim to lands, reefs and waters in *Mabo*. The claimants were depicted by senior government leaders as 'a small group' who lacked the support of their community.[10]

Islanders' remembering, its form, its substance, its timing, may be understood through an account of what had been gained previously and what came under threat later. Islanders' lands had been annexed on behalf of the British Crown in 1879. Like the Irish clans conquered by Britain following the invasion of Ireland in 1169, people were free to live on their own lands subject to the laws of the conqueror.[11] However, although they were mustered by an officer of the Crown in 1879 and told they were now subject to new laws, their experiences led them to conclude that their islands and their seas remained theirs. In the 1990s, historian Henry Reynolds remembered vividly how Eddie Mabo received the news from Reynolds and a colleague in the late 1970s that, in Queensland law, Mer Island belonged to the Crown: 'Eddie stared at us for a long while in silence with a look combining horror and incredulity.'[12]

Holding the sea, by song: Yolŋu people

'HOLDING THE SEA BY SONG' EXPRESSES THE IDEA OF people and the sea belonging together through the journeys of creator beings. It echoes the title of a paper prepared by John Bradley for the Northern Land Council on behalf of Yanyuwa landowners — 'We're holding the land, by song'. On the opening page he wrote: 'To the Yanyuwa their believed-in truths, traditions, history and thoughts are preserved in their songs and the associated rituals.' For the Yolŋu too, as I have said, sacred songs re-enact the journeys of creator beings. Today, recalling these journeys means thinking back to departed kin and land–sea country to reclaim the past for new generations. In the days before the missionaries arrived at Yirrkala in 1935, and before a bauxite mine was established on Yolŋu country in the early 1960s, holding land or sea in this way was 'natural' for Yolŋu people. Their lives were organised and given meaning through sacred songs of creation. Invasion placed upon them a new responsibility to safeguard, nurture and defend an inheritance.

Holding the sea by song is an elemental and powerful form of remembering. By 'song' I mean first sacred song, often accompanied by performance; the singing is a deeply aesthetic experience. While these sacred forms are fairly readily recognisable to the outsider, there are other songs and performance which, because of their non-classical form, appear foreign to so-called traditional cultures. For example, some Torres Strait Islanders composed Christian hymns in their own languages and people sing them to the beat of a New Guinea drum. Some of the words speak resistance and spiritual strengthening; one hymn about Moses and the Red Sea dividing provides a metaphor for the Islanders' situation during the darkest days of colonial rule.

How did you remember in the bad times? I asked George Kaddy, a senior Meriam man, in 1999. 'By dancing and songs about the seas, the currents, the winds, the birds, fishing. These kept people going.' To bear what was happening better and keep their spirits alive, 'You might start whistling a song.' In the traditions of all the saltwater peoples 'dancing the sea' is also an essential part of life. Sea people must keep a connection with the currents, the winds, with all the qualities of the sea. Song and dance activate this connection. George Kaddy calls this 'spirit'; it is what gives a man or woman a sense of being somebody. These acts of remembrance are outward and public expressions of holding the sea by song. They are not merely evocations, they are renewing. New songs may celebrate ancient sites and certainties, in the course of grappling with new experience. *When the tide comes upward against the wind/The waves come higher*: these are the words a song man of Murray Island composed drawing upon ancient knowledge of the waves rolling up at the passage between Mer and Dauar known as Saper Kes, a passage of ring tides and especially rough waves in the south-east season.

Sacred songs or song-cycles follow the paths of the Dreaming figures which, as we have seen, Yanyuwa people refer to as the 'map-makers' who join named localities by a road. These so-called 'maps', as told in song, are bodies of knowledge; to follow a song path or road is to know, where knowing is an aesthetic, emotional — a religious experience. It is conveyed by the way the singers place themselves physically and mentally. John Bradley, who spent many years in the 1980s and 1990s with the Yanyuwa people, explains: 'The singers place themselves into a position where they can convey feelings, thoughts and at times actions which could not be put into spoken language alone.' The listener who inserts himself or herself into the experience is absorbing the knowledge of the song path. Bradley evokes the beauty and the depth of feeling engendered in the way the singers draw 'on the great powers of the Dreaming era, and in so doing . . . receive a feeling of unity with the environment and spiritual ancestors', a 'feeling that should never be underestimated'.[13]

YOLŊU CLANS ARE MAINLY COASTAL PEOPLES. BEFORE missionaries arrived in their area they lived in small bands of 30 to 40 people in widely divergent parts of northeast Arnhem Land. A major line of communication was along the coast, though some groups were connected to one another through inland routes. Three large mission settlements were established on Yolŋu camping grounds: at Milingimbi in 1922, at Yirrkala in 1935 and at Galiwin'ku–Elcho Island in 1942. By the late 1940s, the majority of Yolŋu were spending the wet season in at least one of these settlements.[14]

In 1969, Yolŋu clans based at the village of Yirrkala brought a land claim against the company, Nabalco, and the Commonwealth of Australia — often referred to as the first Aboriginal land rights case. The plaintiffs sought to prevent Nabalco from mining bauxite on Yolŋu land at Nhulunbuy–Gove. In 1971 Justice Blackburn ruled against the Aboriginal claimants, at the same time recognising the existence of a body of Yolŋu law: '[a] system of rules of conduct which is felt as obligatory by the members of a definable group of people'.[15]

That judgment brought forth a surge of energy among Yolŋu. They had been holding ceremonies — for their dead, for their sons and daughters — but in the wake of the Nabalco case they began to actively 'think back' so that new generations might carry on from them. A series of 22 films, made under the general auspices of Film Australia, document a renaissance in Yolŋu culture.[16] Yolŋu landowners, Law men and artists created this unique documentation of their responses to a new wave of dispossession that moved right to the doorstep of the Yolŋu community at Yirrkala. Artist and Law man, the late Narritjin Maymuru, sums up his feelings in his own film, 'One Man's Response'. There he invites the bauxite mining company, Nabalco, to a clan ceremony in an effort to help members of the company understand his cultural tradition.

In the film 'Djuŋguwan at Gurka'wuy' made in 1990, the late Dundiwuy Wanambi explains what he came to think about while he was living at the Yirrkala mission settlement. His mind kept returning to Gurka'wuy, his ancestral homeland 150 kilometres south of Yirrkala. So he left Yirrkala and went to Gurka'wuy, 'because of this important [thing] for my father and my great grandfather'. Gurka'wuy is the place where *djarrka*, the water goanna, arrived from the sea and came onto the shore. *Djarrka* gave his name to a place on the shore, his white bubbles turning to stone: 'And that's why we like to spend our time in this place. I will stay here all my life because of this [rock] telling me ceremony all the time.'

In March 2000, film-maker Ian Dunlop recalled to me his part in the making of these documentary films with Yolŋu people. In 1970 he left Sydney with the suggestion of two people — anthropologist William Stanner and H. C. 'Nugget' Coombs, at that time a member of the Commonwealth Office of Aboriginal Affairs. Both were men with lucid appreciation of the integrity of Aboriginal cultures and the tragic history of dispossession. 'Look out for moves back to clan homelands,' Stanner suggested. 'If films are being made, one should be on the effects of the mine on Yolŋu people,' Dunlop recalled Coombs advising him. Working in close association with Yolŋu people, Dunlop directed these films over two decades. In remembering and re-enacting the creation journeys which gave the Yolŋu people life they were also returning to these places.

Late in 1971 when Wandjuk Marika, a senior Yolŋu man, led his family and clan in a ceremony for his father Mawalan, he said, 'We do this in remembrance of him,' a phrase that strikes a chord with Christian religious ceremony as well as with classical Yolŋu tradition. In 1934 his father and other members of the Rirratjiŋu clan gave permission to the Methodist missionaries to found a church at Yirrkala. In effect, Marika was saying something new: We are letting ourselves know and we are letting you white people know that we are people with a spiritual inheritance. We are celebrating the Yolŋu story of creation. And Marika issued a warning to any *balanda* who 'tries to influence us and . . . take our law from us, wooing us with his flour and sugar'.

Over two generations, life at Yirrkala had been affected by new ways and beliefs. Marika's ceremony was not only in remembrance of Mawalan. It was a statement of cultural pride. It embodied something of the same thinking as that of Meriam priest Reverend Dave Passi in 1976. Dave's comparison of the two cultures had made him proud of his own.

IT WAS MONDAY, 23 AUGUST 1971. MEMBERS OF THE Rirratjiŋu clan were beginning the eight-day ceremony led by senior man Wandjuk Marika, in honour of his father, Mawalan, who had died in 1967. Wandjuk was allowing the public parts of the ceremony to be filmed for the film, 'In Memory of Mawalan' — a memorial to his father. Mawalan had erected a sacred tree known as a *djuta*. It had become old and a new one was being erected to take its place as part of the Yolŋu creation story of the Djan'kawu, the sisters who created sacred wells with their digging sticks, travelling the sea to new lands. Wandjuk Marika's Dreaming ancestors travelled across the seas to a place known as Yalaŋbara on the mainland. The sea was strong; white-capped waves were pushing them into shore. They dug in the sand for water to make the wells, and to create the people who would drink from those wells. The sacred walking stick of the Djan'kawu, known as *mawalan*, also created the sacred *djuta* tree which the clan was now erecting afresh. Giving birth to many children, the two Djan'kawu sisters also gave the group its clan lands, its sacred law, its clan names, its language. The group was the half or moiety of the Yolŋu people known as Dhuwa people; the other complementary half being Yirritja.

This ceremony for Mawalan was not just a memory: it was also a reaffirmation of the law of the land and people it governed. It was tradition being recreated as well as conserved as a living experience.

> *We are not doing this just for*
> *ourselves, it's not a new idea.*
>
> *We've erected this Djuta*
> *to replace the old one.*

The ceremony is about succession, about the remembrance less of things than of an ongoing pledge.

> *This new one will stand strong*
> *for our children to see.*
>
> *This is our law and we're*
> *keeping it strong . . .*

Two generations before, in 1934, Mawalan had given the Reverend Wilbur Chaseling permission to stay at the place where the Yirrkala Creek meets the Arafura Sea. More and more people came into the mission founded by Reverend Chaseling from other clan lands within some two hundred kilometres of Yirrkala. Between 1926 and 1929 American anthropologist Lloyd Warner found them continuing to live 'off the sea and the land' within the yearly cycle of rainy and dry periods. In eastern and northern Arnhem Land he found only half a dozen or so missionaries at three fairly recently established Christian outposts. He found no cattle stations north of Roper River where 'a melancholy and profitless effort' was being made by white people. Few traders visited the mouths of the tidal rivers in their luggers, and in his view 'all other economic efforts' had been found unprofitable.[17]

Unlike the first missionaries to the Torres Strait Islanders, the Methodists who came to Yirrkala in 1934 had not prohibited Yolŋu ceremony and many ceremonial rites continued to be performed. By 1971 the first Aboriginal land rights case had been lost. A bauxite mine was in operation on Yolŋu land. The first hotel at the mining town of Gove–Nhulunbuy was completed. One Yolŋu response was a reassertion of ancestral rights in a religious ceremony. In the film 'In Memory of Mawalan', Wandjuk and his brother, Roy Marika — a plaintiff in the Yolŋu land case — are together. They sing over the walking sticks, teaching the children of the Djan'kawu. The ceremony's importance as remembrance is linked explicitly and totally with the children. Wandjuk Marika says:

> *This is going to be a very*
> *big event . . .*
>
> *This law is very important . . .*

it's not a small thing . . .
not just for our group . . .

not just for us men . . .

and it's not just for these
people here.

It's for the Yolŋu of the future. 'You children, watch what we do in the name of our ancestors.' The right way is being announced and taught as the Djan'kawu are remembered. The Djan'kawu signify the Law. A large circle has been drawn. It is not just 'for our group', not just 'for us men', or even just 'for these people here'. The Law is everywhere for Yolŋu today. But it is succession they are now thinking about. That's why the children are exhorted to learn the Law the proper way, the right way. So those who come later will also know. When the people performing the ceremony sing of Matjarra, the children of the Djan'kawu, the instruction is very explicit. They are remembering in order to teach; and teaching enhances memory. *Learn it properly so you'll/know how it goes in the future.* There is a right way and a wrong way. *Knees and feet . . . keep them in time.* The instruction is explicit and firm. The clan is strengthening itself.

The land rights' case was lost but the Law was strengthening: a reminder not just of Mawalan but of Mawalan's heritage. The words 'In remembrance of Mawalan' have layers of meaning, each one of them 'calling up' another: Mawalan the man, keeper of the Law; the Mawalan of the sacred tree used to create people and fresh water; the strength of the sea denoted by the foam on the waves pushing the ancestors' canoe into the shore.

The clan designs laid down by ancestral beings, in this case the Djan'kawu sisters, reappear in Yolŋu song, dance and prose. The *djuta* tree, a symbol of strength, is being erected afresh; the

School children and teachers at the opening of Buku-Larrŋgay Mulka, arts and cultural centre at Yirrkala, 1996

new is replacing the old so that succession may continue. I am reminded of the sacred ceremony of the Meriam known as Malo-Bomai, where the star-headed stone club of Malo is passed from one dancer to the next. This signifies that the authority of Malo must continue. It is like the laying on of hands, Reverend Dave Passi believes, but hereditarily grounded in ancestral succession.

MORE THAN A DECADE LATER, IN 1995, WANDJUK Marika tells the story of his own life in his book *Wandjuk Marika, Life Story*. He is looking back now on his life, his memories. But in recalling memories he draws not only on his own individual thoughts and experiences: 'I'm keeping myself on same track and line which is the one my father have been teaching me.' He does not see himself as an individual, as Wandjuk 'making his own life'. His is not simply 'free expression'; he is following footprints made by his ancestors. 'I am there walking with my mother and father,' he says in his book. He is remembering making the film.[18] He recalls it as a special film: 'my film is "Memory of Mawalan",' one 'I made by myself'.

He looks back to how the Yolŋu lost the first land rights case in 1971; lost the second time at the Commission into Aboriginal Land rights in 1973 presided over by Mr Justice Woodward; and 'third time we win' with federal legislation, the *Aboriginal Land Rights (Northern Territory) Act* (1976). He reflects upon the long process which began in 1963 with the sending of a petition to the Commonwealth government in Canberra, a petition made up of clan designs painted on bark and accompanied by a typed document. Marika explains how he brought all the sacred emblems which signify his own and others' rights to certain lands from Yalaŋbara, the place which the ceremony honoured in remembrance of his father. 'Why can't they, the *balanda* of the court and the government and Nabalco see what is obvious to the Rirratjiŋu landowners: how the land and sea belong to Yolŋu people.' *We know the trees, the land and the dancing is came from/the land, song and ceremony is came from the land.*[19] He tried to explain to members of the court but they didn't understand. The pain that the lost land case engendered is heightened by feelings of despair in being unable to make non-indigenous people understand. The silence is deep. And the land–sea owners and Law men strengthen themselves for a further attempt in the name of their fathers and mothers, and with their children's inheritance at the forefront of their minds.

In the remembrance ceremonies of the 1970s Yolŋu people were returning to Beginnings; recreating themselves and their world — their cultural way — through the repetition of the actions of their ancestral founding figures. A time of political and social uncertainty can be a time of spiritual strengthening; just what is needed to turn a defeat in a *balanda* court into a victory for the Law of Yolŋu. Their gestures, movements, chants represent a recreation of their identity. Remembering becomes a source of hope. In *Cosmos and History: The Myth of the Eternal Return*, the late Mircea Eliade, a renowned authority on comparative religion, has written of how the 'eternal return to the sources of the sacred', the repetition of the acts of creation, the gestures, and the movements of the figures of creation can be the wellspring of an optimistic vision. This is the locus of Yolŋu existence and belief. The shapes and beings of landscape and seascape, given to them as the condensed experience of ancestral figures, are held in memory and in song as the guiding light of their actions. This is what is meant by 'holding the sea by song'.

Down to the sea in boats: Yanyuwa and Bardi, Jawi peoples

ONE VERSION OF AN OLD ADAGE SAYS: 'YOU CAN TAKE the man away from the sea but you can't take the sea out of the man.' A living example of this can be found in the life of Edward Koiki Mabo, exiled from his homeland at Las on the island of Mer for most of his adult life. His lands, his reefs and waters were imprinted on Koiki Mabo as part of his soul. When he died in January 1992, six months before the nation-shaking victory for native title in the High Court of Australia, he performed the movements of his shark totem, a very sacred sea rite of his clan. In the few years before his death when he visited his island, he could be seen fishing with his metal pronged spear in his section of Las lagoon with a skill passed on to him by his forebears.

Strong memories hold in place a desire to return home. The two slim accounts that follow are mere fragments of the journeys of two peoples who for a time were exiled from their land–sea country, one to an inland site. Both of these exiles were short-lived. The journeys home give a sense of the strength of the people's attachment to saltwater country. Like Koiki Mabo, although their experiences away had changed them, in their fishing and sea hunting activities they seemed, at least to an onlooker, as though they had never been separated from the seas they inherited.

One story of this kind is that of the journey of the Yanyuwa back to their islands, known today as the Sir Edward Pellew Islands. In 1960, without consultation, 133 Yanyuwa were moved from the river estuary township of Borroloola to an inland 'scrub' place called Dangana, on land belonging to 'bush people'. According to John Bradley, who worked with the Yanyuwa community for 22 years and lived with them for three, behind the Welfare Department's decision to move them was the belief that it would give the Department 'total control over the lives of the Yanyuwa people'.[20]

Roddy Harvey, whose mother, brothers and sisters were taken to the inland station, recalled to John Bradley in 1997 the impact on her people:

> Eastwards, they were taken eastwards, it was welfare that did it, they took all of the Yanyuwa people eastwards into that scrub country, into that country of bush, it was not their country, it was another group of people's country. It was Garrwa country, they are the people for that country, we are coastal people, sea people, people of the open country.[21]

Less than two years later the saltwater people left Dangana. In a quiet display of independent spirit and ingenuity, they cut trees and made enough dugout canoes to transport themselves home.

They then paddled downstream along the Robinson River, first visiting some of their islands, and thence on to Borroloola. Yanyuwa people recall this action with pride. 'They cut canoes,' Roddy Harvey continues, 'many canoes, some were big and others small . . . they did not stay in that place of the scrub. They departed downstream to the sea; they were happy . . . they sailed northwest.' Older people who had remained in the islands 'were crying for those people that had come back to their country to the islands and the sea'. Were the cultural memories of the Yanyuwa men and women stirred by their forced move to scrub country, land foreign to them as saltwater people? As we saw earlier, they see themselves as 'dugong hunters of excellence' because they are endowed with special knowledge relating to the Dugong Hunter Spirit Ancestors. Roddy Harvey points to this in her explanation of why they returned to the sea: 'they went down to the sea because they were dugong hunters of excellence, that was their country that sea, those islands, for all of us we are Yanyuwa. We talk Yanyuwa because we are people whose spiritual origins came from the sea.'

People who had visited their country recognised the Yanyuwa as an independent saltwater people. One visitor to part of their country at Borroloola at the beginning of the twentieth century noted their independent stance and affinity with salt water:

> These people live down by the salt-water and don't have much to do with the inland natives . . . [they] are not at all unfriendly but very independent. There is such a supply of food here that they can do without what we have to give them easily, in fact they feed just about as well as we do.[22]

Yanyuwa country is all saltwater country, and reaches no more than ten to twenty kilometres inland from the sea. It begins in the Sir Edward Pellew Islands, named by Matthew Flinders in 1802, and extends to coastal regions on the estuary of the McArthur River. Like their neighbours in Arnhem Land and further west, the Yanyuwa traded fish, turtle meat and shell, as well as their labour for rice, tobacco, arrak, dugout canoes and other goods. A few years after the Macassans were excluded from visiting the northern coasts and islands many Yanyuwa began to move to Borroloola, then an isolated police outpost on the coast some 80 kilometres from their home islands. The McArthur River at Borroloola is tidal up to that point. Long after it had been an isolated police post in the 1880s it became an Aboriginal people's town, not a white man's town. And except on two brief occasions Aboriginal people outnumbered Europeans. The first exception was in 1886 when 1,500 non-Aboriginal people on their way to the Kimberley goldfields passed through over three months with 3,000 horses. The second was 100 years later in 1985 when the Borroloola weekend centenary celebrations attracted many Europeans.[23] In the early days Borroloola was 'the end of the line' for police patrol officers: for white people it seemed there was *nothing* in Borroloola and being sent there felt like exile. Yanyuwa people, however, came into Borroloola in increasing numbers, so that by the beginning of the 1950s the majority of Yanyuwa were 'found', that is, believed by them to be conceived, in Borroloola. Their ongoing spiritual attachment to Borroloola was a major contributor to the acceleration of the process of 'coming in' to this part of their country.[24]

The Second World War years were the last period in which the Yanyuwa were able to move in their customary way over all their islands. The pattern that formed thereafter began with young men being taken away by police, often handcuffed, and then being 'forwarded on to drovers or cattle stations on the Barkly Tablelands'.[25] Bill Harney, who was employed by the Native Affairs Department during the Second World War, commented critically on the wrong done to this 'strong tribe of people who lived by the sea' — being forcibly scattered over nearly 650 kilometres of inland plains and bearing 'the full weight' of wartime pressures.[26]

But Yanyuwa people remembered their sea country, bringing back two or three new canoes on their trucks on return from work on inland stations, work they undertook for the duration of the wet season. They held the seascapes of their home islands in their memories; and 'holding the sea by song' developed a special meaning for Yanyuwa saltwater people. Nostalgia pervades this wistful poem about separation from sea country:

I stand and feel the sea wind,
it refreshes my face; for too long
I have been a woman of the inland 'scrub country'.

Other songs simply evoke the sea hunter's life with the sea, like Yanyuwa poet Jack Baju's song poem of the sea hunter waiting in his canoe for a turtle to surface with the wind.

Silence
A stirring of wind,
Bringing,
The Flat Backed Turtle.[27]

Jack Baju's other poem about the Yanyuwa people — 'Our hair is tightly coiled and heavily oiled' — tells of the strength of the dugong people. He composed it in the 1920s when Yanyuwa people were moving around in the Borroloola area, working on boats along the coast, travelling inland to work on pastoral stations. 'We are the dugong hunters of excellence,' the Yanyuwa continued to affirm to themselves. Through this process of comparison and contrast they situated themselves and contributed to a re-imagined Yanyuwa sea people. Was this the strength they took with them as they paddled down the Robinson River towards home?

THE SEA CULTURE OF THE BARDI AND JAWI PEOPLES, who today live mainly at One Arm Point near Cape Leveque close to the southern Kimberley coast, stretches back to the time when the reef flats were developing up to 3,000 years ago. Their sea environment is a place of whirlpools, and cyclones are common. The tides that rise and fall up to eight metres each day may reach even twelve knots. Like the Meriam of the Murray Islands in the far northeast, long ago the sea peoples of the area built permanent stone fish-traps: today, the fish arriving in the lagoons are trapped at low tide and the people spear the fish or often catch them with their hands. In 1997 twenty-two fish-traps were identified and photographed; men and women were collecting fish in the traps, collecting shellfish and fishing in the area. Moya Smith, a researcher at the Western Australian Museum, prepared a report in cooperation with Bardi and Jawi people that gives a picture of a rich and living sea culture today.[28] People fish with materials different from those of their forebears, but anyone who reads her report of their fishing and hunting prowess without knowledge of their recent past might understandably assume an unbroken history. Yet this is by no means so.

The Bardi and Jawi people's homelands are the myriad islands and the coastal lands on the Dampier Peninsula. Jawi are the original people of Sunday Island; the Bardi's traditional homelands lie on the mainland near One Arm Point. William Dampier noted a little of their heritage as fisherfolk: how they travelled out with the tide on their mangrove rafts, caught fish and returned on the incoming tide. He mistakenly assumed that this activity constituted their whole daily lives and he knew

Bardi people Esther and Sandy Paddy collecting 60 trevally from a stone-wall fish-trap (mayoor), *Lananan*

nothing of their spiritual lives or the spirit beings known to them as *raija* or *ray*: spirit beings who remain invisible but may take human or animal shape. The *raija* live in spirit centres, specific sites in Bardi and Jawi country, moving between 'natural' and human personae and being alternately helpful and harmful. They are like spirit doubles and bring 'dream corroborees' known as *ilma* to the song men, complete with words, music and dance patterns.[29]

The dance icons of the Bardi and Jawi feature whirlpools and ring tides, features which abound in their sea country. Bardi and Jawi people believe that their contact with these spirit doubles is only maintained if they keep in active touch with them, hence receiving new dream corroborees which stamp them as Bardi or Jawi. In other words, their spiritual connections are continually replenished and given living meaning through contact with spirit centres in their country. The total ensemble of their beliefs, their attachments to humans and other species are renewed continually through this contact; it is a relationship tied to *place*. Dances performed by people living away from home are still their dances carried in memory; but as one Meriam elder explained to me, people dance differently at home to the way they dance elsewhere. Their spiritual energies are more intense at home, nuanced by a relationship with the movements of their seas.

In 1948 many Bardi and Jawi people returned to their homelands following war-time evacuation. Moves were soon being made by government authorities to force them to settle around the port of Derby on the mainland. The people resisted. However, by June 1962 the United Aboriginal Mission, which had run the settlement at one of their islands known as Sunday Island since 1899, withdrew its staff under government pressure. These persuasive techniques of the local officer of the Department of Native Welfare to coerce the Bardi and Jawi into moving to Derby met with vocal opposition. Many people refused to leave the Sunday Island settlement and supplies were delivered to the island fortnightly. The local officer emphasised all the advantages of moving, while the Bardi and Jawi enumerated the disadvantages. To resist, he argued, was to selfishly 'deny their children . . . the opportunity to grow with the progress of the Kimberleys'. This manipulative argument met with a 'favourable response' from the Bardi and Jawi, he reported.[30] The older Bardi, who sought to protect their cultural inheritance by keeping their roots in ancestral lands and seas, could do little now. School-age children were taken to Derby and housed in a hostel. Many older people still refused to move; they were forced to do so when the Mission ceased delivering supplies to Sunday Island in May 1964. Not all of them moved to Derby however; some moved to the Catholic Mission at Lombadina, others to the site of a new pearl culture station at Cygnet Bay on the Dampier Peninsula. Still, according to one scholar, by 1968 'most of the Bardi were living in Derby'.[31]

However, their relocation could not extinguish the wish of many Bardi and Jawi to return home. They had been told that transport would be available to take people back to the island for ceremonies held regularly during the northwest rainy season. In a mood of considerable anger, Billy Ah Choo, a senior Bardi, confronted 'the Department' in the Derby office on 5 November 1962, the beginning of the wet season: promises had not been kept, the transport had not been forthcoming, and the Bardi and Jawi were threatening action. As anthropologist A. P. Elkin had observed in 1954, indigenous people who leave their country usually do so with the intention of returning to it, 'especially for ceremonial purposes'.[32] It was the wet season, the time for ceremonies, and Bardi and Jawi in Derby were demanding their right to return to their land–sea country. In seeking this they were implicitly demanding the right to determine their own future. Billy Ah Choo 'said he would get a little boat and take himself and family back to [the] island alone'.[33] This was the beginning of the Bardi and Jawi people's return to their country. Yet even today the story of the move back and its reasons has been little recorded. H. C. Coombs tells the story briefly in his book *Kulinma* in 1978; according to him, by the mid-1970s there were about 160 Bardi people at One Arm Point, close to Sunday Island where the mission had been. Older men and women inspired others to return.[34] But in their absence during the 1960s, outsiders had been preparing to work the reefs off Sunday Island for trochus shell. On 23 June 1969 sixty Bardi and Jawi men and women attended a meeting that advocated action to stop the project. A six-man plea to institute a Bardi fishing project was rejected by one commercial fisherman, but with the assistance of another, in 1969 the Bardi Cooperative Society was formed.[35] Some 30 years later, in February 1999, a land–sea claim was filed under the *National Native Title Act 1993* on behalf of Bardi and Jawi land–sea owners.

In the late 1990s, anthropologist Geoffrey Bagshaw, who prepared a report in support of this claim, found impressive 'the level of fine-grain detail' of people's recollections.[36] Adults remembered very clearly the names of ritual, economic and historical sites, the bodies of land and sea they owned, the journey routes of supernatural beings, even the occupants of old traditional burial places, and old and new bush birth sites. His 130-page report on the character and detail of Bardi and Jawi society has the character of a living memory bank. The people whose recollections are recorded include many of those who spent up to ten years in Derby from the mid-1960s.

We are speaking of something much more than memory. The people who returned to their homelands went on practising their fishing and hunting skills in daily life, and their ceremonial activities were strong. In 1962 Tommy Thomas had confronted the Native Welfare Department in Broome with Billy Ah Choo demanding the fulfilment of the promise that his people return to Sunday Island in the northwest season. In 1979 Thomas made several mangrove rafts for museums. In the 1990s Bardi and Jawi people were obtaining most of their local food from their marine domains, children of five years were casting hand lines, and men and women were again using some of the 39 fish-traps built by their forebears.[37]

It is significant that none of the recent reports on Bardi and Jawi knowledge and practices today refers at all to their absence in the 1960s. Perhaps it does not seem relevant; or perhaps the writers simply do not know. I find the depth as well as the scope and detail of Bardi and Jawi recollections exciting. As early as

1928, anthropologist A. P. Elkin had been struck by the profound knowledge of country which individuals displayed.[38]

Looking back to the brave and forthright actions of those who confronted the administration in Derby in the 1960s to be told they couldn't go back to their homelands and to stop being violent, there is room for reflection on the strength of their memory of seascape. It was not possible to take the seascape out of the senior Jawi and Bardi people. 'Law is first for us' said Khaki Stumpagee Jamaji, and his words offer a clue to the reason. Those who have the Law must make regular contact with their country to replenish their knowledge, for country is a giving place, not merely a physical site. Most importantly, the connection to a specific estate is first and foremost a spiritual one. *Ilma*, the songs and dances brought in dream visits to particular locations, depend on contact with country.[39]

Skippers of their own boats: Kowanyama people

JACK BRUNO IS A FOLK HERO OF KOWANYAMA, AN Aboriginal community with a melancholy past and a confident present. In the worst days of *terra nullius*, indigenous men of independent spirit were often sent to Palm Island, a penal settlement far enough off the coast of Townsville to prevent the prisoners from swimming back to the mainland. Bruno's was a tragic world, softened by what he and his people call 'being grown up by country', strengthened by the voices of the ancestors. His unpublished manuscript, an epic life journey, contains his hymn to creation. It reads in part:

One being created it;
he created it.

He made the heavens.
He made the waves,
constantly moving.

He set them down.

The waves.

He set them down
constantly moving.

His thought extends and completes the thought of the past. As philosopher–poet he remembered the messages of his ancestors and in the Christian era he fashioned his own beliefs about He who placed the stars and the sea in their uniqueness, constantly moving. Bruno is a resilient figure, imaginative, courageous, and incisive. 'They send people [to Palm Island] . . . For them just to die there.' He himself refused this punishment and set his course on returning to country.

I stole a horse.
In the dark
of the night
I stole it . . .

I lit a flame,
a piece of tea-tree bark,
I waved it . . .
Nothing; they don't see.
They're asleep.

'Palm Island Escapes', Jack Bruno's powerful epic poem of many stanzas, translated into English in 1978,[40] is about a land-and-sea highwayman.

I came
back this way, in a boat.
I stole the boat
And went.

This is his epic of a forbidding era. The tension of having to outwit captors, of dangerous deeds and trickery are evoked by Jack's rendering of the landscape of his journey: darkness, sleeping police, silence, stealth — all counterpointed by his wakefulness; his words proceed to the beat of the horse's feet taking him back home. His country is largely river delta land so rich in tributaries that seen from above the waters resemble trees laid out gracefully along the ground. Further afield, a stolen boat takes him along the east coast.

At night.
In the darkness,
I took it
I came this way from there.

He writes of angry waves, 'big angry waves', and he recalls his trickery: he pushed the boat off empty with its sail up, sailing westwards, while Jack himself came eastward to his home country.

In the early 1980s at Kowanyama, the home of about 1,000 people of three language groupings, a small drama took place on a beach at a place called Topsy Creek. Dead fish were found — queen fish, salmon — lying on the sand. A non-Aboriginal commercial fisherman had used mesh too small for the fish he wanted and had thrown the unwanted ones out. Aboriginal people were very angry. Kowanyama people were worried. Wastage stirs deep-seated beliefs about right and wrong, because the law of the land says that if you waste fish you are not *with* the land and it will retaliate by denying you. When the elders said, 'There'll be no fish out there for us,' they were reacting to a violation of their land–sea domain; the commercial fishermen were seen as placing both Kowanyama people's future and the land in jeopardy. John Clarke, senior Ranger, recalled to me how in the early 1980s they 'stood up and said: "Too many boats on the South Mitchell [River] and too many fish being wasted".'

The event triggered a train of memories that inspired action. There were incendiary incidents, both figuratively and literally. Threats were made to burn the boats of commercial fishermen. At a place called Bottle Camp on the northern side of Topsy Creek, a net had been tied by the non-indigenous fishermen blocking the creek. Kowanyama people pulled it out with a vehicle, a few shots were fired by the commercial fishermen and members of the Kowanyama community fired a few back. Kowanyama people have vivid memories of the five years of struggle which followed. They recall with pride how in 1987 the Queensland government ruled the South Mitchell River closed to recreational and commercial fishermen.

Three important steps were then taken by Kowanyama people. First of all they hosted a fisheries conference at Kowanyama in 1988 with government managers and commercial fishermen present. The groups present were wary of each other and the meeting began with some arm-waving and foot-stamping about sea, river and land rights. But at that conference the community succeeded in putting 'Indigenous Fishers' on the Queensland fisheries map for the first time. Secondly, the Kowanyama people found allies among fishers of the barramundi and prawn port of neighbouring Karumba. In 1991 a third step was taken: the creation of a Land and Natural Resources

Management Office (called KLANRO) at Kowanyama, which allowed the community to run the rivers, the rich deltas and the 80 kilometres of sea country on the Gulf of Carpentaria. They could conserve their traditional subsistence fishery, they had the area to themselves, they were able to regulate recreational fishing traffic, and their 'partnership' with the Karumba fishers gave active support to their program to build up fish stocks in their rivers.

Colin Lawrence, an elder of the Kunjen people, one of the three groupings at Kowanyama, summed up 'the law of the land' for his people:

> Long time before white people come here, the black people looked after the land, the rivers and lagoons. Come to this day, we still want to look after this country. For our young people. They going to live on and on and on . . . We gonna take care of this land, we gonna look after him. We don't want the Government to look after him, because, long before, our ancestors looked after it.[41]

This was in 1993, ten years after the elders, the elected Council and the community had taken matters into their own hands.

The Kowanyama story is exciting and unique. The work of the Kowanyama community since 1990 on management of the whole Mitchell River catchment is a wonder; it earned them the reputation among their 'partners' at Karumba as 'the eyes and ears for us of the environment'.[42] Rarely have we seen sustained action of this kind in Australia; even more unusual is the opportunity it offers to gain a sense of underlying indigenous motifs. In speaking of the experience, participants themselves as well as those who inspired them give us a sense of the spiritual inheritance that guided them. The late Jack Bruno and others might trace this to the Creation Ancestor.

The elders are 'up-front' at Kowanyama; they are a presence in daily life. They are most approachable and make time to talk about light-hearted as well as serious things. They chide you for not talking with them. Behind them lie many unhappy memories of the behaviour of white people, but they know there are white people who respect the land, the waters and Aboriginal culture, even though their way of thinking may be rather different. Elder Thomas Bruce, whom I first got to know through Meriam priest Reverend Dave Passi (himself parish priest at Kowanyama in the 1970s), volunteered how Karumba fisherman, Gary Ward, had offered 'a partnership between us and himself'; and how from then on they worked 'evenly side by side'. Bruce was proud of working together with Ward; and as I learnt later, so was Gary.

The link between commercial fishing and custom is made by younger Aboriginal people who have 'custom and fisheries'. The elders teach them everything they can as long as they carry out their work as rangers or fisheries' inspectors on the elders' behalf. John Clarke, who filled this dual role, explains the knowledge the elders 'pushed across' to him. This knowledge, he told me, begins with the law of the land and how to respect it. He explained about 'baptising' newcomers with water so the country knows them, how treating the land respectfully and with good feeling is reciprocated by ancestral spirits who in turn provide for their kin. 'This is your tucker,' the ancestral spirits are saying; what you've got to know about the land, where the sacred places are, which clan comes from each country, which animals may be eaten. It involves 'reading trees' — flowers that are blossoming let you know which animals are getting fat; the right way to cut certain fish; how a stingray becomes fat after lightning flashes on its back; the customs to observe after someone dies (you must keep away from their country for four to six months, an observance that helps bring the wildlife back to the area). This knowledge enables them to do modern things 'our way', the Kowanyama way.

The Kowanyama story is one of strength as well as pain. Some of their forebears were killed in 'the Battle of the Mitchell', as Frank and his brother Alexander Jardine called the massacre at Mitchell River, in which they fired 59 rounds of ammunition at the clanspeople on 18 December 1864 while journeying overland with a herd of cattle through Cape York Peninsula to Somerset.[43] Kowanyama people know this and other parts of the history of invasion. They themselves have experienced servitude and felt despair. They are also people with experience on boats, with cattle and station culture, and the Kowanyama community today owns a cattle station. They have experienced the freedom of sailing and of droving cattle 'up the Cape'. Elders today 'could ride the socks off anyone', as Bill Kehoe, one of their Karumba 'partners', said to me with great respect.

Their readiness to take the reins and ride free in the last two decades was given strength from two other closely linked events. In 1974, following years of struggle from the mid 1960s by the so-called 'Treaty tribes' of northwest Washington State, a rare decision was made in the District Court. *US v. Washington* (1974) was known popularly as 'the Boldt decision' after Justice George Boldt upheld mid-nineteenth-century treaty rights of the tribes of the Pacific seaboard to hunt in all 'usual and accustomed places' on and off reservations, to exclude others from certain fishing grounds in rivers and bays, and to participate in regional fisheries management.[44]

The tribes of the northwestern seaboard had defended their Treaty fishing rights on the Nisqually River in the territory of the Squaxin Island tribe, as well as on other major rivers, for many years, taking direct action in 'fish-ins' where tribal people fished the river together in a public act of civil disobedience. They were upholding fishing rights won by their forebears in the 1850s when the settlers took the fertile lands of the vast river plains around Puget Sound near present-day Seattle. Following the Boldt decision a Northwest Indian Fisheries Commission was established by the associated tribes; at its head were the leaders of the fishing rights struggle: Billy Frank Snr (and later, Billy Frank Jnr), and David Whitener, a Squaxin Island tribal leader and professor at Evergreen College in Washington State. Their local friends during that struggle had been the Quaker body known as The Society of Friends.

Through a non-indigenous friend, Viv Sinnamon who worked with them at Kowanyama for many years, the Kowanyama people learnt of the successful struggle of the Pacific northwest tribes. David Whitener was at Kowanyama at the watershed conference on the management of the Mitchell River catchment area in 1990. In June 1998 he recollected to me how Sinnamon pressed for the establishment of a Counsel of Elders there.

Reflections upon the past: the Meriam example

THE MURRAY ISLAND COMMUNITY AND FAMILY FISHING enterprise, which took shape after the *Mabo* case, was born out of an earlier dream; or more specifically, a frustrated desire of the Meriam to take responsibility for their fishing activities. In 1981 a Murray Island fishing committee had been formed by Ron Day, now the Chairman of the Murray Island Council, and other Meriam. The Meriam had to set up a trial mackerel fishing enterprise after persistent pressure on the local office of the Commonwealth Department of Aboriginal Affairs (DAA) for technical assistance. The project instructor, a professional commercial fisherman, arrived at Mer and taught Meriam fishers some new methods. He also brought new gear. The men went out to sea and returned home with their catches. Records were kept daily. The fish quota set by the project leader was filled far ahead of schedule. Adults today recall memories of their childhood during these months of economic independence when fish-money came regularly into their families. Men and women drank socially at the canteen after the day's work. Community morale was high on the island. 'Maybe our fishing project will happen now,' they said to me then, in 1981. The project instructor departed and the Murray Islanders awaited further news. But there was only silence. When they inquired at the DAA office in Thursday Island they were told there was no support for the real project to begin. No reasons were given. Was there a question of power?

THE MERIAM PEOPLE'S FILM, 'SMALL ISLAND BIG Fight', which screened on 21 December 2000, tells the story of their current efforts to establish an independent fishing economy. Their perceptions of themselves as maritime people with ancient traditions were reinforced by new archaeological discoveries in 1999. As I mentioned in Chapter Four, research at Mer and Dauar indicated that the stone fish-traps on their reef flats were built by their forebears soon after the flats were formed some 3,000 years ago. Their dream to take charge of waters within their traditional maritime boundaries and to develop a cash economy goes hand in hand with their wish to explain to themselves and to the world who they are and what they want their future to be. As illustrated in the dramatic action of several Meriam fishermen at Dugong Reef in 1998 in boarding the boat and removing fish caught by non-indigenous fishermen, they reject totally the idea that outsiders have an equal coexisting right under Australian law to take fish from the waters around the Murray Islands.

As we saw in the Yolŋu's current perceptions of 'Macassan times', the Meriam people look to their past traditions of independence, courage and skill to guide them into the future. In seeing themselves writ large in the refracting mirror of Matthew Flinders' perceptions of them as 'dextrous sailors and formidable warriors', they also know that their traditions have changed in important ways. For instance, the retributive part of their traditional law that says 'Your jaws for [the god] Malo's necklace' is not followed by them today. Yet in the mirror they hold up they see themselves as fearless sea people. This self image lies behind their passionate defence of younger Meriam people's right to make a real living from fishing. This is their answer to a life of long-standing imposed dependence. 'We are not frightened,' Bishop Dave Passi said to me recently with a laugh, speaking of their tempestuous efforts to establish a marine economy over two decades. In taking this stance today, they see themselves as following the seamarks made by their forebears.

10
Old Traditions, New Ways

Riding new waves

A gathering murmur of protest against non-indigenous fishermen intruding into northern saltwater people's marine territories has developed into a decisive call. At the first National Indigenous Sea Rights Conference held in Hobart in September 1999, land–sea owner and claimant in the *Croker Island Seas* case John Kristoffersen voiced the widely held sentiment in a few words. 'All along the coasts we are fighting for rights, we are fighting for responsibilities.' He supported working mutually with others 'as long as we are treated with respect as the first peoples'.

In this view, taking responsibility for sea or land means not only the right to own it but the right to manage it in the name of inherited knowledge, custom and law. In the indigenous perspective, native title is not an end in itself; it includes taking command in the name of significant practices that have been bequeathed to clans and families.

The desire to take responsibility for sea country has been given expression since the early 1980s. Anthropologist Ben Scambary, a colleague who has carried out research in support of native title claims along the Northern Territory coast over the last seven years, finds a consistency on two core attitudes among indigenous people: the need for protection of sacred sites in the sea and on the coast; and a belief that some commercial fishermen misuse the sea and marine resources. Indigenous saltwater people also see the illegal landing of commercial fishers on Aboriginal land and the lack of involvement of Aboriginal persons in marine enterprises as matters of urgency.

Upholders of traditional obligations to sea country speak of a world structured in a way that keeps rights and responsibilities in balance with one another. Greedy or disrespectful actions bring shame to a person, and because avenues for approved ways of acting are built into the system, they serve as powerful regulators of people's conduct towards one another. Indigenous people formed within this system of complementary rights and responsibilities speak honestly when they say, 'We'll look after the environment better than you commercial fishermen.'

These indigenous views moved into the public arena at the end of the century, and are consistent with and often extend those which emerged in the early 1980s. In the 1980–81 hearings before the Aboriginal Land Commissioner on sea closures at coastal communities in parts of Arnhem Land senior Yolŋu witnesses gave these views and their origins strong expression. In their tradition, they said, an outsider to their country must have a message or letter stick, an 'entry permit' brought from their own homeland and people. If you have no letter stick, they explained, 'you stay where you are'. Behind the intransigent stand of land–sea owners lie the broken promises of some commercial barramundi fishermen.

In the 1980–81 hearings witnesses drew upon their relationships with, and basic beliefs about, the sea and themselves in a plea for recognition of primary rights. Witnesses contrasted *balanda* people's relationships with the sea as 'just for enjoyment and the dollar' to their own: the seas are places 'that mean something to our people, something that we belong to'. Significant places are 'linked to you with feelings'. 'The thunder and clouds and birds . . . is the feeling of the people.'[1]

What might be called 'responsibility-based fishing' is part of the accumulated experience of indigenous people who live on their own homelands. As senior people among them have often stated, wasting fish or endangering marine life is upsetting because it disregards their Dreamings and ignores their descendants. A serious and active recognition of responsibility has served these peoples well in the way they live together and many saltwater people today continue to see themselves as bound by it. However, demoralisation, dependency and despair have eaten into those older values and practices that senior people wish to conserve.

More and more saltwater people see sea rights as a stepping stone to a long overdue economic independence. They look across the Tasman and observe Maori business ventures on a scale unheard of in Australia. Over more than a decade, Maori fishing rights, customary and commercial, have been recognised by the Crown and fishing quotas have been allocated to Maori *iwi* or tribes. The most well known of these allocations is the Maori 50 per cent share in Sealord Products. The 30,000-strong Ngai Tahu *iwi*, for example, established Ngai Tahu Fisheries Limited which, by mid-1997 was running its own fisheries, processing and marketing wet fish, abalone and lobster.[2]

Indigenous people in Australia have for so long been denied the opportunity to take part as free agents in marine enterprise, and we can only wish them well in future commercial maritime ventures. But that should not blind us to the truth that the form of property rights and the values in whose name they have fought for native title are not those of conventional business enterprise. Those indigenous people, Aboriginal leader Noel Pearson significant among them, who call for the right to take responsibility in building modern indigenous enterprise stress the need to carry forward the values of reciprocity and responsibility.[3] But values are not innate attributes of people; they are born out of social life, and if that form of social life from which they spring is supplanted these values will eventually be replaced by others. Hence there is no guarantee that obligations to others or to place will survive present market pressures that favour possessive individualism. The power of market-oriented aspiration is enormous. A telling example of global transformative power is its challenge to public rights in the sea, the cornerstone of the Western conception of coastal marine space. There is irony in the fact that at the time when Justice Olney in the *Croker Island Seas* case in 1998 was upholding the public right to fish as the anchoring point of state law and marine policy, various forms of privatisation of sea space were emerging in Australia.

An ethic for modern enterprise

MARKET-BASED FISHING NEEDS TO SEEK NEW structures of obligation or accountability towards others. This is a general problem. In relation to indigenous people the right to take responsibility is being used in two rather different contexts: the first is that of the man and his son sardine fishing at Mer; the second is that of business enterprise. As we saw, the Meriam have *debe tonar*, the good custom of reciprocity and accountability. Business enterprise operates according to rules that relate to individual possessiveness and the aim of profit.

However, as human and environmental ecologists Rettig, Berkes and Pinkerton have noted, there is 'a treasure chest' of examples of self-regulatory fisheries and successful resource management in contemporary times.[4] As we have seen in Chapter Seven, many of these have built upon long-existing and usually unwritten common property situations, at least in places like northern Norway, not all of which were acknowledged by state law.

This is the time and place for questions about potential as well as loss. Have new pathways been formed between indigenous clans and families, along which extended forms of cooperation may flourish? I think of Mer and the community-inspired fishing enterprise pursued in the name of eight clans. A further question follows: Do the common property systems expanded through these pathways provide the soil for self-regulated community enterprise?

Many 'first peoples' have expressed vigorously their right to gain both material and spiritual sustenance from their country and their primary responsibility to care for it. Their call comes under rapidly worsening world conditions not of the first peoples' making; and today indigenous peoples' call goes beyond caring for and managing habitat to participation in marine enterprise on a much wider basis than before. The central question I am posing — how to build in an ethic of accountability to other people and to the environment — cannot be answered without understanding these changing conditions and aspirations.

In the long struggle to survive as distinctive saltwater peoples in the time of *terra nullius*, continuing identification with their saltwater domains played an essential part in keeping indigenous saltwater cultures alive. It would be doing an injustice to the saltwater peoples to end their story at this point. For I believe that the destructive dispossession of the *terra nullius* era may be equalled by the effects of market forces now coming to engulf even the most marginal parts of the world.

People emerging from colonial situations in other countries — Papua New Guinea, for example — have found that even the long-standing cultural values of reciprocity or 'payback' have melted away like snow in the sun, together with the structures that nourish them, in favour of narrowly conceived commercial goals. How might people avoid such tragedies? A positive side to intensifying globalisation is people's ready access to the experiences of others in far-off places.

To a greater or lesser degree today, tropical saltwater peoples are blessed with the long-standing competence and experience to sustain themselves, their places of habitation and their marine territories. *Eburlem es maolem*, the Meriam say — this means: don't exploit the land or sea, take only what you need, don't waste fish or garden produce. New knowledge and skills are required to develop habitat protection and enhancement and to run marine enterprises. As we have seen, on parts of their coasts, islands and waters saltwater people have taken part in pearling, trepanging and fishing industries for more than a century. However, a question being posed here and in other places — on the coasts of Ireland, the marine areas of Troms and Finnmark of arctic Norway, the fisheries of Ireland, of Nova Scotia, of Vancouver — is, can community survive?[5] To help identify the various forces operating to destroy community goals, and the kind of responses indigenous peoples elsewhere are making to resist this destruction, we need to look outside Australian experience.

The death rattle of public rights

MOVES BY INDIGENOUS PEOPLES TO TAKE PRIMARY responsibility for their inherited lands and seas are being accompanied by moves to care for and replenish their country. Building up fish stocks in the rivers around Kowanyama, and turtle identification and conservation activities by the Yolŋu land management body Dhimurru, both exemplify this trend. They are important initiatives, particularly when the path to development is costing the environment and local people dearly. However, the main response to the devastation of so many marine species has been a move towards the privatisation of fishing and marine space.

Behind government regulation and privatisation lies an economically rational way of relating to the world. Today the outcome is devastation of many species. The fate of the albatross is symbolic of present dangers. Cook's men shot albatrosses in the ice-islands visited by the *Resolution* in the 1770s; they did so for sport and some of them felt remorse about it. In the poet Coleridge's hands their actions spoke ill omens. Today as many as seventeen varieties of albatross are listed as endangered or vulnerable; adding to their vulnerability, these birds take bait on the long-lines of trawlers and then get pulled in with the fish and drowned. But threats to sea birds are just the visible tip of a vast iceberg — although some believe the danger may have abated since the days of the unregulated long-line trawlers of the 1970s. The development of factory production in fishing, however, and the narrow-minded pursuit of money goals — where fishers and others simply pursue their own interests without concern for others or for habitat — have been a major cause of exhaustion of fish supplies in many waters. Unfortunately, it seems that government regulation has failed to reverse this effect.

Market-driven moves towards privatisation of coastal fishing rights are challenging long-standing open access marine rights. A transformation in rights to coastal waters, now becoming visible in Australia, is occurring rapidly within major fishing nations. Pointing to the failure of government regulation to stem the tide of resource depletion and habitat destruction in the 1980s and 1990s, advocates of privatisation have rejoiced in the 'death rattle' of open access. Public rights are, in practice, being supplanted by a private property right in fishing known within the fishing industry today as 'rights-based fishing'.

Writing in the 1996 winter issue of the international journal *Marine Resource Economics*, marine economist Francis Christy documents the decline of practices based on open access fishing in coastal waters by the citizens of a state, and its accompanying regulation by government bodies. He points to an inexorable process of privatisation of fisheries, a trend which he advocates in his article. He also notes the lack of international awareness of the speed of privatisation, and places Individual Transferrable Quotas and Total Available Catch categories as a stage within a larger process: a move from licensing to private rights.[6] Individual Transferable Quotas or ITQs came into being some twenty years ago as a response to the failure of government regulation to regulate 'free riding' within open access regimes. The quota system grew out of the attempt to limit licence-holders and so prevent over-exploitation of the sea. To reiterate an Australian example: barramundi fishers at Karumba, a port on the Gulf of Carpentaria, speak with satisfaction about how they eliminated 'the cowboy element' from the industry at the beginning of the 1980s. Between 1981 and 1987 the numbers of licensed fishers were reduced from 276 to 112.[7] As Canadian marine economist Anthony Scott observed at the end of 1999, there has been a move from licensing to ITQs to property rights in fishing, even though this transition was not planned.[8] Whatever its origins, this transition may be creating what a leader of the Shetland Islands Fish Producers' Organisation referred to in 1999 as 'a seismic shift in attitudes' on property rights in fishing among fishers in the United Kingdom.[9] However, in Australia belief in open access still remains entrenched in the fishing industry and in public opinion. Ninety-seven per cent of Australians favour open access, Nigel Scullion,

Darwin-based President of the Seafood Industry Council, contended in 1997 on the ABC radio program 'Late Night Live'.

In his 1996 article, Christy accepted the fact that 'the need to reduce over-capacity will lead to a concentration of rights' in fewer hands. Privatisation may mean greater power to exploit, to disregard habitat and declare communities redundant in the name of efficiency. Rights-based fishing sanctions the primacy of economic goals driven by the market. Christy argued that stock mining is not necessarily a bad thing. 'For stocks which are subject to wide natural fluctuations, the best approach may be to fish them out when they are abundant and move to another stock when they are not.'[10]

The trend towards concentration of ownership of marine space has proceeded apace in Canada in the 1990s. In 1994 the Fisheries Council of Canada proposed a partnership between the government and fish processors with the appealing title of 'A Vision for Atlantic Fisheries . . .' under the rubric of co-management. That kind of partnership may be the model for future inshore fisheries on the Pacific coast to the detriment and ultimate exclusion of small scale community-based fishers in the Vancouver region of British Columbia.[11] As a third-generation fisherman remarked at the 1998 Seventh International Conference for the Study of Common Property in Vancouver, 'If the current alliance between indigenous and non-indigenous fishers in this region fails to hold back the tide of dispossession, many of us will soon be history.'

The end of community?

WHILE PROPERTY RIGHTS-BASED FISHING IS ONLY beginning in Australia, it is well advanced on a world scale. John Phyne, a sociologist based at St Francis Xavier University in Nova Scotia, Canada reported in 1997 on his major study of the contemporary concentration process. He examined critically the way in which transnationally based industrial fish farming — he calls it 'capitalist aquabusiness' — has taken hold on the coasts of the United Kingdom, especially in Scotland and also in the Irish Republic. He uses the term 'the new enclosures' to designate a process of privatisation of coastal marine space with close parallel to that of the land enclosures in Britain in the seventeenth and eighteenth centuries. The distinguishing feature of 'enclosed' land is the transition to absolute individual ownership. Phyne documents the ways in which coastal farmer–fisher people's vision of having a few fish-rearing trays at the bottom of the crofts or farms that abut the sea was overtaken by the reality of a few companies coming to divide up the fish farming business among themselves.[12]

In Australia aquaculture, still in its early stages, is a major growth area in marine enterprise. It is one that may have the same initial appeal to indigenous land–sea owners as it did to some Irish and Scottish coastal inhabitants. According to official statistics, in 1996–97 a little over half of the value of fish production in the Northern Territory was contributed by aquaculture. The Australian Democrats, sensing danger, made a public call at the beginning of January 2000 for the right of 'the public at large' to be consulted on any new aquaculture projects on the grounds that 'the sea belongs to everybody'. Yet there has been little discussion on the effects of aquaculture on the marine environment, or on indigenous communities along the coasts. Among traditional owners, the expressed concern has been about moves by commercial interests acquiring leases for aquaculture to pre-empt their rights to marine territories while their native title claims are pending.[13]

Given the relatively small size of the Australian fishing industry, the loss of marine resources is not vast; spokesmen responsible for commercial fishing report healthy northern waters. As a consequence, there is relatively little competition for, or takeover of, resources comparable with the concentration of ownership evident in Canadian Atlantic and Pacific (Vancouver) fisheries. Nor has the Australian fishing industry undergone radical changes like those in countries of the European Union. I have already drawn attention to some of the negative effects of an over-emphasis on technical efficiency in some Norwegian fisheries. There fishing entitlements were reconstructed according to criteria of technical efficiency. One effect was to make people catch more rather than fewer fish than in the pre-1990 days of a real but informal sea commons. In the days of an informal sea commons people fished for fish rather than quotas, following a very long-standing code of fishing custom and informal rules of give and take.

Irish sociologist Brendan Connolly's 1997 comparative study of fishers on the west coast of Ireland and the Netherlands (like Norway, both members of the European Union) found that it was the 'old timers' who possessed the greatest knowledge of, and concern for, the marine environment.[14] In Teelin, southwest Donegal and on the Dingle Peninsula in County Kerry in May 1998, I found people whose judgments drew upon a sense of the past, a sound knowledge of the local marine environment, and a feeling for the future of their children. I have already mentioned the campaign of the inhabitants of the area bordering the Glen River estuary at Teelin in defence of their primary right to fish, and to follow long-established fishing custom where each boat must have its turn. In 1998 at Dunquin, a mainland village across from the renowned Blaskett or Western Islands, I talked with a senior fisherman. An authority on salmon fishing and habitat, he was leading a move to induce the Fisheries Council of Ireland to take decisive measures to revive the fishing industry in his neighbourhood. He spoke in the name of the local community on the Dingle Peninsula where 'the parents of more than half the school children depend on fishing for their livelihood'.

The move towards ownership rights-based fishing upholds and perpetuates the individualistic ethic and therefore constitutes no solution in itself to the problem of over-exploitation. The idea that the concentration of ownership, even with the explicit burden of certain environmental protection requirements, will solve problems created by human predation on dwindling sea populations is at best wishful thinking. One may build in 'safeguards' on habitat protection, but there is little use appealing to a sense of moral obligation to habitat among those whose economic success depends on putting the economy and profit before everything else.

Where may one look for possible alternatives? The 'Treaty tribes' of the Pacific seaboard of Washington State provide an exemplary illustration of habitat management, resource development and economic independence over more than two decades. The fishing cooperatives of Japanese inshore marine enterprise are a long-standing example of how responsibility may be built into economic projects.

Before turning to these examples, I wish to suggest that where strong territorially based use rights are vested in a community, or where a producers' organisation represents a community of fishers, ITQs may be modified according to joint or collective ownership rights. In other words, where community in one or another form remains strong, the latter may provide a form of organisation based upon and geared to cooperation rather than to individually based competition. Contemporary Shetland fisheries organisation and practices point in this direction. Quotas are community-held, in this case by the fish producers' association, a move designed to protect the rights of younger fishers. Since quotas are tradeable commodities and can be sold outside the Shetland islands 'never to return', community quotas provide some defence of national independence.[15]

In a quite striking reversal of his advocacy of property rights-based fishing in 1996, three years later Francis Christy made a surprise plea for recognition of self-regulating community-based fisheries. In a paper titled 'Common Property Rights: An Alternative to ITQs' presented to the 1999 international conference on Property Rights in Fisheries Management in Fremantle, Christy pointed to a failure to accommodate informal rules among fishers already in existence.[16] Reflecting upon the deprivation of small-scale fishing communities, to which lack of recognition of their benefits by national governments has contributed, Christy noted the importance of self-regulation. He argued that community-based fisheries management is founded upon exclusive rights over the resources in the area adjacent to the community, which is what the Croker Islanders and the Meriam are seeking.

Many experiences drawn from different eras and locales illustrate what Christy is now advocating. One is the world-famed fishery operating in the Lofoten area off the coast of Norway in the twentieth century, which was praised by Norwegian government officials as a model of enterprise and accountability. Fundamental to the fishery's success was the fishermen's ethic of equality, their sense of fairness and their tradition of cooperation. Lofoten is known widely as the site of the maelstrom where the *Nautilus* in Jules Verne's novel *Twenty Thousand Leagues under the Sea* met its fate at the 'Navel of the Ocean', a whirlpool which carried it along at a 'giddy speed'.

The Lofoten cod fishery, in which as many as 30,000 men participated, has a long history going back to the seventeenth century and with lessons for fisheries in the twenty-first. After 1857 when a law was enacted declaring open access to Lofoten waters, large-scale boats came to dominate the fishing grounds. In 1890 a direct clash occurred when some large operators blocked the entrance to the Trollfjord by tying four steamships together. But the fishermen managed to get through the entrance. This event led directly to the 1897 'Lofoten Law', legislation favouring smallholders. The smaller-boat fishermen grasped their opportunity to decide the rules of the fishery. As Norwegian marine sociologists Svein Jentoft and Trond Kristoffersen have observed, they placed the give and take embedded in the 'equal distribution of opportunities' at the centre of their lives as fishermen. 'Maximizing the total catch' was secondary.[17]

In the 1980s, some scholars from overlapping disciplines saw the potential in this self-regulatory impulse within local communities, and its relevance to the defence of habitat in the circumstances of an unprecedented fish tragedy. For example, the concluding essay of the 1989 book *Co-operative Management of Local Fisheries* combines scholarship with moral concern. R. Bruce Rettig, Fikret Berkes and Evelyn Pinkerton, human ecologists with a concern for habitat and community survival, argue there that where long-existing cultures with customary norms and values largely independent of national cultures continue, they are in a good position to develop an ongoing commitment to conservation practices.

Nearly half a century ago, the eminent French anthropologist Claude Lévi-Strauss wrote *Triste Tropiques*. It left an indelible mark on me, less for its account of a world on the wane as for its melancholy sensibility. At the end of the twentieth century, new and perhaps more sinister events than those Lévi-Strauss identified have begun to overtake the world. The cod, once prolific in the seas and rivers of the northern hemisphere, have vanished from many waters. From the two 'sides' of the Atlantic travelling westward to the Pacific coast one is caught up in a situation of tragic affliction: the wild salmon, a silvery leaping fish which inhabits the temperate and arctic zones of the northern hemisphere, has also become uncommon. A senior student in his twenties I met at the University of British Columbia interrupted his studies there to work with indigenous and non-indigenous fishing communities in the Vancouver region of Canada. The fish blues song he sang at an impromptu concert in June 1998 catches the prevailing mood:

Let the bell keep ringing
There were fish hooks, gear and clothes there
But can't find fish any more.
So I was blue
There was food down there on the beach
But there was no fish.

Habitat as the key

It was June 1998 and I was in the office of the Northwest Indian Fisheries Commission, Olympia, the capital of Washington State. Its President Billy Frank Junior was speaking to me. Stopping fishing forever won't bring the salmon back, he said, because the habitat for wild salmon spawning and rearing continues to disappear. It's being paved over. It's being degraded by water pollution. It's disappearing as a result of the demands for water and space from the millions who live in this region now and the thousands who move to it each month. Protection and enhancement of habitat is the key. Twenty years earlier Frank's father, Billy Frank Senior, led a tumultuous and often bitter struggle to defend the primary right of the tribes to fish the Nisqually River. The story of their long action, which passed into history as a landmark victory in the 1974 case of *US v. Washington*, I have referred to as 'the Boldt decision'.

Taking the reins, the associated tribes moved rapidly to self-governance after 'the Boldt decision'. Energies devoted to defence of their rights could now be redirected towards the task of building a life that protected and enhanced the environment for the benefit of 'Indian and non-Indian alike'.[18] Self-governance provided the basis of their leadership role in the protection and enhancement of the habitats of the fish on every river within their territories. Their project is exemplary. They provided the Kowanyama people of northern Cape York Peninsula with the inspiration and the energy to take their own road to self-governance.

In June 1998 I visited two of the reservations and tribal fish hatcheries of the associated tribes of the northwest region of Washington State. I was the guest of the Northwest Indian Fisheries Commission, which the tribes established in 1974 to give them a single voice on issues of habitat protection and fisheries management. The tribes' projects today are on a vast scale. They have come to conduct a range of fisheries including hatcheries and growing ponds: in 1996 they released more than 40 million hatchlings from their tribal hatcheries into streams and rivers around western parts of Washington State. Their goal is to supplement not replace wild salmon stocks and they have a long-term program for the recovery of the salmon, the tribes' long-standing fish staple.

The senior spokespeople for the 'treaty tribes', as they are known, say they have always conducted their fisheries responsibly, respecting the sea and the fish. Like the saltwater peoples of the Australian tropics their lives followed seasonal and other cycles. Salmon, and their spawning and maturing times, lay at the heart of these Indian people's lives. The first two months of their year were spawning times for steelhead salmon; the ninth month, the time for black chinook salmon; the tenth for silver salmon. Even two varieties of berries important to the tribes are named salmonberries, their sprouts ready in April, the berries in May. Images of fish permeate the Indian people's star knowledge and patterns. The seven Pleiades — half the crew of the sea hero Tagai's canoe in the Torres Strait, and part of a vast reindeer constellation among the arctic Chukchi herders — are to these tribes a species of fish with large heads and small tails. According to Fay Cohen in her book, *Treaties on Trial*, in the ceremony for the first salmon of the season held by the 'treaty tribes' to this day, sharing rites are performed and the salmon bones returned to the sea. In the past one group believed that salmon people lived to the west beyond the ocean and when caught their souls returned to the salmon homelands, becoming fish for the next year's run.

The associated tribes manage to keep their cultures alive and at the same time engage with complex contemporary problems of habitat recovery, rebuilding stocks, and fish production. For example, since 1997 the Northwest Indian Fisheries Commission has begun inquiring into negative effects of fish hatchery practices followed by the tribes and others on wild salmon in their competition for nutriment.

Marine cooperatives: The Japanese example

A CONTEMPORARY EXAMPLE WITH A VERY OLD BACKground in marine common property is the ongoing success story of Japanese inshore fisheries. Drawing upon traditions which go back almost a thousand years, modern residentially based cooperatives are linked together through Fisheries Co-operative Associations. Traditionally finding expression in fishing guilds, the unit of fisheries organisation, cooperatives were restricted to persons born in a particular village. There are certain key features of these Co-operative Associations still operating today: the fishing community creates its own plans, the cooperatives have the right to manage all aspects of the fisheries with the exception of habitat matters, including questions of quality level for the high-standard domestic market. Since the Second World War exclusive rights to fish are vested in the fishing cooperative and these rights are inalienable. Importantly, and in contrast to Individual Transferable Quotas, a person cannot sell rights to fish; these rights do not lie with the individual and they are not saleable anyway. Moreover, the cooperatives remain close to the fishing ground so that local fishers' knowledge allows the co-operative to respond to its members' experiences and problems in all aspects of fishing. Japanese inshore fishing plans 'have a different feel' to Canadian fishing plans, as Martin Weinstein, a Canadian scholar, observed in 1998 in a reflective account of Japanese fishing cooperatives. He saw the importance of the association between rights vested in the people who do the fishing, know the resource and then make the decisions, and their shouldering of responsibility for mistakes as well as successes. He concludes: 'Because the fishery has a local territory structure, the mistakes are borne by the people who make them. This is surely the most powerful form of accountability.'[19]

Japan's history of experimentation with different models, which established, disbanded and then re-established fishing cooperatives over a long period, has lessons for others. When inshore waters were declared open access areas around 1876 — a replication of the free use of the 'unownable seas' formula of Western capitalist states — the familiar pattern of outsiders and absentee fishers buying into particular fisheries created chaos. It also led to the impoverishment of some local resident fishers. Only when non-transferable rights were vested in the fishing cooperative was a cycle of enrichment at one extreme and impoverishment at the other reduced significantly. Moreover, the association of planning rights, feedback on fish resources, fishing experiences and management accountability point a way towards embedding obligation and rights, allowing no place for either top-down bureaucratic direction or free riding of the waves:

a timely message for others who seek forms of modern marine enterprise that rely on an ethic of obligation and accountability. This account may seem tinged with the image of frictionless and harmonious Japanese fishers. The reality is quite different. Japanese fishing life has been interspersed with times of emotion and conflict. Within fishing communities no majority vote is taken; differences are talked through often with emotion. But the resolution of a dispute calls for celebration and, according to one account, this is the appropriate time to order food and rice wine for all the members.[20]

Don't shoot the albatross

When Billy Frank Jnr, president of the Northwest Indian Fisheries Commission, said to non-Indian people, 'Come, break bread with us; let us talk together,' he was speaking from a position of strength. After years of seemingly endless struggle, the associated tribes of the Pacific Northwest had taken command. They had a unique court decision upholding the treaty rights negotiated by their forebears a century before. In the 1980s they also won a second legal case interpreting their treaty right to hunt in 'all usual and accustomed places', on and off their reservations, as a right to take responsibility for habitat. The right to hunt presupposes that the hunted have not been destroyed directly or by loss of habitat; salmon will die if the river forests are destroyed because their breeding grounds lie in the rivers.[21]

The two-score associated tribes are like nations within nations; the keynote of their life is self-governance. Although their colonial history is different, their victory in court rather spectacular and perhaps unimaginable in Australia, the principles upon which the argument for self-governance rest and their fundamental aspirations seem to be much the same as those of indigenous communities in Australia. They also contend with powerful forces which actively seek to undermine their achievements and their possibilities. In the political arena of Washington State, Senator Slade Gordon made a move to legislate what is called tribal sovereign immunity out of existence. According to Billy Frank, his success would mean the end of the tribes.

In the Australian tropics the marine situation has many healthy characteristics. First is the fact that indigenous saltwater peoples have gone on and in many cases revived and intensified their food-getting and nurturing activities. Their return to their homelands beside the sea, often known as 'outstations', has helped. Second is the developing interest among indigenous and non-indigenous people in coast and sea care. The Kowanyama Land and Natural Resources Management Office, and the Yolŋu land and sea care projects, initiated and carried through by the land and resources management body Dhimurru, are noteworthy examples of indigenous projects which seek to care for the environment. Third is the development of environmental concern among non-indigenous fishers. The 'Saving the albatross' project is a nice example. According to the ABC's 'The 7.30 Report' on 4 July 2000, some Australian fishermen have initiated the 'save-a-tross' trial, where long-liners are fitted with a chute which serves to keep baited hooks at a depth of six metres. This means the baits, a hundred million of which are cast on hooks by the world's long-liners, are out of reach of the albatross and other sea birds.

Environmental concern may be misdirected as in the following story, told to me by Gary Ward, a leading commercial fisherman at the port of Karumba. It's about a fisherman who accidentally caught a dugong, a prohibited species, in his net. By the time he hauled it on to the beach to disentangle it, the dugong had died. He buried it with the aid of a back-hoe. But the media got hold of the story and the dugong was dug up and photographed; an accusatory finger was pointed at the fisherman. Such was his personal anguish that the man gave up fishing for good.

It is healthy to have exchange between different cultural viewpoints and experiences: the Kowanyama experience of cooperation and cross-cultural respect, and the change it generated, is exemplary. I recall talking with Bill Kehoe at his home in Karumba in June 1997. 'I came out of the Kowanyama experience a better person. I learnt to sympathise with Aboriginal people and how they feel about their land and waters.' Bill is a senior non-indigenous fisherman from Karumba and he was reflecting on how experience of cooperation had changed his outlook on Aboriginal people and on life.

Mixed systems are beneficial. They nourish people's sense of who they are and bring to the surface underlying value systems usually taken for granted. Moreover, the interplay between two peoples may create individuals who embody the best of each. Ranger and fisheries inspector at Kowanyama during the 1990s, John Clarke is first and foremost an Aboriginal person; he is also a man who appreciates and interprets non-indigenous standpoints and ways of acting that respect his people and their rights. Finally, the underlying different senses of morally based obligation towards others may reinforce and strengthen one another, facilitating what Yolŋu people call 'travelling together' like salt and fresh waters at the river mouth.

Reclaiming memory

'TRAVELLING TOGETHER' MEANS WHAT ONE ELDER AT Kowanyama referred to as 'working evenly together'. This book has sought to foster this kind of understanding. Two saltwater men, the late Wandjuk Marika, the Yolŋu man and the late Edward Koiki Mabo, the Meriam man, each expressed a wish for this to happen — on terms of equality and reciprocity. Marika spoke this well in his autobiography, *Wandjuk Marika, Life Story*, published in 1995: 'Can we work together, not only just like we are now, but know each other, hand in hand, side by side.' Koiki Mabo went south and broke bread with white people. That journey followed the tradition of the sea god Malo: Sow your ideas everywhere and bring back the harvest to the Meriam people. Native title 'against the whole world' was gifted to all indigenous Australia. Marika and Mabo are each following in the footsteps — or the seamarks — of their ancestors. Each of them took hold of their traditions in ways which gave them the confidence, the inspiration and the strength to meet contemporary challenges.

A sense of tradition is enabling because it gives people the confidence to become active agents of change. The waves of memory may wash back and forth on familiar terrain, bringing new knowledge and altering tradition in the name of its unchangeability. People with cultural pride will be of inestimable importance in recasting 'good custom' to meet the needs of younger people.

The challenge of the future for saltwater people is about problems not only for them, or even for the whole fishing industry, but for us all. We live in a world where, in the name of economic growth, whole cultures may be destroyed. In the new context 'working evenly together', even 'side by side', has an urgency. The man from Arnhem Land for whom the sea was part of his 'blood and body', telling him 'what to do', meant it told him how to fish, how to read the signs on sea and land that tell of danger, and above all, how to respect his sea and land Dreamings. Fortunately there are many non-indigenous people whose thoughts and actions are also shaped by feeling and emotion. The poet Judith Wright was the embodiment of that imagination; her words about land, 'beloved and imperilled and my own blood and bone', come from an early poem. Her poetic imagination grew over a life-time, coming to know no bounds. Her sphere of concern encompassed the land, the forests, the wildlife, the Reef, the indigenous people — the whole imperilled earth. That sensibility was grounded in the here and now of concern for suffering and for achievement. Twelve days before Koiki Mabo died in January 1992, she wrote: 'please tell Koiki that not only I but a lot of other people who know him only as a hero will be wishing and hoping for him.'

Like the man from Arnhem Land and others among the saltwater people, Wright's imagination carries intense feeling; and it implies a way of living tempered by knowledge and respect for the land and the sea. These are exemplars for others to follow.

But follow where? To a world losing forests and species and imperilled by rising seas? Fortunately, this is not the only story. There are people everywhere who seek sustainable use of resources and the survival of local communities. What Dutch fishers refer to critically as 'the horsepower race' strikes a chord with coastal communities in many places.[22] As we have seen, many successful self-regulatory fisheries are grounded in geographical locality. In an overexploited world, sea tenure — where each group of residents takes responsibility for its patch of foreshore, reef and home seas — may be a godsend. There is an intimate connection between joint or common ownership of land or sea and knowing well that particular area and the other people who share it. For those of us who live in the mainstream of competitive individualism, understanding those who live otherwise can help renew our own humanity.

Notes

1 Two Traditions of the Sea

1 Rebecca Bliege Bird and Douglas W. Bird, Gendered Fishing among the Meriam: Implications for the Sexual Division of Foraging Labor, ms, University of Utah, January 2001, p. 19.
2 W. H. R. Rivers, 'Vision', in A. C. Haddon ed., *Reports of the Cambridge Anthropological Expedition to Torres Straits*, vol. 2, Cambridge University Press, 1901, p. 44.
3 A. C. Haddon, 'Science', in *Reports of the Cambridge Anthropological Expedition to Torres Straits*, vol. 4, 1912, p. 229.
4 Anthony Wilkin, 'Property and Inheritance', in *Reports of the Cambridge Anthropological Expedition to Torres Straits*, vol. 6, 1908, p. 167.
5 As cited in Hugo Grotius, *The Freedom of the Seas or the Right which Belongs to the Dutch to Take Part in the East Indian Trade*, Orno Press, New York, 1972, p. 30 (1st Latin edition 1633).
6 See Chapter 7. In Australia in 1999, according to one dissenting judgment in the *Croker Island Seas case*, the common law is capable of recognising the existence of exclusive rights, so displacing the public right to fish. (See Justice Merkel, *Commonwealth v. Yarmirr* (1999), S629, p. 138.)
7 William Blackstone, *Commentaries on the Laws of England*, Clarendon Press, Oxford, vol. 2, 1979, p. 18 (Facsimile of first edition 1765–69).
8 *The Commonwealth v. Yarmirr; Yarmirr v. Northern Territory* (2001), High Court of Australia HCA 56 (11 October 2001), Gleeson CJ, Gaudron, Gummow and Hayne JJ, para. 98, p. 26. <http://www.austlii.edu.au/au/cases/cth/high_ct/2001/56.html>

9 *Calder v. Attorney-General of British Columbia* (1973), 8 *Dominion Law Reports* (3d), 61.
10 B. Solow, 'A New Look at the Irish Land Question', *Economic and Social Review*, vol. xii, no. 4, p. 303, as cited in O. MacDonagh, *States of Mind: Two Centuries of Anglo-Irish Conflict*, Pimlico, London, 1992, p. 39.
11 W. E. H. Stanner, The Yirrkala Case: Some General Principles of Aboriginal Landholding, unpub. paper, 1969, p. 3, in possession of author; with thanks to Dr Nancy Williams for sending me a copy of this paper.
12 Howard Morphy, 'From Dull to Brilliant: The Aesthetics of Spiritual Power among the Yolŋu', *Man*, 1989, vol. 24, no. 1, pp. 21–39.
13 Dula Ŋurruwuthun, 'Declaration', in *Saltwater: Yirrkala Bark Paintings of Sea Country, Recognising Indigenous Sea Rights*, Jennifer Isaacs Publishing, Sydney, 1999, p. 9.
14 Mr Weluk, Aboriginal Land Commission, Sea Closure, Transcript of Proceedings before Justice Toohey, Darwin, 1981, p. 143.
15 *Yarmirr v. Northern Territory of Australia* (1998), 771 Federal Court of Australia, Transcript of Proceedings, Darwin, 23 April 1997, pp. 62–63. The name *Croker Island Seas* case is used by Ron Levy, solicitor for the Croker Island claimants. See Ron Levy. The Croker Island Decision and other Major Cases, Northern Land Council, Casuarina, Northern Territory, 29 September 1999, pp. 1–8.
16 Tim Bonyhady, *The Law of the Countryside: The Rights of the Public*, 1987, p. 244 cites S. A. and H. S. Moore, *The History and Law of Fisheries*, 1903, p. 406 on the multitude of several fisheries on tidal rivers and estuaries.
17 S. D. Cole, 'The Highways of the Sea', in *Transactions of the Grotius Society*, vol. iv, *Problems of War*, Sweet and Maxwell, London, p. 17.
18 *Moore v. Attorney-General 1934*, per Justice Fitzgibbon, in J. C. W. Wylie, *A Case Book on Irish Law*, Professional Books, Oxford, 1981, p. 24.
19 Sir Tipene O'Regan, pers. comm. with author, Wellington, New Zealand, 27 December 1996.
20 Noel Pearson, Our Right to take Responsibility. Discussion Paper prepared for the Cape York Land Council, Trinity Beach, Queensland, 1999, p. 7. Others are now addressing the question of indigenous economic independence; see for example, Jon Altman, Development Dilemmas on Aboriginal Lands; Sustainable Options for the Twenty-first Century, paper given to The Power of Knowledge, the Resonance of Tradition — Indigenous Studies Conference 2001, AIATSIS, Canberra, 2001.
21 See Peter Jull, 'Inuit and Nunavut: Renewing the New World', in Jens Dahl, Jack Hicks and Peter Jull, eds, *Inuit Regain Control of their Lands and Their Lives*, International Work Group for Indigenous Affairs, Document no. 102, Copenhagen, 2000, pp. 118–141.
22 Greg Dening, *Readings/Writings*, Melbourne University Press, Carlton South, 1998, p. 111.
23 W. E. H. Stanner, *After the Dreaming: The 1968 Boyer Lectures*, Australian Broadcasting Commission, Sydney, 1969, p. 27.
24 Nicolas Peterson and Bruce Rigsby, eds, 'Introduction', *Customary Marine Tenure in Australia*, Oceania Monograph 48, University of Sydney, Sydney, 1998, p. 1. This book, unique in Australia, contains a set of essays rich in ethnographic material about a range of coastal communities. They list

ethnographic and other published work relating to sea estates on pages 2–3; on the existence of an ethnographic literature since the 1960s, see pages 2–9.

25 Dermot Smyth, 'Fishing for Recognition: The Search for an Indigenous Fisheries Policy in Australia', *Indigenous Law Bulletin*, vol. 4, no. 29, April–May 2000, p. 8, cites Belinda Lawson, Aboriginal Fishing and Ownership of the Sea, Fisheries Division, Department of Primary Industries, Canberra, 1984. See also the following: John Cordell, Managing Sea Country: Tenure and Sustainability of Aboriginal and Torres Strait Islander Marine Resources, Report on Indigenous Fishing, Ecologically Sustainable Development Fisheries Working Group, 1991; Dermot M. Smyth, *A Voice in all Places: Aboriginal and Torres Strait Islander Interests in Australia's Coastal Zone*, Resource Assessment Commission, Canberra, 1993; Commonwealth of Australia, *Coastal Zone Inquiry: Final Report*, Resource Assessment Commission, Canberra, 1993; Peter Jull, *A Sea Change: Overseas Indigenous–Government Relations in the Coastal Zone*, Consultancy Report, Resource Assessment Commission, Coastal Zone Inquiry, Canberra, 1993.

26 Bernard Nietschmann, 'Traditional Sea Territories, Resources and Rights in Torres Strait', in John Cordell, ed., *A Sea of Small Boats*, Cultural Survival Report 26, Cambridge, Massachusetts, 1989, p. 70.

2 *Saltwater Peoples*

1 *Yarmirr v. Northern Territory of Australia* (1998), 771 Federal Court of Australia, Transcript of Proceedings, pp. 62–63.

2 Michael V. Robinson, Change and Adjustment Among the Bardi of Sunday Island, North-Western Australia, unpub. MA Thesis, Anthropology Department, University of Western Australia, Perth, 1973, p. 221.

3 Mr Gaykamanu, Aboriginal Land Commission, Sea Closure, Transcript of Proceedings before Justice Toohey, Darwin, 1981, p. 185.

4 S. O'Cathain, 'The Folklore of the Sea', in J. de Courcy Ireland, ed., *Ireland and the Sea*, Cuman Merriman, Dublin, 1983, p. 136. Writing of the four cycles in early Irish literature, Marie Heaney recounts that part of the mythological cycle on the conquest of the Tuatha de Danaan by the Milesians (*Over Nine Waves: A Book of Irish Legends*, Faber and Faber, London, 1994, pp. 50–54).

5 B. O'Floinn, 'Sionnach ar do Dhuán', in P. O'Héalai, ed., *Béaloideas*, An Cumann le Béaloideas Eireann, Dublin, 1980–81, p. 98.

6 J. Drever, '"Taboo" Words among Shetland Fishermen', *Old-Lore Miscellany of Orkney, Shetland, Caithness and Sutherland,* vol. 10, Viking Society for Northern Research, University College, London, 1935–46, pp. 235–40. Cf. J. Spence, 'The Days of the Old Shetland Sixern', *Old-Lore Miscellany of Orkney Shetland Caithness and Sutherland*, Old-Lore Series, vol. III, pp. 36–41.

7 J. Conrad, *The Mirror of the Sea: Memories and Impressions*, Methuen, London, 1924, p. 47.

8 David H. Lewis, *The Voyaging Stars: Secrets of the Pacific Island Navigators*, Collins, Sydney, 1978, p. 135.

9 Kingsley Palmer, 'Customary Marine Tenure at Groote Eylandt', in Nicolas Peterson and Bruce Rigsby, eds, *Customary Marine Tenure in Australia*, Oceania Monograph 48, University of Sydney, Sydney, 1998, p. 149.

10 O. W. Brierly, *Rattlesnake Journals*, 16 October 1848, cited in David R. Moore, *Islanders and Aborigines at Cape York*, Australian Institute of Aboriginal Studies, Canberra, 1979, pp. 48, 45.

11 Donald F. Thomson, 'Notes on Some Primitive Watercraft in Northern Australia', *Man*, no. 52, pp. 1–5.

12 Donald F. Thomson, 'The Dugong Hunters of Cape York', *Journal of the Royal Anthropological Institute*, no. 64, 1934, p. 238; Bruce Rigsby and Athol Chase, 'The Sandbeach People and Dugong Hunters of Eastern Cape York Peninsula: Property in Land and Sea Country', in *Customary Marine Tenure in Australia*, pp. 192–218.

13 Marsden Hordern, *Mariners are Warned! John Lort Stokes and HMS* Beagle *in Australia 1837–1843*, Melbourne University Press, Melbourne, 1989, p. 253.

14 R. and H. Walker, *Curtin's Cowboys: Australia's Secret Bush Commandos*, Allen & Unwin, Sydney, 1986, p. 51.

15 See Nonie Sharp, 'Following in the Seamarks?', *Indigenous Law Bulletin*, vol. 4, no. 29, 2000, pp. 4–7.

16 John Bradley, '"We Always Look North": Yanyuwa Identity and the Maritime Environment', *Customary Marine Tenure in Australia*, p. 131.

17 Khaki Stumpagee to Geoffrey Bagshaw 1997, as cited in Geoffrey Bagshaw, Anthropologist's Report, Native Title Claim WAG 49/98, prepared for the Kimberley Land Council on behalf of the native title claimants, February, 1999, p. 28.

18 Bagshaw, Anthropologist's Report, s6.3, pp. 71–73. See Kim Akerman, 'The Double Raft or *Kalwa* of the West Kimberley', *Mankind*, no. 10, pp. 20–23.

19 Charlie Wardaga, as cited in Nicolas Peterson and Bruce Rigsby, eds, *Customary Marine Tenure in Australia*, p. 6.

20 Stephen Davis, Aboriginal Tenure and the Use of the Coast and Sea in Northern Arnhem Land, MA thesis, University of Melbourne, Melbourne, 1984, p. 43, as cited in Geoffrey Bagshaw, '*Gapu Dhulway, Gapu Maramba*: Conceptualisation and Ownership of Saltwater among the Burrara and Yannhaŋu Peoples of Northeast Arnhem Land', *Customary Marine Tenure in Australia*, p. 157. Bagshaw writes of how these patterns are created by 'alternating moiety affiliations' (p. 157).

21 Anna Shnukal, Kulkalgal 'Roads': Central Torres Strait Islander Responses to Contact 1870–1920, Hons thesis, Department of Sociology, Anthropology and Archaeology, University of Queensland, St Lucia, November 2000.

22 Peter Veth, pers. comm., on Bardi and Jawi, Townsville, 1999.

23 Wandjuk Marika, *Wandjuk Marika, Life Story*, as told to Jennifer Isaacs, University of Queensland Press, St Lucia, 1995, p. 17.

3 *Seascape and Memory*

1 Michael Walsh, Ten Years On: A Supplement to the 1979 Kenbi Land Claim Book, Northern Land Council, Stuart Park, Northern Territory, April 1989, p. 29.

2 W. B. Kirkland, Report of a Visit to the Administrator by Larrakia People, Darwin, 1936, as cited in Samantha J. Wells, Town Camp or Homeland? A History of the Kulaluk Aboriginal Community, Report to the Australian Heritage Commission, Darwin, 8 November 1995, p. 26.

3 A. E. Woodward, Justice, Aboriginal Land Rights Commission, First Report, *Parliamentary Paper no. 69*, Government Printer, Canberra, 1973, paras 157–160; Wells, Town Camp or Homeland?, pp. 1–114; Sue Jackson, Dreaming, Planning and Judging: The Kenbi Land Claim, Geographies of Coexistence: Native Title, Cultural Difference and the Decolonisation of Planning in North Australia, unpub. PhD thesis, Macquarie University, North Ryde, 1998, Chapter 4.

4 S. Coleridge, *Biographia Literaria*, J. Shawcross, ed., Oxford, 1907, p. 79, as cited in Bernard Smith, *Imagining the Pacific*, Melbourne University Press, Parkville, 1992, p. 170.

5 Geoffrey Bagshaw, Native Title Claim WAG 49/98, Anthropologist's Report prepared for the Kimberley Land Council on behalf of native title claimants, February 1999, s6.4.

6 Captain C. Pennefather, Report of a Cruise, in Queensland State Archives (QSA) COL/A288, 19 December 1879.

7 Announcement of removal of Murray Island school from the Department of Public Instruction, 30 January 1903, in QSA EDU/Z1993; Nonie Sharp, *Stars of Tagai: The Torres Strait Islanders*, Aboriginal Studies Press, Canberra, 1993, pp. 127–129.

8 John J. Bradley, We're Holding the Land, by Song, unpub. report, Northern Land Council, 1984, p. 1.

9 Murray Island Court Reports, Transaction no. 83, Council Office, Mer-Murray Island; see also *Mabo and Others v. The State of Queensland and the Commonwealth*, no. 12 of 1982, Particulars including Reports (two vols).

10 David Lawrence, *Customary Exchange across Torres Strait*, *Memoirs of the Queensland Museum*, vol. 34, no. 2, Queensland Museum, Brisbane, 1984, p. 279.

11 Lloyd Warner, *A Black Civilization: A Social Study of an Australian Tribe*, Harper and Brothers, New York, 1969, p. 4.

12 Patrick J. Killoran, *Mabo and Others v. Queensland*, Supreme Court of Queensland, Transcript of Proceedings, 1989, p. 3062.

13 Baldwin Spencer, Diary 1901, S and G2 1901, no. 4, 1901, p. 97, held in National Museum of Victoria, as cited in Richard Baker, *Land is Life: From Bush to Town, The Story of the Yanyuwa People*, Allen & Unwin, Sydney, 1999, p. 57.

14 Athol Chase and Peter Sutton, 'Australian Aborigines in a Rich Environment', in W. H. Edwards, ed., *Traditional Aboriginal Society: A Reader*, Macmillan, Melbourne, 1987, p. 69.

15 C. W. M. Hart and A. R. Pilling, *The Tiwi of North Australia*, Holt, Rinehart and Winston, New York, 1965, pp. 34–35.

16 See Bruce Rigsby and Athol Chase, 'The Sandbeach People and Dugong Hunters of Eastern Cape York Peninsula: Property in Land and Sea Country', in *Customary Marine Tenure in Australia*, esp. pp. 196–199 on classical and contemporary social organisation. See also below, Chapter 6, n10.

17 Daymbalipu Munuŋgurr, as cited in Nancy M. Williams, *The Yolŋu and their Land: A System of Land Tenure and the Fight for its Recognition*, Australian Institute of Aboriginal Studies, Canberra, 1986, pp. 6–7.

18 Fiona Magowan, Waves of Knowing: Polymorphism and Co-Substantive Essences in Yolŋu Sea Cosmology, paper presented to Australian Anthropological Society conference, Magnetic Island, Queensland, 1997, p. 19, cf p. 16.

19 Fiona Magowan, 'Crying to Remember: Reproducing Personhood and Community', in B. Attwood and F. Magowan, eds, *Telling Stories: Indigenous History and Memory in Australia and New Zealand*, Allen & Unwin, Sydney, 2001, pp. 41–60.

20 Michael Lloyd, ed., *Turner*, National Gallery of Australia, Canberra, 1996, p. 34.

21 Cézanne, 'Cézanne's Doubt' as cited in M. Merleau-Ponty, *Sense and Nonsense*, Northwestern University Press, Evanston, 1964, p. 17.

22 John J. Bradley, pers. email comm. with author, 23 August 1999.

23 Howard Morphy, 'Colonialism, History and the Construction of Place: The Politics of Landscape in Northern Australia', in Barbara Bender, ed., *Landscape, Politics and Perspectives*, Berg, Oxford, 1993, p. 207.

24 Sylvie Poirier, 'Kukatja Country and Identity in the Native Title Era', paper presented to the Eighth CHAGS Conference, Osaka, 1998, p. 10.

25 Charles Manydjarri, statement before the Aboriginal Land Commissioner Justice Toohey, Sea Closure, Bathurst Island, Melville Island and Milingimbi Land Claim, Transcript of Proceedings, Darwin and Milingimbi, 1980–81, p. 145.

26 Smith, *Imagining the Pacific*, p. 143.

27 Smith, *Imagining the Pacific*, p. 156.

28 Matthew Flinders, *A Voyage to Terra Australis*, C. & W. Nicol, London, vol. 1, 1814, p. ii.

4 Living Connections

1 Andrish Saint-Clare, *Trepang* program description, Festival of Darwin, September 1999; Lisa Palmer, 'Trepang Opening Night', *Arena Magazine*, no. 45, March 2000, pp. 9–10.

2 Radio carbon dates suggest regular contact up to 800 years ago. C. C. Macknight, an authority on Macassan voyaging, gives the year such contact began as around 1720 AD. See C. C. Macknight, *The Voyage to Marege': Macassan Trepangers in Northern Australia*, Melbourne University Press, Parkville, 1976, p. 98; C. C. Macknight, 'Macassans and the Aboriginal Past',

Archaeology in Oceania, no. 21, 1986, pp. 69–75; on Macassan influence on art forms, see Macknight, *The Voyage to Marege'*.

3 Donald F. Thomson, *Economic Structure and the Ceremonial Exchange Cycle in Arnhem Land*, Macmillan, Melbourne, 1949, Plate 5 with text, facing p. 58, cf. pp. 89–90.

4 Thomson, *Economic Structure and the Ceremonial Exchange Cycle in Arnhem Land*, pp. 59–60.

5 Thomson, *Economic Structure and the Ceremonial Exchange Cycle in Arnhem Land*, p. 91.

6 Seamus Deane, *Civilians and Barbarians*, Field Day Theatre Co., Derry, 1983, p. 19.

7 Macknight, *The Voyage to Marege'*, p. 90.

8 Donald F. Thomson, 'The Hero Cult, Initiation and Totemism on Cape York', *Journal of the Royal Anthropological Institute*, no. 63, July–December 1933, pp. 453–537.

9 John J. Bradley, '"We always look North": Yanyuwa Identity and the Maritime Environment', in Nicolas Peterson and Bruce Rigsby, eds, *Customary Marine Tenure in Australia*, Oceania Monograph 48, University of Sydney, Sydney, p. 131.

10 Roddy Harvey, 25 May 1997, recorded by John Bradley, pers. email comm. with the author, 25 January 1999.

11 Donald F. Thomson, 'The Dugong Hunters of Cape York', *Journal of the Royal Anthropological Institute*, no. 64, 1934, p. 238.

12 See especially Donald F. Thomson, *The Seasonal Factor in Human Culture: Illustrated from the Life of a Contemporary Nomadic Group*, Proceedings of the Prehistoric Society, Paper no. 10, pp. 209–221.

13 Deborah Bird Rose, *Dingo Makes Us Human: Life and Land in an Aboriginal Culture*, Cambridge University Press, Cambridge, 1992, p. 118.

14 John J. Bradley, 'We Always Look North', in *Customary Marine Tenure in Australia*, p. 131.

15 D. Roe, 'Maritime, Coastal and Inland Societies in Island Melanesia: The Bush Saltwater Divide in Solomon Islands and Vanuatu', in S. O'Connor and P. Veth, eds, *East of Wallace's Line: Studies of Past and Present Maritime Societies in the Indo-Pacific Region*, Modern Quaternary Research in South East Asia 16: V–VI, A. A. Balkema, Rotterdam, p. 99.

16 Moya Smith, Fish-Capture Sites and the Maritime Economies of some Coastal Australian Communities, Anthropology Dept, Western Australian Museum, Perth, 1997, p. 89.

17 Nicholas Peterson and Bruce Rigsby, 'Introduction', *Customary Marine Tenure in Australia*, p. 6. See also Rigsby, 'Property Theory and Tenure Types', *Customary Marine Tenure in Australia*, pp. 37–38, note 15.

18 Nicolas Peterson and Bruce Rigsby, 'Introduction', *Customary Marine Tenure in Australia*, p. 6.

19 Roe, 'Maritime, Coastal and Inland Societies in Island Melanesia', p. 99.

20 Roe, 'Maritime, Coastal and Inland Societies in Island Melanesia', p. 99; Roe cites R. M. Keesing, In the Mountains: Towards a Systemic View of Southeast Solomons Prehistory, unpub. paper.

21 Richard Baker, *Land is Life: From Bush to Town, The Story of the Yanyuwa People*, Allen & Unwin, Sydney, 1999, p. 235.

22 Baker, *Land is Life*, p. 140; this in no way contradicted their self-perception as saltwater people (see p. 59).
23 Rebecca Bliege Bird and Douglas W. Bird, Gendered Fishing Among the Meriam: Implications for the Sexual Division of Foraging Labor, Dept of Anthropology, University of Utah, ms, Jan. 2001, p. 13.
24 Torres Strait Protected Zone Joint Authority, *Annual Report 1997–1998*, Commonwealth of Australia, Australian Fisheries Management Authority, Barton, ACT, 1999, pp. 26, 24.
25 Rebecca Bliege Bird, Douglas W. Bird and John M. Beaton, 'Children and Traditional Subsistence on Mer (Murray Island), Torres Strait', *Australian Aboriginal Studies*, no. 1, 1995, pp. 1–17.
26 See H. Allen and G. Barton, 'Ngarradj Warde Djobkeng: White Cockatoo Dreaming and the Prehistory of Kakadu', *Oceania Monograph* no. 37, 1989, p. 7, cited in S. C. Taçon, M. Wilson and C. Chippindale, 'Birth of the Rainbow Serpent in Arnhem Land Rock Art and Oral History', *Archaeology in Oceania*, vol. 31, no. 3, October 1996, p. 116.
27 Paul Memmott and David Trigger, 'Marine Tenure in the Wellesley Islands Region, Gulf of Carpentaria', in *Customary Marine Tenure in Australia*, p. 120.
28 S. O'Connor and P. Veth, 'The World's First Mariners: Savanna Dwellers in an Island Continent', in S. O'Connor and P. Veth, eds, *East of Wallace's Line*, p. 111.
29 O'Connor and Veth, 'The World's First Mariners', p. 129.
30 O'Connor and Veth, 'The World's First Mariners', p. 101. Cf. S. O'Connor, 'The Timing and Nature of Prehistoric Island Use in Northern Australia', *Archaeology in Oceania*, no. 27, 1992, pp. 49–60.
31 P. Veth, 'Aridity and Settlement in Northwest Australia', *Antiquity*, no. 69, 1995, p. 743.
32 Moya Smith, Fish-Capture Sites and the Maritime Economies of Some Coastal Australian Communities, pp. 22, 21.
33 Matthew Flinders, *A Voyage to Terra Australis*, C. and W. Nicol, London, 1914, vol. 2, p. 108.
34 Robert Johannes, marine biologist and authority on marine tenures among Pacific Islanders, noted the unique practice of subdividing the traps among owners. See Johannes, *Mabo and Others v. Queensland*, Supreme Court of Queensland, Transcript 1989, p. 2789, cited in Nonie Sharp, *No Ordinary Judgment: Mabo, the Murray Islanders' Land Case*, Aboriginal Studies Press, Canberra, 1996, p. 197.
35 Veth, pers. comm., July 1999.
36 Taçon, Wilson and Chippindale, 'Birth of the Rainbow Serpent in Arnhem Land Rock Art and Oral History', esp. p. 116.
37 Darrell Lewis, *The Rock Paintings of Arnhem Land: Social, Ecological, and Material Culture Change in the Post-Glacial Period*, BAR International Series 415, Oxford, 1988, pp. 90–91; Taçon, Wilson and Chippindale, 'Birth of the Rainbow Serpent in Arnhem Land Rock Art and Oral History', p. 116.
38 John Bradley, '"We Always Look North"', *Customary Marine Tenure in Australia*, p. 132.
39 Charlie Wardaga, Croker Island, cited in Nicolas Peterson and Bruce Rigsby, eds, 'Introduction', *Customary Marine Tenure in Australia*, p. 6.

40 Rose, *Dingo Makes Us Human*, p. 118, is writing here of Yarralin people, but Dreaming tracks overlay much of the continent; see Peter Sutton, 'Icons of Country: Topographic Representations in Classical Aboriginal Traditions', in D. Woodward and G. M. Lewis, eds, *The History of Cartography*, vol. 2, University of Chicago Press, Chicago, 1998, p. 361.
41 Cited in Michael V. Robinson, Change and Adjustment among the Bardi of Sunday Island, North-Western Australia, unpub. MA thesis, University of Western Australia, Perth, 1973, p. 221.
42 Nicolas Peterson, pers. comm., 23 October 2001.
43 Michael Alexander (translated and introduced), *The Earliest English Poems*, Penguin Books, Harmondsworth, 1966, pp. 74, 76. *The Seafarer* is included in a book of early Anglo-Saxon poetry now called the Exeter Book (fol 81b–83a). The first bishop of Exeter (who died c 1072) is recorded as having given this book to his cathedral. See S. A. J. Bradley, transl. and ed., *Anglo-Saxon Poetry*, Dent, London, 1982, pp. 201–202.
44 D. McDinny, Nyilba, 1984 field diary, cited in John J. Bradley, *Li-Anthawirriyarra*, People of the Sea: Yanyuwa Relations with their Maritime Environment, unpub. PhD thesis, Northern Territory University, Darwin, 1997, pp. 124–125.
45 Joseph Conrad, *The Mirror of the Sea: Memories and Impressions*, Dent, London, 1946, p. 56.
46 C. Edwards, *The Oldest Laws in the World*, Watts, London, 1906, p. 38.
47 Don Miller, ms, 1991, p. 88, cited in Bradley, *Li-Anthawirriyarra*, People of the Sea, p. 291.
48 A. C. Haddon, *Reports of the Cambridge Anthropological Expedition to the Torres Straits*, Cambridge University Press, Cambridge, vol. 6, 1908, p. xix; on the complexities of the subject, see Nonie Sharp, *Stars of Tagai: The Torres Strait Islanders*, Aboriginal Studies Press, Canberra, 1993, p. 267, n14.
49 Sharp, *Stars of Tagai*, pp. 106–110; 'Malo's Law in Court: The Religious Background to the Mabo Case', in Max Charlesworth, ed., *Religious Business: Essays on Aboriginal Spirituality*, Cambridge University Press, Cambridge, 1998, pp. 176–202.
50 A. C. Haddon, *Reports of the Cambridge Anthropological Expedition to the Torres Straits*, vol. 1, 1935, p. 183.

5 Sea Dreamings and Seamarks

1 Patricia Excell, 'Dancings of the Sound: A Study of Francis Webb's Eyre All Alone', *Occasional Paper* 13, English Department, Australian Defence Force Academy, nd, p. 84.
2 John J. Bradley, We're Holding the Land, by Song, unpub. report, Northern Land Council, 1984, pp. 16–17.
3 John J. Bradley, *Li-Anthawirriyarra*, People of the Sea: Yanyuwa Relations with their Maritime Environment, unpub. PhD thesis, Northern Territory University, Darwin, 1997, p. 137.

4 See Donald Thomson's classic study of the seasonal cycle of the Wik Muŋkan (1946) showing how their lives were 'in step with the seasonal cycles themselves': D. F. Thomson, *The Seasonal Factor in Human Culture: Illustrated from the Life of a Contemporary Nomadic Group*, Proceedings of the Prehistoric Society, Paper no. 10, pp. 209–221. Seasonal calendars for groups mentioned frequently in this book include: K. Palmer and M. Brady, A Report prepared in Support of an Application to Control Entry onto Seas adjoining Aboriginal Land: Croker Island and other Islands, Northern Land Council, Darwin, 1984, p. 88, Table 10.1; M. Smith and A. Kalotas, Bardi Plants: An Annotated List of Plants and their Use by the Bardi Aborigines of Dampier Land, North Western Australia, Records of the Western Australian Museum, vol. 12, no. 3, p. 323; B. Nietschmann, 'Traditional Sea Territories, Resources and Rights in Torres Strait', in J. Cordell, ed., *A Sea of Small Boats*, Cultural Survival, Mass., 1989, p. 68; Bradley, *Li-Anthawirriyarra,* People of the Sea, pp. 115–120 and Table 2; R. Baker, *Land is Life: From Bush to Town*, Allen & Unwin, Sydney, 1999, pp. 45–50.

5 Nonie Sharp, *Stars of Tagai: The Torres Strait Islanders*, Aboriginal Studies Press, Canberra, 1993, pp. 52–63.

6 Bradley, *Li-Anthawirriyarra*, People of the Sea, esp. pp. 179–183.

7 W. E. H. Stanner, *On Aboriginal Religion*, Oceania Monographs, Sydney, 1963, p. 63.

8 Howard Morphy, 'From Dull to Brilliant: The Aesthetics of Spiritual Power Among the Yolŋu', *Man*, vol. 24, no. 1, p. 24. For an interpretive discussion of clan designs, see Howard Morphy, *Ancestral Connections: Art and an Aboriginal System of Knowledge*, University of Chicago Press, Chicago and London, 1991, pp. 169–180.

9 Peter Sutton, 'Icons of Country: Topographic Representations in Classical Aboriginal Traditions', in David Woodward and G. Malcolm Lewis, eds, *The History of Cartography*, vol. 2, *Cartography in Traditional African, American, Arctic, Australian, and Pacific Societies*, University of Chicago Press, Chicago and London, 1998, p. 371. See 'Squid and Turtle Dreamings', 1972, South Australian Museum, Adelaide, as reproduced in Sutton, 'Icons of Country', p. 372, Fig. 9.13.

10 W. E. H. Stanner, 'Some Aspects of Aboriginal Religion', in Max Charlesworth, ed., *Religious Business: Essays on Australian Aboriginal Spirituality*, Cambridge University Press, Cambridge, 1998, pp. 16, 6.

11 Howard Morphy, *Journey to the Crocodile's Nest*, Australian Institute of Aboriginal Studies, Canberra, 1984, p. 39.

12 Fiona Magowan, Waves of Knowing: Polymorphism and Co-Substantive Essences in Yolŋu Sea Cosmology, ms, Adelaide, 2000, p. 3.

13 Morphy, *Journey to the Crocodile's Nest*, p. 41.

14 Donald F. Thomson, unpub. field notes held in the National Museum of Victoria, Melbourne.

15 Peter Sutton, ed., *Aboriginal Dreamings*: *The Art of Aboriginal Australia*, Viking-Penguin, Ringwood, 1989; Peter Sutton, Chapter 3, 'The Morphology of Feeling', pp. 60–61; Howard Morphy, 'From Dull to Brilliant: The Aesthetics of Spiritual Power Among the Yolŋu', pp. 21–39.

16 Morphy, *Ancestral Connections: Art and an Aboriginal System of*

Knowledge, p. 299; cf. Morphy, 'From Dull to Brilliant: The Aesthetics of Spiritual Power among the Yolŋu', esp. pp. 28–33.

17 Sutton, *Aboriginal Dreamings*, p. 61.

18 Morphy, 'From Dull to Brilliant', p. 31, cites Wandjuk Marika's translation.

19 Ronald Berndt, *Love Songs of Arnhem Land*, Nelson, Melbourne, 1976, p. 159.

20 Magowan, Waves of Knowing, p. 10. Cf. H. C. Coombs, *Aboriginal Autonomy*, Cambridge University Press, Cambridge, 1994, p. 230.

21 John J. Bradley, An Unchanging Law, unpub. report for the Sacred Sites Authority, Darwin, 1984, cited in Baker, *Land is Life*, p. 59.

22 Geoffrey Bagshaw, '*Gapu Dhulway, Gapu Maramba*: Conceptualisation and Ownership of Saltwater Among the Burarra and Yan-nhangu Peoples of Northeast Arnhemland', in Nicolas Peterson and Bruce Rigsby, eds, *Customary Marine Tenure in Australia*, Oceania Monograph 48, University of Sydney, Sydney, 1998, p. 165.

23 Stephen Davis and J. R. V. Prescott, *Aboriginal Frontiers and Boundaries in Australia*, Melbourne University Press, Melbourne, 1992, p. 52; Bagshaw, '*Gapu Dhulway, Gapu Maramba*', in *Customary Marine Tenure in Australia*, p. 159.

24 Dula Ŋurruwuthun, 'Declaration', in Buku-Larrŋgay Mulka Centre, *Saltwater: Yirrkala Bark Paintings of Sea Country, Recognising Indigenous Sea Rights*, Jennifer Isaacs Publishing, Sydney, 1999, p. 11.

25 Bagshaw, '*Gapu Dhulway, Gapu Maramba*', p. 159.

26 Bagshaw, '*Gapu Dhulway, Gapu Maramba*', p. 159.

27 Ginytjirrang Mala/ADVYZ, Manbuyŋa ga Rulyapa, Arafura Sea, Marine Strategy, Darwin, 1994, p. 1; Bagshaw '*Gapu Dhulway, Gapu Maramba*', p. 159.

28 *Yarmirr v. Northern Territory of Australia* (1998) 771, Federal Court of Australia, Transcript of Proceedings, 25 April 1997, p. 273.

29 John J. Bradley, '"We Always Look North": Yanyuwa Identity and the Marine Environment', in *Customary Marine Tenure in Australia*, p. 131.

30 The song-cycle of the Djan'kawu is sung and performed in the film 'In Memory of Mawalan'; through it, Howard Morphy suggests, one may 'glimpse the power of Yolŋu aesthetics' (Morphy, 'From Dull to Brilliant', p. 38, n7).

31 Bradley, *Li-Anthawirriyarra*, People of the Sea, p. 244.

32 Donald F. Thomson, 'The Dugong Hunters of Cape York', *Journal of the Royal Anthropological Institute*, no. 63, 1934, pp. 238, 243.

33 Bradley, *Li-Anthawirriyarra*, People of the Sea, pp. 136–137.

34 Thomson, 'The Dugong Hunters of Cape York', p. 251.

35 Thomson, 'The Dugong Hunters of Cape York', p. 251.

36 Bradley, '"We Always Look North"', *Customary Marine Tenure in Australia*, p. 130; cf Bagshaw, '*Gapu Dhulway, Gapu Maramba*', pp. 162–163. Bagshaw uses the word 'consubstantiation', being of the same essence.

37 A. C. Haddon, ed., *Reports of the Cambridge Anthropological Expedition to the Torres Straits*, vol. 4, Cambridge University Press, Cambridge, 1912, pp. 167, 168.

38 Bernard Nietschmann, 'Traditional Sea Territories, Resources and Rights in

Torres Strait', in John Cordell, ed., *A Sea of Small Boats*, Cultural Survival, Cambridge, Mass., 1989, p. 69; cf. pp. 70–73.

39 David H. Lewis and Mimi George, 'Hunters and Herders: Chukchi and Siberian Eskimo Navigation across Snow and Frozen Sea', *The Journal of Navigation*, vol. 44, no. 1, January 1991, pp. 1–10. See R. M. Downs and D. Stea, *Maps in the Minds*, Harper and Row, New York, 1977, cited in Lewis and George, 'Hunters and Herders', note 4.

40 David H. Lewis, *The Voyaging Stars: Secrets of the Pacific Island Navigators*, Collins, Sydney, 1978, p. 123.

41 Arthur Francis Grimble, *Tungaru Traditions: Writings on the Atoll Culture of the Gilbert Islands*, H. E. Maude, ed., Melbourne University Press, Parkville, 1989, pp. 48–51.

42 Geoffrey Bagshaw, Native Title Claim WAG 49/98, Anthropologist's Report, prepared for Kimberley Land Council on behalf of the native title claimants, 1999, s6.3 and pers. comm., January 2000.

43 Lewis, *The Voyaging Stars*, pp. 76–77.

44 Nonie Sharp, *Stars of Tagai: The Torres Strait Islanders*, Aboriginal Studies Press, Canberra, 1993, pp. 55–56.

45 In cognitive mapping of the sea, the image of a fish and the star are key elements. See Tomoya Akimichi, 'Image and Reality at Sea: Fish and Cognitive Mapping in Carolinean Navigational Knowledge', in Roy Ellen and Katsuyoshi Fukui, eds., *Redefining Nature: Ecology, Culture and Domestication*, Berg, Oxford, 1996, pp. 496, 500–503.

6 Owning and Belonging

1 David Haigh, '"Fishing War" in the Torres Strait: *The Queen v. Benjamin Ali Nona and George Agnew Gesa*', *Indigenous Law Bulletin*, vol. 22, no. 4, 1999, p. 20; 'Fishing War in the Torres Strait – Round Two', *Indigenous Law Bulletin*, vol. 24, no. 4, p. 18.

2 State Reporting Bureau, Transcript of Proceedings, Indictment no. 583 of 1998, *The Queen v. Benjamin Ali Nona and George Agnew Gesa*, District Court, Cairns, 31 January 2001, Day 3, p. 152 (with thanks to Rosemary Hesp).

3 *The Commonwealth v. Yarmirr*; *Yarmirr v. Northern Territory* (2001), HCA 56 (11 October 2001), per Gleeson CJ, Gaudron, Gummow and Hayne JJ, para 85, 22–23; judgments made by McHugh and Callinan JJ did not recognise native title rights to the sea. <http://www.austlii.edu.au/au/cases/cth/high_ct/2001/56.html>

4 *The Commonwealth v. Yarmirr*; *Yarmirr v. Northern Territory* (2001), per Kirby J, para 244, 53. Only Justice Kirby took the view that the native title rights to the sea contain the right to exclude access to others. See especially paras 289 and 290, p. 63, which give his reasons.

5 Sea Closure, Transcript of Proceedings, Darwin and Milingimbi 1980–81, pp. 143–144; Telegram, Ramingining community to Justice Toohey, cited by Parsons, Transcript of Proceedings, 20 October 1980, p. 138.

6 In the second judgment the Court concluded that the 1760 treaty rights were confined to areas traditionally used by each of three communities (Mi'kmaq, Maliseet and Passamaquody); they belonged to communities, not individuals; and they were gathering rights for basic necessaries. (See Peter H. Russell, in P. H. Russell, R. Knopff and F. L. Morton, eds, *Federalism and the Charter: Leading Decisions on the Constitution*, McGill-Queens University Press, forthcoming, 2002; *R v. Marshall J*, Supreme Court of Canada (1999) 3 SCR 533.)

7 *Torres News*, 31 December 1993 to 6 January 1994; Nonie Sharp, *No Ordinary Judgment: Mabo, The Murray Islanders' Land Case*, Aboriginal Studies Press, Canberra, 1996, esp. pp. 203–204, including map of traditional boundaries; Ron Day, 'The 7.30 Report' 1999; 'Small Island, Big Fight', Documentary film, dir. Aven Noah, Film Australia, Sydney, 2000.

8 Bruce Rigsby and Athol Chase, 'The Sandbeach People and Dugong Hunters of Cape York', *Customary Marine Tenure in Australia*, p. 196, write of these landowning groups as 'perpetual corporations of people'.

9 Athol Chase, *Wuthati: Ten Islands Land Claim*, Cape York Land Council, 1996, cited in Bruce Rigsby and Athol Chase, 'The Sandbeach People and Dugong Hunters of Eastern Cape York Peninsula: Property in Land and Sea Country', *Customary Marine Tenure in Australia*, p. 196.

10 W. E. H. Stanner, The Yirrkala Case: Some General Principles of Aboriginal Landholding, mimeograph, 1969, p. 2.

11 Nonie Sharp, *No Ordinary Judgment*, p. 14.

12 Bruce Rigsby and Athol Chase, 'The Sandbeach People and Dugong Hunters of Eastern Cape York Peninsula: Property in Land and Sea Country', *Customary Marine Tenure in Australia*, p. 200.

13 Fiona Magowan, A Sea has many Faces: Multiple Continuities in Yolŋu Coastal Waters, Paper presented to Australian Institute of Aboriginal and Torres Strait Islander Studies, The Power of Knowledge and the Resonance of Tradition — Indigenous Studies: Conference 2001, Australian National University, Canberra, pp. 7, 9–10; see also Muwarra Ganambarr, in Buku-Larrŋgay Mulka, *Saltwater: Yirrkala Bark Paintings of Sea Country*, Jennifer Isaacs Publishing, Sydney, 1999, p. 18.

14 Peterson and Rigsby, *Customary Marine Tenure in Australia*, p. 4.

15 Statement by Bardi claimant, in Geoffrey Bagshaw, Native Title Claim WAG 49/98, Anthropologist's Report prepared for the Kimberley Land Council on behalf of native title claimants, February 1999, s8.3, s5.5.

16 *Mabo v. Queensland*, Supreme Court of Queensland, Transcript of Proceedings, p. 1643 as cited in Sharp, *No Ordinary Judgment*, p. 193; Justice Moynihan, Determination of Issues of Fact, 16 November 1990, pp. 184–185.

17 Maningrida Seas Native Title Meeting, videotape, courtesy Northern Land Council, 16 May 1997.

18 Peter Sutton, 'Icons of Country: Topographic Representations in Classical Aboriginal Tradition', in David Woodward and G. Malcolm Lewis, eds, *The History of Cartography*, vol. 2, *Cartography in the Traditional African, American, Arctic, Australian, and Pacific Societies*, University of Chicago Press, Chicago and London, 1998, p. 384 (emphasis added).

19 Sutton, 'Icons of Country', p. 363 (emphasis in original).

20 See Deborah Bird Rose, *Dingo Makes Us Human: Life and Land in an*

Aboriginal Australian Culture, Cambridge University Press, Cambridge, 1992, p. 55. She is referring to Gurindji and Ngaliwurru people.

21 John J. Bradley, *Li-Anthawirriyarra*, People of the Sea, p. 303.
22 John J. Bradley, We're Holding the Land, by Song, mimeograph, Northern Land Council, Casuarina, 1984, pp. 8–9.
23 Bradley, *Li-Anthawirriyarra*, People of the Sea, p. 303.
24 Bradley, *Li-Anthawirriyarra*, People of the Sea, p. 273. Cf Martin Duwell and R. M. V. Dixon, eds, *Little Eva at Moonlight Creek and Other Aboriginal Song Poems*, University of Queensland Press, Brisbane, 1994, p. 49.
25 Rose, *Dingo Makes Us Human*, p. 52; cf p. 55.
26 Sutton, 'Icons of Country', p. 364.
27 Barbara Glowczewski, ed., *Yapa: Peintres Aborigènes de Balgo et Lajamanu*, Baudoin Lebon, Paris, 1991, p. 166, as cited in Sutton, 'Icons of Country', p. 363, n41.
28 Peter Sutton, *Country: Aboriginal Boundaries and Land Ownership in Australia*, Aboriginal History Monograph 3, Canberra, 1995, p. 55.
29 Nonie Sharp, *Stars of Tagai: The Torres Strait Islanders*, Aboriginal Studies Press, Canberra, 1993, pp. 49–78.

7 *The Freedom of the Seas*

1 *Queensland Votes and Proceedings for the Year 1885*, Government Printer, Brisbane, 1885.
2 Report of the Commission on the Pearl-Shell and Bêche-de-Mer Fisheries, Queensland, 1897, p. 1316.
3 Ian Kirkegaard, Assessment of the Northern Territory Fishing Industry, Forestry, Fisheries, Wildlife, Environment and National Parks Branch, Northern Territory, 19 July 1974. I thank Dr Rex Pyne for lending me this Report.
4 Kirkegaard, Assessment of the Northern Territory Fishing Industry, pp. 17–18.
5 Kirkegaard, Assessment of the Northern Territory Fishing Industry, p. 2Q, 1.
6 Justice Olney, *Yarmirr v. Northern Territory* (1998) 156, *ALR* 370, s141, p. 71.
7 Cited in *Yarmirr v. Northern Territory* (1998), s145, p. 73.
8 *Attorney-General for British Columbia v. Attorney-General for Canada* (1914), AC 153, p. 169.
9 *Yarmirr v. Northern Territory* (1998), Transcript of Proceedings, p. 50.
10 *Yarmirr v. Northern Territory* (1998), Transcript, p. 945.
11 Justice Olney, *Yarmirr v. Northern Territory* (1998), s162.5, p. 80. See also Graham Hiley QC, Fishing in the Seas off Croker Island, paper given to the Past and Future of Land Rights and Native Title Conference, Townsville, 28–30 August 2001, pp. 1–5. Graham Hiley was Counsel for the 'Fishing Industry Parties' in the *Croker Island Seas* case.
12 'Anglers asked to Surrender Licence. Udazas Request Condemned as "Censorious"', *Donegal Democrat*, 2 October 1997.

13 Lawrence Taylor, '"Man the Fisher": Salmon Fishing and the Expression of Community in a Rural Irish Fishing Settlement', *American Ethnologist*, 1981, vol. 8, no. 4, pp. 774–788; Lawrence Taylor, '"The River would run Red with Blood": Community and Common Property in an Irish Fishing Settlement', in B. McCay et al, eds, *The Question of the Commons*, University of Arizona Press, Tucson, pp. 296–304; Nonie Sharp, 'Australian Native Title and Irish Marine Rights', *Law in Context*, vol. 16, no. 2, 1999, pp. 34–48.

14 Justice Boldt, *United States v. Washington* (1974), 384, F. Supp. 312. For an able account of that case, its historical setting and its consequences, see Fay Cohen, *Treaties on Trial: The Continuing Controversy on Northwest Fishing Rights*, University of Washington Press, Seattle, 1986.

15 Hugo Grotius, *The Freedom of the Seas or the Right Which Belongs to the Dutch to Take Part in the East Indian Trade*, Orno Press, New York, 1972, p. 38 (Facsimile of Oxford University Press, New York, 1916. Ruan Deman Magoffin transl. *Mare Liberum*, 1st Latin edition 1633).

16 See *De Jure Belli ac Pacis Libri, The Law of War and Peace*, Bobbs-Merrill, Indianapolis, 1925, pp. 209–10, where Grotius revises his main contention on the freedom of the seas and does not exclude occupation of coastal waters bound by land. B. Telders, *Verszamelde Geschriften*, II, p. 121 refers to this reversal as a 'volte face' in Grotius' system of ideas; as cited in F. De Pauw, *Grotius and The Law of the Sea*, l'Institut de Sociologie, Brussels, 1965, p. 68.

17 John Selden, *Mare Clausum: The Right and Dominion of the Sea*, 2 vols, Andrew Kembe & Edward Thomas, London, 1663, Preface.

18 As cited in Grotius, *The Freedom of the Seas*, pp. 28–30.

19 W. S. M. Knight, 'Grotius in England', in *Transactions of The Grotius Society*, vol. V, *Problems of Peace and War* (Papers Read before the Society in the Year 1919), Sweet & Maxwell, London, 1920, p. 9, following Seneca *Nat. Quaest*, vol. 5, p. 18.

20 *Hall on the Sea-shore*, 1875, p. 42 as cited in Justice Merkel, *Commonwealth of Australia v. Yarmirr* (1999), Federal Court of Australia (FCA) 1668, 3 December 1999, p. 121.

21 Cited in Justice Merkel, *Commonwealth v. Yarmirr* (1999) FCA, 3 December 1999, s544.

22 S. D. Cole, 'The Highways of the Sea', in *Transactions of the Grotius Society*, vol. IV, *Problems of War* (Papers Read before the Society in the Year 1918), Sweet & Maxwell, London, 1919, p. 17.

23 Cf Knight, 'Grotius in England', *Transactions of the Grotius Society*, p. 4.

24 Hale, *De Jure Maris* 1787: Chapter 4, as cited in Merkel J., 1999: s529, 120.

25 See Tim Bonyhady, *The Law of the Countryside, The Rights of the Public*, Professional Books, Abington, 1987, Chapter 8. Concluding that 'a several fishery does not conflict with the skeletal principle of freedom of the seas', Justice Merkel draws the important conclusion that 'native title can burden the Crown's sovereign rights by a several fishery in much the same manner as a several fishery established by prescription or custom . . . limited the Crown's prerogative rights prior to Magna Carta' (*Commonwealth v. Yarmirr* [1999], 3 December 1999 FCA 1668 s629, 138). In other words, according to this interpretation, the public right to fish offers no

impediment to the recognition of exclusive native title to fisheries in offshore areas.

26 Justice Merkel, *Commonwealth v. Yarmirr* [1999], FCA 1668 3 December 1999, S629, p. 138. Cf Bonyhady, *The Law of the Countryside*, Chapter 8.

27 As cited in Justice Merkel, *Commonwealth v. Yarmirr* [1999], FCA 1668 S529–S545. The King's role in sixteenth-century France is interesting. In 1543 the French monarchy incorporated the sea-shore into the domain of the Crown, the latter's inalienability having been established by edict on 30 June 1539. This domain includes the zone of 50 geometric paces ('the King's footsteps') in France and 80 paces in New Caledonia (see Marie Hélène Teulières, 'The Law of the Sea and Kanak Fishermen: Property and Usage Rights', in C. R. South, D. Goulet, S. Tuqiri and M. Church, eds, *Traditional Marine Tenure and Sustainable Management of Marine Resources in Asia and the Pacific*, University of the South Pacific, Suva, 1994, p. 107 and notes 5 and 6.

28 P. T. Fenn, 'Origins of the Theory of Territorial Waters', *American Journal of International Law*, no. 20, 1926, pp. 468–469.

29 See Chief Justice Kennedy, *Moore v. Attorney-General for Soarstát Éireann* (1934), IR 44 68 ILTR 55, in J. C. W. Wylie, *A Case Book of Irish Law*, Professional Books Ltd, Oxford, 1984, p. 12.

30 *Moore v. Attorney General* (1934), pp. 24, 14.

31 See Nonie Sharp, *Reimagining Sea Space in History and Contemporary Life: Pulling Up Some Old Anchors*, Discussion Paper no. 5, North Australia Research Unit, Australian National University, Canberra, pp. 1–31; 'Why Indigenous Sea Rights are not Recognised in Australia: "The Facts" of *Mabo* and their Cultural Roots', Australian Aboriginal Studies, no. 1, pp. 28–37; 'Terrestrial and Marine Space in Imagination and Social Life', *Arena Journal* no. 10, 1998, pp. 51–68; 'Reimagining Sea Space: From Grotius to Mabo', in N. Peterson and B. Rigsby, eds, *Customary Marine Tenure in Australia*, Oceania Publications, Sydney, 1998, pp. 47–65.

32 Garrett Hardin, 'The Tragedy of the Commons', *Science*, no. 163, 1968, p. 1244.

33 S. V. Ciriacy-Wantrup and R. C. Bishop, 'Common Property as a Concept in Natural Resources Policy', *Natural Resources Journal*, vol. 15, no. 4, 1975: 713–27; F. Berkes, D. Feeny, B. McCay and J. Acheson, 'The Benefits of the Commons', *Nature*, no. 34, 1979, pp. 91–3; B. J. McCay and J. M. Acheson, eds, *The Question of the Commons*, University of Arizona Press, Tucson, 1987; F. Berkes, ed., *Common Property Resources: Ecology and Community-Based Sustainable Development*, London, Belhaven Press, 1989, pp. 1–18; D. W. Bromley, 'Commons, Property and Common-Property Regimes', in Bromley, ed., *Making the Commons Work: Theory, Practice and Policy*, International Center for Self-Governance, San Francisco, 1992; C. Ford Runge, 'Common Property and Collective Action in Economic Development', in D. W. Bromley, ed., *Making the Commons Work: Theory, Practice and Policy*, San Francisco, International Center for Self-Governance, 1992: 18–9; Bruce Rigsby, 'A Survey of Property Theory and Tenure Types', in Nicolas Peterson and Bruce Rigsby, eds, *Customary Marine Tenure in Australia*, Oceania Monograph 48, University of Sydney, 1998, pp. 22–46; on Aboriginal Australia, see Deborah Bird Rose, 'Common Property Regimes in

Aboriginal Australia: Totemism Revisited', in Peter Larmour, ed., *The Governance of Common Property in the Pacific Region*, Pacific Policy Paper 19, Australian National University, Canberra, 1997, pp. 127–144.

34 Runge, 'Common Property and Collective Action in Economic Development', in *Making the Commons Work*, p. 18.

35 Bromley, 'Introduction', *Making the Commons Work*, p. 11 (emphasis added).

36 See Nonie Sharp, *No Ordinary Judgment: Mabo, the Murray Islanders' Land Case*, Aboriginal Studies Press, Canberra, 1996.

37 Bonnie McCay, 'Sea Tenure and the Culture of the Commoners', in J. Cordell, ed., *A Sea of Small Boats*, Cultural Survival, Cambridge, MA, 1989, p. 205.

38 A. Macfarlane, *The Origins of English Individualism*, Cambridge University Press, New York, 1979, p. 63 (emphasis added); see also C. B. Macpherson, *The Political Theory of Possessive Individualism*, Oxford University Press, Oxford, 1977.

39 John Phyne, 'Capitalist Aquaculture and the Quest for Marine Tenure in Scotland and Ireland', *Studies in Political Economy*, no. 52, Spring 1997, p. 78; see also pp. 73–109.

40 H. S. A. Fox, 'The Chronology of Enclosure and Economic Development in Medieval Devon', *Economic History Review*, 2nd Ser., no. 28, 1975, p. 182.

41 Nonie Sharp, 'Journeys of Reconciliation', *Arena Magazine*, no. 33, 1998, pp. 31–36; Nonie Sharp, 'Open Access, Common Property and the Return of Responsibility? Reimagining Northern Seascapes in Australia', Paper prepared for the Seventh International Conference for the Study of Common Property, Vancouver, 10–14 June 1998.

42 *Mabo and Others v. Queensland*, Transcript of Proceedings, Supreme Court of Queensland, TQ, pp. 2108, 1892.

43 Geoff Sharp, 'Constitutive Abstraction and Social Practice', *Arena*, no. 70, 1985, pp. 48–82; Geoff Sharp, 'Extended Forms of the Social', *Arena Journal*, new series, no. 2, pp. 21–37.

44 Runge, 'Common Property and Collective Action in Economic Development' in *Making the Commons Work*, p. 18.

45 E. P. Thompson, *Whigs and Hunters: The Origin of the Black Act*, Allen Lane, London, 1975, p. 21.

46 Thompson, *Whigs and Hunters*, pp. 63–64.

47 Thompson, *Whigs and Hunters*, p. 136.

48 McCay, 'Sea Tenure and the Culture of the Commoners', in *A Sea of Small Boats*, p. 206.

49 Anthony Netboy, *The Atlantic Salmon: A Vanishing Species?*, Houghton Mifflin, Boston, 1968, p. 97.

50 Cf. McCay, 'Sea Tenure and the Culture of the Commoners', in *A Sea of Small Boats*, p. 207.

51 Bonnie McCay, 'The Culture of the Commoners', in B. J. McCay and M. Acheson, eds, *The Question of the Commons: The Culture and Ecology of Communal Resources*, University of Arizona Press, Tucson, 1987, pp. 2–5, 198–199.

52 See Te Runanga o Ngai Tahu, Information pack, Wellington, August 1997. On islands of New Caledonia, see Libération Kanak Socialiste, ed., *Une Totalité en Négation*, Noumea, January 1995, pp. 1–11.

53 John Cordell, 'Introduction', in *A Sea of Small Boats*, p. 7.
54 Cordell, 'Introduction', in *A Sea of Small Boats*, p. 12.
55 Nicolas Peterson and Bruce Rigsby, 'Introduction', in *Customary Marine Tenure in Australia*, Oceania Monograph 48, University of Sydney, Sydney, 1998, p. 2.
56 These were James Acheson in Maine (1972), John Cordell in Brazil (1972), R. Andersen and G. Stiles in Newfoundland (1973). See Cordell, *A Sea of Small Boats*, p. 16.
57 John M. Lightwood, *A Treatise on Possession of Land*, Stevens and Sons Ltd, London, 1894, p. 12.
58 Netboy, *The Atlantic Salmon: A Vanishing Species?*, pp. 131, 97.
59 Peter Örebech, Public and Common Private Property Rights: How to Protect and Preserve Inalienable Rights?, Paper given at Researcher Training Course, Legal Change in North/South Perspective, Copenhagen, 22–25 November 1995, p. 4 (copy in possession of the author).
60 Peter Örebech, The Legal Right to Norwegian Fisheries Participation with a Special Emphasis on the Lofoten Cod Fisheries, Paper given to the Man and Biosphere Conference, 21 February 1993, p. 4.
61 Anita Maurstad, 'To Fish or not to Fish: Small-Scale Fishing and Changing Regulations of the Cod Fishery in Northern Norway', *Human Organization*, vol. 59, no. 1, 2000, pp. 37–47.
62 Anita Maurstad, Customs in Commons–Commons in Court: Fishermen's Customary Practice and Statutory Law Concerning the Cod-Fishery in North Norwegian Waters, Paper given to the Fifth Common Property Conference of the International Association for the Study of Common Property, Bodø, Norway, 24–28 May 1995, pp. 5, 25, 61; Anita Maurstad, Closing the Commons — Opening the 'Tragedy': Regulating North-Norwegian Small-Scale Fishing, Paper given to Third Common Property Conference of the International Association for the Study of Common Property, Washington DC, 17–20 September, 1992; Who Should have a Voice in Management of Local Marine Resources?, Paper given to the Fifth Common Property Conference, Reinventing the Commons, Bodø, Norway, 24–28 May 1995.

8 *Flinders' Journey into Sea Space*

1 Australia's Oceans, New Horizons, incl. Maps, 1997. The distances of the three respective maritime zones are given in nautical miles in accordance with the convention on the International Law of the Sea.
2 J. R. V. Prescott, *Australia's Maritime Boundaries*, Department of International Relations, ANU, Canberra, 1985, p. 6.
3 P. T. Fenn, 'Origins of the Theory of Territorial Waters', *American Journal of International Law*, no. 20, 1926, pp. 480–481.
4 International Commission of Jurists, Report 116, p. 160, as cited in C. R. Symmons, *Ireland and the Law of the Sea*, The Round Hall Press, Dublin, 1993, p. 45.

5 Fenn, 'Origins of the Theory of Territorial Waters', p. 478.
6 H. S. K. Kent, 'The Historical Origins of the Three Mile Limit', *American Journal of International Law*, 1954, no. 48, pp. 537–553.
7 J. R. V. Prescott, *The Political Geography of the Oceans*, David and Charles, Devon, 1975, pp. 39–42.
8 Michel De Certeau, *The Practice of Everyday Life*, University of California Press, Berkeley, 1984, pp. 12–21.
9 Ernest Scott, *The Life of Captain Matthew Flinders, RN*, Angus and Robertson, Sydney, 1914.
10 Scott, *The Life of Captain Matthew Flinders*, RN, p. 206.
11 Matthew Flinders, *A Voyage to Terra Australis*, 2 vols, plus Charts, C. and W. Nicol, London, 1814, vol. 1, p. 73.
12 Flinders, *A Voyage to Terra Australis*, vol. 1, p. xxix.
13 Flinders, *A Voyage to Terra Australis*, vol. 2, p. 198.
14 Flinders, *A Voyage to Terra Australis*, vol. 1, p. xxiii.
15 Flinders, *A Voyage to Terra Australis*, vol. 1, pp. 60–61.
16 Flinders, *A Voyage to Terra Australis*, vol. 2, p. 199.
17 J. M. Holmes, *Australia's Open North*, Angus and Robertson, Sydney, 1963, p. 5. Holmes notes that settlements in the north based on sea transport failed (p. 31).
18 G. Williams and A. Frost, '*Terra Australis*: Theory and Speculation', *From Terra Australis to Australia*, Oxford University Press, Melbourne, 1988, p. 98 (see their note 34).
19 Jan Carstensz, ARA VOC 1080, records of the United East India Company — Dutch, as cited in Williams and Frost, *From Terra Australis to Australia*, p. 91.
20 Holmes, *Australia's Open North*, p. 9.
21 C. W. M. Hart and A. R. Pilling, *The Tiwi of North Australia*, Holt, Rinehart and Winston, New York, 1965, pp. 9, 27.
22 Holmes, *Australia's Open North*, p. 9.
23 Nonie Sharp, *Footprints along the Cape York Sandbeaches*, Aboriginal Studies Press, Canberra, 1992.
24 Kenneth Ruddle, 'A Guide to the Literature on Traditional Community-Based Fishery Management in the Asia-Pacific Tropics', FAO Fisheries Circular no. 869, Rome, 1994, pp. 47–51.
25 Law Commission, 'The Treaty of Waitangi and Maori Fisheries', Prelim. Paper no. 9, Wellington, 1989, pp. 26–32, 68–73.
26 Tom Bennion, 'Protecting Fishing Rights — Recent Fisheries Settlements in New Zealand', in *Turning the Tide: Indigenous Peoples and Sea Rights*, Law Faculty, Northern Territory University, Darwin, 1993.
27 Anthony Wilkin, 'Property and Inheritance', in *Reports of the Cambridge Anthropological Expedition to Torres Straits*, vol. 6, *Sociology, Magic and Religion of the Eastern Islanders*, Cambridge University Press, Cambridge, 1908, p. 167 n1 (emphasis added).
28 Justice Moynihan, Determination pursuant to reference of 27 February 1986, by the High Court of Australia to the Supreme Court of Queensland to hear and determine all issues of fact raised by the pleadings, particulars and further particulars in High Court action B12 of 1982, unreported, Brisbane, 16 November 1990, p. 186.

29 See Nonie Sharp, *No Ordinary Judgment: Mabo, the Murray Islanders' Land Case*, Aboriginal Studies Press, Canberra, 1996, pp. 189–206.
30 Wilkin, 'Property and Inheritance', p. 167.
31 R. E. Johannes and J. W. McFarlane, *Traditional Fishing in the Torres Strait Islands*, Commonwealth Scientific and Industrial Research Organisation, Division of Fisheries, Hobart, 1991, p. 81 citing J. R. Beckett, pers. comm., nd.
32 Transcript of proceedings, Supreme Court of Queensland, 1989, p. 2753; Sharp, *No Ordinary Judgment*, p. 197.
33 Cited in Sharp, *No Ordinary Judgment*, p. 198.
34 Howard Morphy, 'The Ownership of the Sea in North-east Arnhem Land', *Hansard of the Joint Committee on Aboriginal Land Rights in the Northern Territory*, Commonwealth Government Printer, Canberra, 3 May 1977, pp. 1100–1103. See also Ian Keen, *Report on the Milingimbi Closure of Seas Hearing*, Submission to the Aboriginal Land Commissioner, 1980.
35 De Certeau, *The Practice of Everyday Life*, p. 120.
36 John J. Bradley, We're Holding the Land, by Song, mimeograph, Northern Land Council, 1984, p. 8.
37 Sue Jackson, Geographies of Coexistence: Native Title, Cultural Difference and the Decolonisation of Planning in North Australia, unpub. PhD thesis, Macquarie University, North Ryde, 1998, p. 376.
38 Peter Sutton, 'Aboriginal Maps and Plans', in David Woodward and G. Malcolm Lewis, eds, *Cartography in the Traditional African, American, Arctic, Australian, and Pacific Societies*, vol. 2, Book 3, University of Chicago Press, Chicago and London, pp. 398–399.
39 John J. Bradley, *Li-Anthawirriyarra*, People of the Sea: Yanyuwa Relations with their Maritime Environment, unpub. PhD thesis, Northern Territory University, Darwin.
40 Peter Sutton, 'Icons of Country: Topographic Representations in Classical Aboriginal Traditions', in *Cartography in the Traditional African, American, Arctic, Australian, and Pacific Societies*, p. 364 and notes 44–47. See also n38 above.
41 Sylvie Poirier, Ontology, Ancestral Order and Agencies among the Kukatja (Australian Western Desert), ms, nd., p. 27, takes an example of a painting by a Western desert artist, suggesting that his 'painted spatial stories are not "maps"' but journeys 'within a named, personified land'.
42 See Sutton, 'Icons of Country', in *Cartography in the Traditional African, American, Arctic, Australian, and Pacific Societies*, esp. p. 364.

9 *Waves of Memory*

1 C. O'Leary, Preliminary Report of Deputy Chief Protector of Aboriginals to Chief Protector, 22 February 1936, Queensland State Archives, 36/4579, p. 3.
2 Nonie Sharp, *Stars of Tagai: The Torres Strait Islanders*, Aboriginal Studies Press, 1993, Chapter 7.

3 J. Chalmers, reported in Butcher, London Missionary Society Records Relating to the South Seas, 4 January 1907; Sharp, *Stars of Tagai*, p. 129.
4 T. Austin, 'F.W. Walker and Papuan Industries Ltd', *Journal of the Papua New Guinea Society*', vol. 6, no. 1, pp. 38–62; Sharp, *Stars of Tagai*, pp. 158–161.
5 See for example, Annual Report of the Chief Protector of Aboriginals to the Under Secretary, *Queensland Parliamentary Papers*, 1911, p. 20; Sharp, *Stars of Tagai*, pp. 162–164.
6 Chief Protector of Aboriginals to the Minister for Health and Home Affairs, 16 August 1937, enclosed with 37/9577 in Queensland State Archives A/3941; Sharp, *Stars of Tagai*, p. 211.
7 Report on Horn Island as at 6 July 1965, Department of Native Affairs, Thursday Island, unpub. report, p. 1 (copy in possession of the author); Nonie Sharp, *Footprints along the Cape York Sandbeaches*, Aboriginal Studies Press, Canberra, 1992, pp. 116–118.
8 Oliver Lyttleton, *From Peace to War: A Study in Contrast, 1857–1918*, 1968, p. 152, cited in Paul Fussell, *The Great War and Modern Memory*, Oxford University Press, New York and London, 1975, p. 327.
9 Relevant correspondence contained in Queensland State Archives 36/5997 was marked 'Away B'. See Nonie Sharp, Springs of Originality among the Torres Strait Islanders, PhD thesis, La Trobe University, Bundoora, 1984, p. 31, note 27.
10 W. Gunn, Second Reading Speech, The Queensland Coast Islands Declaratory Act 1985, *Queensland Parliamentary Debates, Hansard of the Legislative Assembly*, 1985, p. 4740.
11 *Queensland Parliamentary Debates*, *Hansard of the Legislative Assembly*, p. 4740.
12 Henry Reynolds, *The Law of the Land*, Penguin, Ringwood, 1992, pp. 185–186.
13 John J. Bradley, We're Holding the Land, by Song, Northern Land Council, unpub. report, 1984, pp. 7, 8, 9.
14 Howard Morphy, *Ancestral Connections: Art and an Aboriginal System of Knowledge*, University of Chicago Press, Chicago and London, 1991, p. 40.
15 *Milirrpum v. Nabalco Pty Ltd and the Commonwealth of Australia* (1971), *Federal Law Reports*, no. 17, per Blackburn J., p. 266.
16 Yirrkala Film Project, A Collection of Twenty-Two Films made with the Yolŋu of Northeast Arnhem Land, Film Australia, Sydney, 1979–1996. Citations from the films mentioned are taken from the respective scripts; with thanks to Ian Dunlop. Film Australia was preceded by the Commonwealth Film Unit.
17 Lloyd Warner, *A Black Civilization*, Peter Smith, Gloucester, Mass., 1969, pp. 4, 3.
18 Wandjuk Marika, *Life Story, as Told to Jennifer Isaacs*, University of Queensland Press, St Lucia, 1995, p. 13.
19 Marika, *Life Story*, p. 108.
20 John J. Bradley, *Li-Anthawirriyarra*, People of the Sea, unpub. PhD thesis, Northern Territory University, Casuarina, 1997, p. 81.
21 Roddy Harvey, 25 May 1997, recorded by John Bradley; pers. email comm. with the author, 25 January 1999.

22 Baldwin Spencer, Diary 1901, S and G2 1901, no. 4, p. 97, held in National Museum of Victoria, as cited in Richard Baker, *Land is Life*, Allen & Unwin, Sydney, 1999, p. 57.
23 Baker, *Land is Life*, p. 54.
24 Baker, *Land is Life*, p. 57.
25 Bradley, *Li-Anthawirriyarra*, People of the Sea, p. 79.
26 Bill Harney, Report on Movement of Natives from Borroloola, Australian Archives, NT Region CRSFI, Item 44.275, pp. 1–2, cited in Bradley, *Li-Anthawirriyarra*, People of the Sea, p. 79.
27 Bradley, *Li-Anthawirriyarra*, People of the Sea, p. 113. The song was composed by Elma Brown.
28 Moya Smith, Fish-Capture Sites and the Maritime Economies of some Coastal Australian Communities, Anthropology Department, Western Australia Museum, Perth, 1997, pp. 1–95.
29 Michael V. Robinson, Change and Adjustment among the Bardi of Sunday Island, North-Western Australia, unpub. MA thesis, University of Western Australia, Perth, 1973, pp. 219–221; cf Bagshaw, Anthropologist's Report, pp. 32–33, 36–37.
30 Report of K. I. Morgan, Department of Native Welfare, 23-11-4, 31 October 1962, cited in Robinson, Change and Adjustment among the Bardi of Sunday Island, p. 189.
31 Robinson, Change and Adjustment among the Bardi of Sunday Island, p. 26.
32 A. P. Elkin, *The Australian Aborigines: How to Understand Them*, Angus and Robertson, Sydney, 1954, p. 60.
33 As reported in R. S. Manger, Journal, Dept of Native Welfare, 5 November 1962, 23-11-1, cited in Robinson, Change and Adjustment among the Bardi of Sunday Island, p. 192.
34 H. C. Coombs, *Kulinma: Listening to Aboriginal Australians*, Australian National University Press, Canberra, 1978, pp. 54–57.
35 Robinson, Change and Adjustment among the Bardi of Sunday Island, p. 255.
36 Bagshaw, Anthropologist's Report, s6.4.
37 Smith, Fish-Capture Sites and the Maritime Economics of Some Coastal Australian Communities, 1997, pp. 17–24.
38 A. P. Elkin, 'Social Organisation in the Kimberley Division, North-Western Australia', *Oceania*, vol. 11, no. 3, pp. 296–333.
39 Bagshaw, Anthropologist's Report, s6.4.
40 Jack Bruno, Palm Island Escapes, unpub. ms, ed. and transl. Barry Alpher, Kowanyama, Queensland, 1978; with thanks to Barry Alpher for permission to cite this ms.
41 Colin Lawrence, as cited in Viv Sinnamon, Co-Management and Self-Governance: Contemporary Indigenous Natural Resource Management, Paper prepared for conference on Conservation Outside Nature Reserves, University of Queensland, Brisbane, 5–8 February, 1996, p. 11.
42 Gary Ward, pers. comm., Karumba, Queensland, June 1997. See Nonie Sharp, 'Handing on the Right to Fish: The Law of the Land and Cross-Cultural Co-operation in a Gulf Community in Australia', *Pacific Conservation Biology*, vol. 4, pp. 95–104.

43 F. Byerley, ed., *Narrative of the Overland Expedition of Messrs Jardine*, Buxton, Brisbane, 1867, p. 36.
44 *US v. Washington* (Phase I) 1974, 384 F. Supp. 312; *US v. Washington* (Phase II) 1980, 506, F. Supp. 187.

10 Old Traditions, New Ways

1 Statement by claimant, Mr Weluk, Aboriginal Land Commission, Sea Closure, Bathurst Island, Melville Island and Milingimbi Land Claim, Transcript of Proceedings, 1980, p. 143.
2 Ngai Tahu Fisheries Ltd, Annual Report, Wellington, 1997.
3 Noel Pearson, Our Right to take Responsibility, Discussion Paper prepared for the Cape York Land Council, Trinity Beach, Queensland, 1999, pp. 1–84.
4 R. Bruce Rettig, Fikret Berkes, and Evelyn Pinkerton, 'The Future of Fisheries Co-Management: A Multi-Disciplinary Assessment', in Evelyn Pinkerton, ed., *Co-operative Management of Local Fisheries*, University of British Columbia Press, Vancouver, 1989, p. 286.
5 Laura Loucks, Tony Charles, Mark Butler, eds, *Managing Our Fisheries, Managing Ourselves*, Gorsebrook Research Institute for Atlantic Canadian Studies, Halifax, Nova Scotia, 1998, pp. 1–83. Cf Nonie Sharp, 'New Waves Across the Seascapes', *Arena Journal*, no. 13, 1999, pp. 51–66.
6 Francis T. Christy, 'Thalassorama: The Death Rattle of Open Access and the Advent of Property Rights Regimes in Fisheries', *Marine Resource Economics*, vol. 11, no. 4, Winter 1996, pp. 287–304. Christy acknowledges Anthony Scott as at 'the forefront in the study of property rights in fishing' (p. 291). See Anthony Scott, 'Conceptual Origins of Rights Based Fishing', *Rights Based Fishing: Proceedings of a Workshop on the Scientific Foundations for Rights Based Fishing*, P. Neher, R. Arnason and N. Mollett, eds, Reykjavik, Iceland, 27 June–1 July 1988, Kluwer Academic Publishers, Netherlands, 1989.
7 Gary Ward, pers. comm., Karumba, June 1997.
8 Anthony Scott, Introducing Property in Fishery Management, Paper presented to the conference on The Use of Property Rights in Fisheries Management, Fremantle, 15–17 November 1999, p. 14.
9 John Goodland, Industry Perspective on Rights Based Management: The Shetland Experience, Paper presented to the conference on The Use of Property Rights in Fisheries Management, p. 11.
10 Christy, 'Thalassorama', p. 298.
11 The full title is *A Vision for the Atlantic Fisheries — Building a Fishery that Works*, Fisheries Council of Canada, Ottawa, 1994; cited and critiqued in L. Loucks, T. Charles and M. Butler, eds, *Managing Our Fisheries, Managing Ourselves*, see esp. pp. 32–36.
12 John Phyne, 'Capitalist Aquaculture and the Search for Marine Tenure in Scotland and Ireland', *Studies in Political Economy*, no. 52, Spring 1997, pp. 73–109.

13 G. McIntyre and G. Carter, Future Acts Affecting Native Title Offshore and Injunctive Relief, Paper presented at the Native Title in the New Millennium Representative Bodies Legal Conference, Melbourne, 16–20 April 2000.

14 Brendan Connolly, *Traditional Fishery Knowledge and Practice for Sustainable Marine Resources Management in Northwestern Europe: A Comparative Study in Ireland and the Netherlands*, Final Report, Human Capital and Mobility Programme of the European Union, University College Galway, 1997.

15 Kevin MacEwen Short, 'Self-Management of Fishing Rights, by Japanese Cooperative Associations: A Case Study from Hokkaido', in John Cordell, ed., *A Sea of Small Boats*, Cultural Survival, Cambridge, Mass., 1989, pp. 371–387.

16 Francis T. Christy, Common Property Rights: An Alternative to ITQs, Paper presented to the conference on The Use of Property Rights in Fisheries Management, pp. 1–8.

17 Svein Jentoft and Trond Kristoffersen, 'Fishermen's Co-Management: The Case of the Lofoten Fishery', *Human Organization*, vol. 48, no. 4, 1989, pp. 355–365.

18 Billy Frank Jnr, 'Habitat is the Key', *Northwest Indian Fisheries Commission News*, vol. 17, no. 4, Fall, 1997, p. 2.

19 Martin S. Weinstein, Pieces of the Puzzle: Getting to the Solution for Community-Based Coastal Zone Management in Canada, Keynote Address, Coastal Zone Canada 98, Victoria, British Columbia, 30 August–3 September 1998, p. 14.

20 Short, 'Self-Management of Fishing Rights', in *A Sea of Small Boats*, pp. 378–379.

21 See D. A. Grinde and B. E. Johansen, *Ecocide of Native America: Environmental Destruction of Indian Lands and Peoples*, Clear Light Publishers, Sante Fe, New Mexico, 1995, Ch. 6, 'Fishing Rights: The Usual and Accustomed Places', pp. 145–170.

22 Connolly, *Traditional Fishery Knowledge*, Conclusions. See also web at: http://homepage.eircom.net/~eufisheries/.

Select Bibliography

The references listed are of key source material. References to works quoted are given in notes to each chapter and these include books, journals, newspapers, films, videos and audio cassette recordings.

Aboriginal Land Commission Sea Closure. *Bathurst Island, Melville Island and Milingimbi Land Claim*, Transcript of Proceedings before His Honour Mr Justice Toohey, Aboriginal Land Commissioner, Darwin, 1980.

Alexander, M. *The Earliest English Poems*, Penguin, Harmondsworth, 1957.

Allen, D. Salt-Water Dreaming, Paper given to *Surviving Columbus:* Indigenous Peoples, Political Reform and Environmental Management in North Australia Conference, North Australia Research Unit, Darwin, 1992.

Bagshaw, G. Anthropologist's Report, Native Title Claim WAG 49/98, prepared for Kimberley Land Council on behalf of the native title claimants, 1999.

Berkes, F. ed. *Common Property Resources and Community-based Sustainable Development*, Belhaven Press, London, 1989.

Blackstone, Sir W. *Commentaries on the Laws of England*, 4 vols, Clarendon Press, Oxford, 1979 (Facsimile of the first edition, University of Chicago Press, 1765–69).

Bradley, J. *Li-Anthawirriyarra*, People of the Sea: Yanyuwa Relations with their Maritime Environment, unpub. PhD thesis, Northern Territory University, Darwin, 1997.

Bromley, D. W. ed. *Making the Commons Work: Theory, Practice and Policy*, San Francisco: International Center for Self-Governance, 1992.

Buku-Larrŋgay Mulka. *Saltwater: Yirrkala Bark Paintings of Sea Country, Recognising Indigenous Sea Rights*, Jennifer Isaacs Publishing, Sydney, 1999.

Ciriacy-Wantrup, S. W. and R. C. Bishop. ' "Common Property" as a Concept in

Natural Resources Policy', *Natural Resources Journal*, vol. 15, no. 4, 1975, pp. 713–727.

Conrad, J. *The Mirror of the Sea: Memories and Impressions*, Dent, London, 1946.

Cordell, J. ed. *A Sea of Small Boats*, Cultural Survival, Cambridge, MA, 1989.

De Certeau, M. *The Practice of Everyday Life*, University of California Press, Berkeley, 1984.

Fenn, P. T. Jnr. 'Origins of the Theory of Territorial Waters', *American Journal of International Law*, no. 20, 1926, pp. 465–482.

Flinders, M. *A Voyage to Terra Australis*, 2 vols, plus Charts, C. and W. Nicol, London, 1814.

Grotius, H. *The Law of War and Peace, De Jure Belli ac Pacis Libri,* Bobbs-Merrill, Indianapolis, 1925.

—— *The Freedom of the Seas or the Right which belongs to the Dutch to take part in the East Indian Trade,* Orno Press, New York, 1972 (Latin and English texts on opposite pages). Facsimile of Oxford University Press, New York, 1916. Ruan Deman Magoffin transl. *Mare Liberum.* 1st Latin edition 1633.

Haddon, A. C. ed. *Reports of the Cambridge Anthropological Expedition to the Torres Straits*, vols 1–6, Cambridge University Press, Cambridge, 1904–1935.

Hardin, G. 'The Tragedy of the Commons', *Science,* no. 163, 1968, pp. 1243–1248.

Jackson, S. E. Geographies of Coexistence: Native Title, Cultural Difference and the Decolonisation of Planning in North Australia, unpub. PhD thesis, Macquarie University, North Ryde, 1998.

Jentoft, S. and T. Kristoffersen. Fishermen's 'Co-Management: The Case of the Lofoten Fishery', *Human Organization,* vol. 48, no. 4, 1989, pp. 355–365.

Jull, P. *A Sea Change: Overseas Indigenous-Government Relations in the Coastal Zone,* Consultancy Report, Resource Assessment Commission, Coastal Zone Inquiry, Canberra, 1993.

Kent, H. S. K. 'The Historical Origins of the Three Mile Limit', *American Journal of International Law,* no. 48, 1954, pp. 537–553.

Kirkegaard, I. Assessment of the Northern Territory Fishing Industry Report, Forestry, Fisheries, Wildlife, Environment and National Parks Branch, Darwin, July 1974, pp. 1–177.

Knight, W. S. M. 'Grotius in England', in *Transactions of the Grotius Society,* vol. 5, *Problems of Peace and War* (Papers Read before the Society in the Year 1919), Sweet and Maxwell, London, 1920, pp. 1–38.

Lewis, D. *The Voyaging Stars: Secrets of the Pacific Island Navigators*, Collins, Sydney, 1978.

—— *We, the Navigators: The Ancient Art of Landfinding in the Pacific*, Hawaii University Press, Honolulu, 1987.

Lewis, D. H. and M. George. 'Hunters and Herders: Chukchi and Siberian Eskimo Navigation across Snow and Frozen Sea', *The Journal of Navigation,* vol. 44, no. 1, January 1991, pp. 1–10.

Lightwood, J. M. *A Treatise on Possession of Land,* Stevens and Sons, London, 1894.

Mabo and Others v. the State of Queensland and the Commonwealth of Australia, in the High Court of Australia, No. 12 of 1982. Transcripts of

Proceedings before High Court of Australia, Supreme Court of Queensland 1984–89. Determination pursuant to reference of February 1986 by High Court to Supreme Court of Queensland to hear and determine all issues of fact raised by the pleadings, particulars and further particulars in High Court action B12 of 1982, 16 November 1990 (Determination). *Eddie Mabo v. State of Queensland* (1992), 175 *Commonwealth Law Reports* 1 (High Court, Full Bench, 3 June 1992).

McCay, B. 'The Culture of the Commoners', in B. J. McCay, and J. M. Acheson, *The Question of the Commons: The Culture and Ecology of Communal Resources,* University of Arizona Press, Tucson, 1987, pp. 195, 216.

—— 'Sea Tenure and the Culture of the Commoners', in *A Sea of Small Boats*, J. Cordell, ed., Cultural Survival, Cambridge, MA, 1989, pp. 203–227.

Macknight, C. C. *The Voyage to Marege': Macassan Trepangers in Northern Australia,* Melbourne University Press, Parkville, 1976.

Magowan, F. A Sea has many Faces: Multiple Continuities in Yolŋu Coastal Waters, Paper presented to Australian Institute of Aboriginal and Torres Strait Islander Studies, The Power of Knowledge, the Resonance of Tradition–Indigenous Studies: Conference 2001, Australian National University, Canberra, pp. 1–15.

Marika, W. *Life Story, as Told to Jennifer Isaacs*, University of Queensland Press, St Lucia, 1995.

Maurstad, A. Closing the Commons — Opening the 'Tragedy': Regulating North-Norwegian Small-Scale Fishing. Paper given to Third Common Property Conference of the International Association for the Study of Common Property, Washington DC, 17–20 September 1992.

—— Customs in Commons — Commons in Court: Fishermen's Customary Practice and Statutory Law concerning the Cod-Fishery in North Norwegian Waters. Paper given to the Fifth Common Property Conference of the International Association for the Study of Common Property, Bodø, Norway, 24–28 May 1995.

—— 'To Fish or not to Fish: Small-Scale Fishing and Changing Regulations of the Cod Fishery in Northern Norway', *Human Organization*, vol. 59, no. 1, 2000, pp. 37–47.

—— 'Trapped in Biology: An Interdisciplinary Attempt to Integrate Fish Harvesters' Knowledge into Norwegian Fisheries Management', in Barbara Neis and Lawrence Felt, eds, *Finding our Sea Legs: Linking Fishery People and their Knowledge with Science and Management*, Memorial University, St John's, Newfoundland, 2000, pp. 135–152.

Morphy, H. *Journey to the Crocodile's Nest*, Australian Institute of Aboriginal Studies, Canberra, 1984.

—— 'From Dull to Brilliant: The Aesthetics of Spiritual Power among the Yolŋu', *Man*, vol. 24, no. 1, 1989, pp. 21–39.

—— *Ancestral Connections: Art and an Aboriginal System of Knowledge*, University of Chicago Press, Chicago and London, 1991.

Netboy, A. *The Atlantic Salmon: A Vanishing Species?*, Houghton Mifflin, Boston, 1968.

O'Connor, S. and P. Veth. eds, *East of Wallace's Line: Studies of Past and Present Maritime Cultures in the Indo-Pacific Region*, Modern Quarternary Research in South East Asia 16, V–VI, A. A. Balkema, Rotterdam, 2000.

Örebech, P. The Legal Right to Norwegian Fisheries Participation with a Special Emphasis on the Lofoten Cod Fisheries, Paper given to the Man and Biosphere Conference, 21 February 1993.

Palmer, K. 'Status of Documentary Information on Aboriginal and Islander Fishing and Marine Hunting in Northern Australia', in Great Barrier Reef Marine Park Authority, ed., *Workshop on Traditional Knowledge of the Marine Environment in North Australia,* Great Barrier Reef Marine Park Authority, Townsville, 1985, pp. 4–18.

Pearson, N. Our Right to Take Responsibility, Discussion Paper prepared for Cape York Land Council, Trinity Beach, Queensland, 1999, pp. 1–84.

Peterson, N. and B. Rigsby eds, *Customary Marine Tenure in Australia,* Oceania Monograph 48, University of Sydney, Sydney, 1998.

Prescott, J. R. V. *The Political Geography of the Oceans,* David and Charles, Devon, 1975.

Resource Assessment Commission (RAC). *Coastal Zone Inquiry: Final Report,* Resource Assessment Commission, Canberra, 1993.

Robinson, M. V. Change and Adjustment among the Bardi of Sunday Island, North-Western Australia, MA thesis, University of Western Australia, Perth, 1973.

Rose, D. B. *Dingo Makes Us Human: Life and Land in an Aboriginal Culture,* Cambridge University Press, Cambridge, 1992.

Schama, S. *Landscape and Memory,* Knopf, New York, 1995.

Schilder, G. 'New Holland: The Dutch Discoveries', in C. Williams and A. Frost, eds, *Terra Australis to Australia,* Oxford University Press, Melbourne, 1998.

Selden, J. *Mare Clausum. The Right and Dominion of the Sea,* 2 vols, Andrew Kembe and Edward Thomas, London, 1663.

Sharp, N. *Stars of Tagai: The Torres Strait Islanders,* Aboriginal Studies Press, Canberra, 1993.

—— *No Ordinary Judgment: Mabo, The Murray Islanders' Land Case,* Aboriginal Studies Press, Canberra, 1996.

—— *Reimagining Sea Space in History and Contemporary Life: Pulling Up Some Old Anchors,* Discussion Paper no. 5, North Australia Research Unit, Australian National University, Canberra, 1996, pp. 1–31.

—— 'Why Indigenous Sea Rights are not Recognised in Australia: "The Facts" of *Mabo* and their Cultural Roots', *Australian Aboriginal Studies,* no. 1, 1997, pp. 28–37.

—— 'Terrestrial and Marine Space in Imagination and Social Life', *Arena Journal,* no. 10, 1998, pp. 51–83.

—— 'Handing on the Right to Fish: The Law of the Land and Cross-Cultural Co-operation in a Gulf Community in Australia', *Pacific Conservation Biology,* vol. 4, 1998, pp. 95–104.

—— 'Australian Native Title and Irish Marine Rights', *Law in Context,* vol. 16, no. 2, 1999, pp. 34–48.

Sinnamon, V. Co-Management and Self-Governance: Contemporary Indigenous Natural Resource Management, Paper prepared for conference on Conservation Outside Nature Reserves, University of Queensland, Brisbane, 5–8 February 1996.

Smith, B. *Imagining the Pacific, In the Wake of the Cook Voyages,* Melbourne University Press, Parkville, 1992.

Smyth, D. *A Voice in All Places: Aboriginal and Torres Strait Islander Interests in Australia's Coastal Zone*, Consultancy Report, Resource Assessment Commission, Coastal Zone Inquiry, Canberra, 1993.

Stanner, W. E. H. The Yirrkala Case: Some General Principles of Aboriginal Landholding, mimeograph, 1969, pp. 1–12, in possession of author; my copy from Dr Nancy Williams.

Sutton, P. *Country: Aboriginal Boundaries and Land Ownership in Australia*, Aboriginal History, Canberra, 1995.

—— 'Icons of Country: Topographic Representations in Classical Aboriginal Tradition; Aboriginal Maps and Plans', in D. Woodward and G. M. Lewis, eds, *Cartography in the Traditional African, American, Arctic, Australian, and Pacific Societies*, vol. 2, Book 3, University of Chicago Press, Chicago and London, 1998, Chapters 9 and 10.

Thompson E. P. *Whigs and Hunters*, Allen Lane, London, 1975.

Thomson, D. F. 'The Hero Cult, Initiation and Totemism on Cape York', *Journal of the Royal Anthropological Institute of Great Britain and Ireland* LXIII, July–December 1933, pp. 453–537, with Plates XXVII–XXXVI.

—— 'Dugong Hunters of Cape York', *Journal of the Royal Anthropological Institute of Great Britain and Ireland*, no. 64, 1934, pp. 237–262.

—— *The Seasonal Factor in Human Culture: Illustrated from the Life of a Contemporary Nomadic Group*, Proceedings of the Prehistoric Society, Paper no. 10, 1946, pp. 209–221.

—— *Economic Structure and the Ceremonial Exchange Cycle in Arnhem Land*, Macmillan, Melbourne, 1949.

Veth, P. 'Aridity and Settlement in Northwest Australia', *Antiquity*, no. 69, 1995, pp. 733–746.

Williams, G. and A. Frost, eds, '*Terra Australis*: Theory and Speculation', *From Terra Australis to Australia*, Oxford University Press, Melbourne, 1988.

Woodward, Justice A. E. Aboriginal Land Rights Commission, First Report, *Parliamentary Paper No. 69*, Government Printer, Canberra, 1973.

Wylie, J. C. W. *A Case Book on Irish Land Law*, Professional Books, Oxford, 1981.

Yarmirr v. Northern Territory of Australia (1998), 771 FCA (6 July 1998); *Commonwealth v. Yarmirr* (1999) FCA 168 ALR 426; *Commonwealth v. Yarmirr*; *Yarmirr v. Northern Territory* (2001), HCA 56 (11 October 2001).

Yirrkala Film Project. *A Collection of Twenty-Two Films made with the Yolŋu of Northeast Arnhem Land*, Film Australia, Sydney, 1979–1996; Films and Scripts as cited.

INDEX